M000121799

Keyboarding, Word Processing, & Communication

Using Microsoft® Office Word and Outlook 2007

Boston, Massachusetts   Chandler, Arizona   Glenview, Illinois   Upper Saddle River, New Jersey

This text has been prepared with the assistance of Gleason Group, Inc., Norwalk, CT.

Editorial Director	Gerald Gleason
Project Manager	Pamela Ross
Assistant Editor	Marilyn Young
Copyeditor	Malinda McCain
Composition	PDS Associates
Interior Design	Vicki A. Lamb

Copyright © 2009 by Pearson Education, Inc., or its affiliates. All rights reserved. Printed in the United States of America. This publication is protected by copyright, and permission should be obtained from the publisher prior to any prohibited reproduction, storage in a retrieval system, or transmission in any form or by any means, electronic, mechanical, photocopying, recording, or likewise. For information regarding permissions, write to Pearson Curriculum Rights & Permissions, One Lake Street, Upper Saddle River, New Jersey 07458.

Pearson® is a trademark, in the U.S. and/or in other countries, of Pearson plc or its affiliates.

Prentice Hall® is a trademark, in the U.S. and/or in other countries, of Pearson Education, Inc., or its affiliates.

Microsoft, Windows, and Office are either registered trademarks or trademarks of Microsoft Corporation in the United States and/or other countries. Microsoft Office Word 2007 and Microsoft Office Outlook 2007 may be registered trademarks or trademarks of Microsoft Corporation in the United States and/or in other countries. Google is either a registered trademark or a trademark of Google, Inc., in the United States and/or in other countries.

Use of the trademarks implies no relationship, sponsorship, endorsement, sale, or promotion on the part of Pearson Education, Inc., or its affiliates.

Information in this text, including URLs, and other Internet Web site references, is subject to change without notice.

ISBN-13: 978-0-13-363984-1
ISBN-10: 0-13-363984-3

3 4 5 6 7 8 9 10   V003   12 11 10

PEARSON

CONTENTS

Introduction 1

Keyboarding 28

ALPHABET AND PUNCTUATION KEYS 29

Word Processing and Communication

COMMUNICATION   277

About Your Book

The second part of the Introduction is called Keying Correctly. It teaches you the basic keying posture and helps break any bad keying habits you may have.

Your book is divided into 3 sections:
- Introduction
- Keyboarding
- Word Processing and Communication

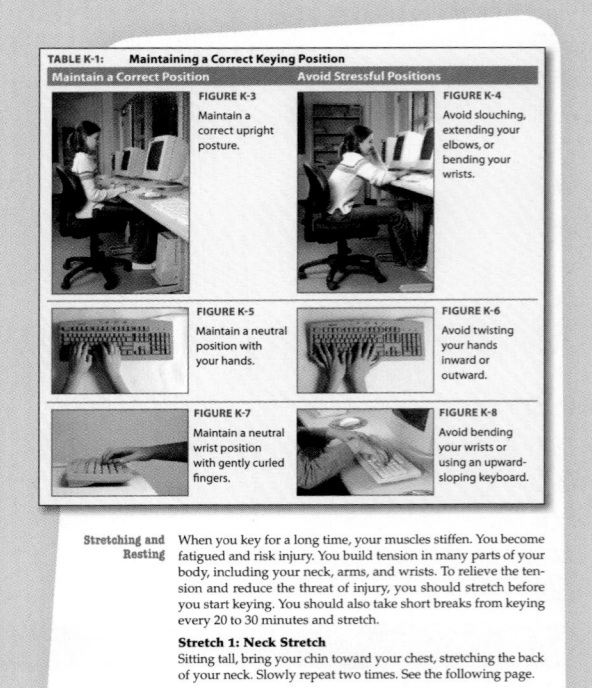

TABLE K-1:	Maintaining a Correct Keying Position		
Maintain a Correct Position		**Avoid Stressful Positions**	
	FIGURE K-3 Maintain a correct upright posture.		**FIGURE K-4** Avoid slouching, extending your elbows, or bending your wrists.
	FIGURE K-5 Maintain a neutral position with your hands.		**FIGURE K-6** Avoid twisting your hands inward or outward.
	FIGURE K-7 Maintain a neutral wrist position with gently curled fingers.		**FIGURE K-8** Avoid bending your wrists or using an upward-sloping keyboard.

Stretching and Resting — When you key for a long time, your muscles stiffen. You become fatigued and risk injury. You build tension in many parts of your body, including your neck, arms, and wrists. To relieve the tension and reduce the threat of injury, you should stretch before you start keying. You should also take short breaks from keying every 20 to 30 minutes and stretch.

Stretch 1: Neck Stretch
Sitting tall, bring your chin toward your chest, stretching the back of your neck. Slowly repeat two times. See the following page.

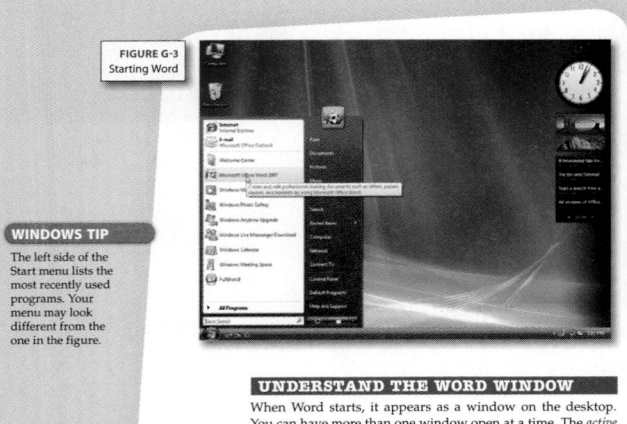

FIGURE G-3 Starting Word

WINDOWS TIP
The left side of the Start menu lists the most recently used programs. Your menu may look different from the one in the figure.

UNDERSTAND THE WORD WINDOW

When Word starts, it appears as a window on the desktop. You can have more than one window open at a time. The *active window* is the window in which you are working. The *title bar* displays the name of the current document open in the active window. Word always starts with a blank document titled "Document1." At the bottom of the screen, the taskbar shows which programs or windows are currently open.

Resize the Word Window — When you work in Word, you can reduce the size of the window to reveal other items on the desktop or maximize the window to cover the desktop completely.

To resize the window by using Window buttons or the mouse:

1. Click the Minimize button ⬚ on the title bar to reduce the window to a button on the taskbar. The button is labeled with the name of the current window, "Document1 – Microsoft Word." See Figure G-4 on the next page.
2. Click the Word taskbar button to maximize the window.
3. Click the Restore Down button ⬚ on the title bar to reduce the size of the window. When a window is reduced, the Restore Down button ⬚ changes to a Maximize button ⬚.

The first part of the Introduction is called Getting Started. It gives you a basic introduction to Microsoft Windows and to Word.

In the Keyboarding section there are two types of Lessons:
- Lessons about new keys (yellow pages)
- Review Lessons (blue pages)

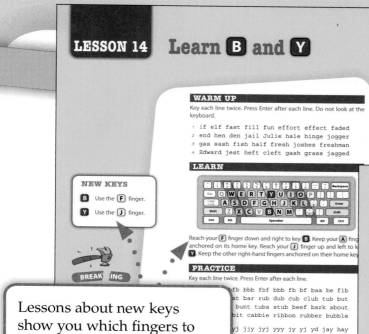

LESSON 14 Learn **B** and **Y**

WARM UP

Key each line twice. Press Enter after each line. Do not look at the keyboard.

1 if elf fast fill fun effort effect faded
2 end hen den jail Julie hale hinge jogger
3 gas sash fish half fresh joshes freshman
4 Edward jest heft cleft gash grass jagged

LEARN

NEW KEYS

B Use the **F** finger.
Y Use the **J** finger.

Reach your **F** finger down and right to key **B**. Keep your **A** fing[er] anchored on its home key. Reach your **J** finger up and left to k[ey] **Y**. Keep the other right-hand fingers anchored on their home key[s.]

PRACTICE

Key each line twice. Press Enter after each line.

LESSON 14 Learn **B** and **Y**

Lessons about new keys show you which fingers to use for the new keys and give you plenty of practice.

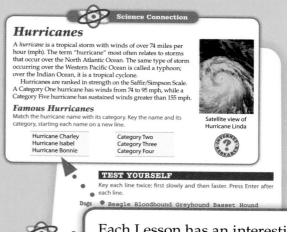

Science Connection

Hurricanes

A *hurricane* is a tropical storm with winds of over 74 miles per hour (mph). The term "hurricane" most often relates to storms that occur over the North Atlantic Ocean. The same type of storm occurring over the Western Pacific Ocean is called a typhoon; over the Indian Ocean, it is a tropical cyclone.

Hurricanes are ranked in strength on the Saffir/Simpson Scale. A Category One hurricane has winds from 74 to 95 mph, while a Category Five hurricane has sustained winds greater than 155 mph.

Famous Hurricanes

Match the hurricane name with its category. Key the name and its category, starting each name on a new line.

Hurricane Charley   Category Two
Hurricane Isabel   Category Three
Hurricane Bonnie   Category Four

Satellite view of Hurricane Linda

TEST YOURSELF

Key each line twice: first slowly and then faster. Press Enter after each line.

Dogs   Beagle Bloodhound Greyhound Basset Hound

12 The boa had beady eyes and a blunt tail.

TIME YOURSELF

13 Moby brings Ben a toy rabbit.
14 Becky enjoyed yoga yesterday.
15 Rob blabbed about your story.
| 1 | 2 | 3 | 4 | 5 | 6 | WPM: 18

57

Each Lesson has an interesting "Connection" to Language Arts, Science, Social Studies, or Mathematics.

Every Lesson offers you the chance to Time Yourself. It's your best way of "knowing how you are doing." Your speed is measured in "Words per Minute" (or "WPM").

LESSON 9 Review **T O G N** Left Shift and Period

REVIEW

The keyboard shows the keys you have learned so far. This lesson focuses on the keys highlighted in purple.

WARM UP

K[ey each line] t[wice.] Pre[ss] Enter after each line. Concentrate on press-

[n]ote got gotten tote
[Ja]ke; Kids like Jake.
[K]ane. Kane is kin.
[Ai]den. Lana looks on.

[aft]er each line.

[t]o toot tot toe tote
[t]t lot jot rote goat
[t] stones toes ghost

; gone; genes; sign
[l]onging song singing
; gig agog; gotten

[g]. Lg. Kg. Jds. Hd.
[h]otel. Otis loiters.
[J.] I. I. I. Hi. No.

[N]o one going. Ogden
Left Shift   15 green gnarl great gross gnats grain gilt
and Period   16 N.J.L. L.J.K. J.I.N.; Old Ohio. Old Hat.

LESSON 9 Review **T O G N** Left Shift and Period   46

The keyboard shown in every Lesson helps you keep track of keys as you learn them. The dark purple keys are the ones you are learning in the Lesson. The slanted color bars help you remember what fingers to use. Keys you haven't learned yet are grayed out.

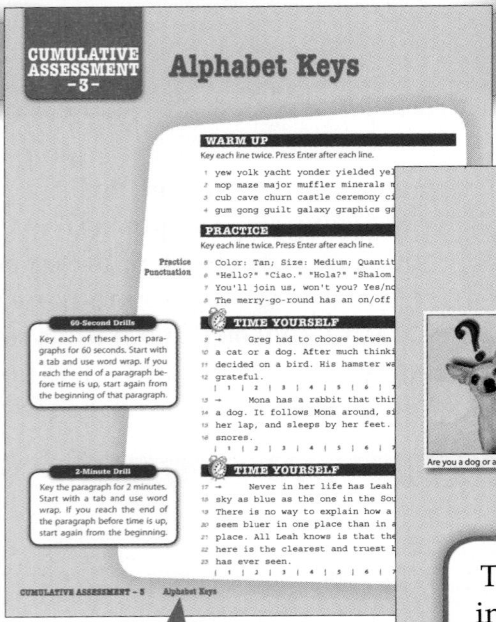

After finishing the Keyboarding section your target is to type 35 words per minute.

In Word Processing and Communication you learn about:
- Letters, memos, and reports
- Tables and columns
- Drawing tools
- Special word processing effects
- E-mail and instant messaging
- The Internet
- Web pages and blogs

The report topics are interesting. You research topics, but you also share your opinions.

Cumulative Assessments give you a chance to see what you have learned. There are 8 Cumulative Assessments in the Keyboarding section.

One of the most important things you learn early in the Word Processing and Communication section is the correct format for reports, letters, memos, and other types of documents.

CUMULATIVE ASSESSMENT -3- **Alphabet Keys**

WARM UP
Key each line twice. Press Enter after each line.
1 yew yolk yacht yonder yielded ye
2 mop maze major muffler minerals m
3 cub cave churn castle ceremony ci
4 gum gong guilt galaxy graphics ga

PRACTICE
Key each line twice. Press Enter after each line.

Practice Punctuation
5 Color: Tan; Size: Medium; Quantit
6 "Hello?" "Ciao." "Hola?" "Shalom.
7 You'll join us, won't you? Yes/no
8 The merry-go-round has an on/off

60-Second Drills
Key each of these short paragraphs for 60 seconds. Start with a tab and use word wrap. If you reach the end of a paragraph before time is up, start again from the beginning of that paragraph.

2-Minute Drill
Key the paragraph for 2 minutes. Start with a tab and use word wrap. If you reach the end of the paragraph before time is up, start again from the beginning.

TIME YOURSELF
9   Greg had to choose between
10 a cat or a dog. After much thinki
11 decided on a bird. His hamster wa
12 grateful.
   1 | 2 | 3 | 4 | 5 | 6 | 7
13   Mona has a rabbit that thin
14 a dog. It follows Mona around, si
15 her lap, and sleeps by her feet.
16 snores.
   1 | 2 | 3 | 4 | 5 | 6 | 7

TIME YOURSELF
17   Never in her life has Leah
18 sky as blue as the one in the Sou
19 There is no way to explain how a
20 seem bluer in one place than in a
21 place. All Leah knows is that the
22 here is the clearest and truest b
23 has ever seen.
   1 | 2 | 3 | 4 | 5 | 6 | 7

CUMULATIVE ASSESSMENT – 3   Alphabet Keys

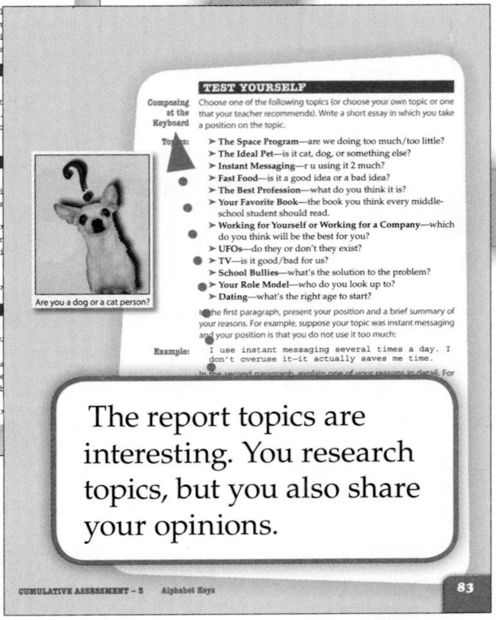

TEST YOURSELF

Composing at the Keyboard
Choose one of the following topics (or choose your own topic or one that your teacher recommends). Write a short essay in which you take a position on the topic.

Topics:
➤ **The Space Program**—are we doing too much/too little?
➤ **The Ideal Pet**—is it cat, dog, or something else?
➤ **Instant Messaging**—r u using it 2 much?
➤ **Fast Food**—is it a good idea or a bad idea?
➤ **The Best Profession**—what do you think it is?
➤ **Your Favorite Book**—the book you think every middle-school student should read.
➤ **Working for Yourself or Working for a Company**—which do you think will be the best for you?
➤ **UFOs**—do they or don't they exist?
➤ **TV**—is it good/bad for us?
➤ **School Bullies**—what's the solution to the problem?
➤ **Your Role Model**—who do you look up to?
➤ **Dating**—what's the right age to start?

In the first paragraph, present your position and a brief summary of your reasons. For example, suppose your topic was instant messaging and your position is that you do not use it too much:

Example:
I use instant messaging several times a day. I don't overuse it—it actually saves me time.

In the second paragraph, explain one of your reasons in detail. For

Are you a dog or a cat person?

CUMULATIVE ASSESSMENT – 3   Alphabet Keys

83

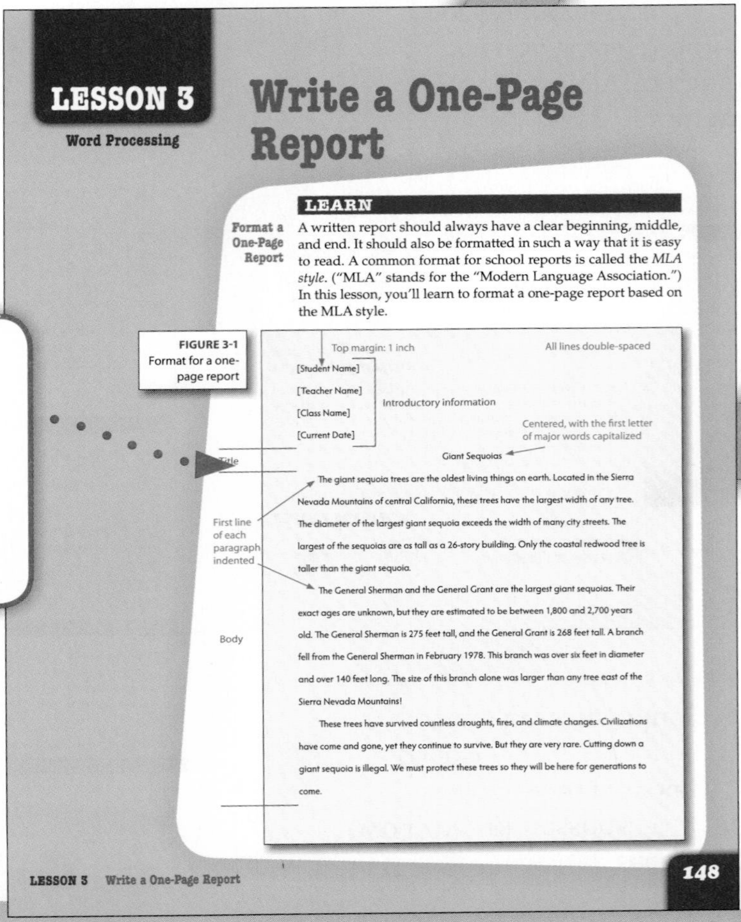

LESSON 3
Word Processing
Write a One-Page Report

LEARN

Format a One-Page Report
A written report should always have a clear beginning, middle, and end. It should also be formatted in such a way that it is easy to read. A common format for school reports is called the *MLA style*. ("MLA" stands for the "Modern Language Association.") In this lesson, you'll learn to format a one-page report based on the MLA style.

FIGURE 3-1
Format for a one-page report

Top margin: 1 inch   All lines double-spaced

[Student Name]
[Teacher Name]
[Class Name]   Introductory information
[Current Date]
                                    Centered, with the first letter
                                    of major words capitalized

Title   Giant Sequoias

First line of each paragraph indented
The giant sequoia trees are the oldest living things on earth. Located in the Sierra Nevada Mountains of central California, these trees have the largest width of any tree. The diameter of the largest giant sequoia exceeds the width of many city streets. The largest of the sequoias are as tall as a 26-story building. Only the coastal redwood tree is taller than the giant sequoia.

Body
The General Sherman and the General Grant are the largest giant sequoias. Their exact ages are unknown, but they are estimated to be between 1,800 and 2,700 years old. The General Sherman is 275 feet tall, and the General Grant is 268 feet tall. A branch fell from the General Sherman in February 1978. This branch was over six feet in diameter and over 140 feet long. The size of this branch alone was larger than any tree east of the Sierra Nevada Mountains!

These trees have survived countless droughts, fires, and climate changes. Civilizations have come and gone, yet they continue to survive. But they are very rare. Cutting down a giant sequoia is illegal. We must protect these trees so they will be here for generations to come.

LESSON 3   Write a One-Page Report

148

Your goal for the Word Processing and Communication section is to become familiar with Microsoft Word and Microsoft Outlook as well as with the Internet.

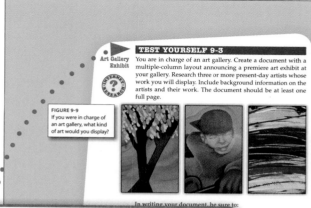

Art Gallery Exhibit

TEST YOURSELF 9-3. You are in charge of an art gallery. Create a document with a multiple-column layout announcing a premiere art exhibit at your gallery. Research three or more present-day artists whose work you will display. Include background information on the artists and their work. The document should be at least one full page.

FIGURE 9-9
If you were in charge of an art gallery, what kind of art would you display?

In writing your document, be sure to:

There are 3 Test Yourself exercises in each Lesson. The first should be easy for you. The second is a bit more challenging. The third one is the most interesting—and the most challenging. It may ask you to do research and to share your opinions with the class.

Practice exercises walk you through every step of the way.

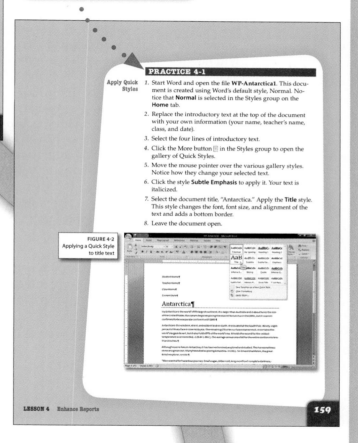

PRACTICE 4-1

Apply Quick Styles

1. Start Word and open the file **WP-Antarctica1**. This document is created using Word's default style, Normal. Notice that **Normal** is selected in the Styles group on the **Home** tab.
2. Replace the introductory text at the top of the document with your own information (your name, teacher's name, class, and date).
3. Select the four lines of introductory text.
4. Click the More button in the Styles group to open the gallery of Quick Styles.
5. Move the mouse pointer over the various gallery styles. Notice how they change your selected text.
6. Click the style **Subtle Emphasis** to apply it. Your text is italicized.
7. Select the document title, "Antarctica." Apply the **Title** style. This style changes the font, font size, and alignment of the text and adds a bottom border.
8. Leave the document open.

FIGURE 4-2
Applying a Quick Style to title text

Microsoft Word

Using Undo and Redo

Two command buttons frequently used when editing text are the Undo and Redo buttons. Use the Undo button to reverse an action you have just done, such as cutting or formatting text.

After using the Undo button, you can change your mind and use the Redo button. Undo and Redo are only available for immediately performed commands. Both command buttons are on the Quick Access toolbar at the top of the document window, and you can also access them with keyboard shortcuts.

TABLE 4-2	Undo and Redo
Ribbon Command	**Keyboard Shortcut**
Undo	Ctrl + Z
Redo	Ctrl + Y

PRACTICE 4-3

Cut, Copy, and Paste

You can have more than one document open at a time. The active window is the window in which you are currently working. You use the taskbar at the bottom of the screen to switch from one document to another. It contains the Start button and buttons for all the open documents.

The text walks you through all the general procedures you need to know.

Each Lesson in the Word Processing and Communication section is divided into general procedures (in boxes) and Practice exercises.

Teacher Advisory Board

Microsoft Windows XP, Microsoft Office 2003 Edition

Larry Bailey
Lauderhill Middle School
Lauderhill, FL

Gloria Belsich
Aledo Middle School
Aledo, TX

Kathy Brittain
Henry Winkelman School
Glenview, IL

Valerie Carter
Ponce de Leon Middle School
Coral Gables, FL

Vaughn Denton
Orchard School/Julia Dyckman Andrus Memorial School
Yonkers, NY

Ann Dilts
St. Charles Borromeo School
Bloomington, IN

Ann Farrington
Holy Name of Jesus School
Indialantic, FL

Maureen Fisher
Hilda Walker Intermediate School
Tinley Park, IL

David Galliher
Carmichael Middle School
Richland, WA

Patty Hernandez
Hacienda Heights Communications Magnet School
El Paso, TX

Pshaun Hopkins
Francis Scott Key Middle School
Houston, TX

Kent Hurlburt
Smith Elementary School
West Hartford, CT

Jill Knight
West Texas Middle School
Stinnett, TX

Sandy Kon
Liberty Junior Middle School
Richardson, TX

Heidi Leventhal
Burbank Middle School
Houston, TX

Natalie Price
Hamilton Middle School
Houston, TX

Adrienne Renner
Presentation High School
San Jose, CA

Noreen Ranallo
Sunnymead School
Hillsborough, NJ

Rose Roth
Cottage Hill Elementary School
Grass Valley, CA

Jacquelle Sconiers
Juvenile Justice Center School
Miami, FL

Heli Shelley
Blythewood Middle School
Blythewood, SC

Mary Jean Smith
St. Genevieve School
Flourtown, PA

Samantha Stewart
Harnett Primary School
Dunn, NC

Kris Umek
Chief Joseph Middle School
Richland, WA

Nancy Williams
George Washington Elementary School
Kingsport, TN

Microsoft Windows (Vista), Microsoft Office 2007 Edition

Pshaun Hopkins
Francis Scott Key Middle School
Houston, TX

Jill Knight
West Texas Middle School
Stinnett, TX

Kathi Mendoza
Hacienda Heights Communication Magnet Elementary School
El Paso, TX

Natalie Price
Hamilton Middle School
Houston, TX

Noreen Ranallo
Sunnymead School
Hillsborough, NJ

Nancy Williams
George Washington Elementary School
Kingsport, TN

Introduction

4. At the bottom of your Web page, create a blog entry.

5. Assume that you have updated the page twice, and add two additional blog entries. Make sure you use different dates and list the entries with the most recent date first.

6. Format the page, the text, and the picture attractively.

7. Save the document as *[your initials]*Test17-3 using the **Single File Web Page** file type. Include an appropriate Web page title.

8. Open the Web page in your browser to view it. Test the links. Print the Web page in the browser and then close the browser.

9. Close the Word document.

Getting Started

OBJECTIVES

After completing this portion of the Introduction, you will be able to:

☑ Start Microsoft Windows and use the mouse to navigate in Windows.

☑ Start Microsoft Word and resize a window.

☑ Create a new document.

☑ Open an existing document.

☑ Name and save a document.

☑ Print a document.

☑ Close a document.

☑ Close Word and return to Windows.

START WINDOWS

Microsoft Windows is the operating system or software that runs your computer. You must start Windows before you can use any other program on your computer.

Log on to Your Computer

When you turn on your computer, Windows begins to load, and the Log On screen appears.

To log on to Windows, you typically must enter a *user password*, a string of characters that you enter by using the keyboard. Your instructor will give you your user password.

You enter your password in a text box that contains a vertical blinking line. This line is called the *insertion point*. It indicates the specific point that is currently active on-screen, where the computer is waiting for you to input information.

To log on to your computer:

1. Turn on the computer, if it is not turned on.

2. When the opening Windows screen appears, key your password in the **Password** text box.

3. Press the Enter key.

WINDOWS TIP

If you make a mistake keying your password, you will see an error message. Press the Enter key (or click OK) and start again.

2. Starting with the first musical style in the document, use your Web browser to find one Web site about Andean music. You might use the following location as a starting point: **www.google.com/Top/Arts/Music/Styles/R/ Regional_and_Ethnic**

3. Write a short paragraph about Andean music in the Word document.

4. In the browser, copy the Web address of the page you used to research Andean music. In the document, select the heading "Andean" and link the text to the Web address. (Use the **Insert** tab, **Hyperlink** command, and paste the Web address in the text box.)

5. Follow the same procedure for the remaining two styles of music: find a Web site, write a short description, and link the Web address to the heading of the musical style in the document.

6. Include at least one picture that you copy from one of the Web sites used in your research. Link the picture to the Web page it came from. Include a ScreenTip with text that describes the picture.

7. Apply a style to the picture. Make sure all the text in the document is consistently formatted.

8. Save the document as *[your initials]*Test17-2 using the **Single File Web Page** file type. Use the **Change Title** command to include an appropriate Web page title.

9. Open the Web page in your browser to view it. Test the links, then close the browser.

10. Print the Word document; then close it.

TEST YOURSELF 17-3

Your Blog What's important to you? What do you feel strongly about? What topic do you know a lot about? Create a Web page that offers information or expresses your point of view on a particular subject. Add blog posts to the Web page.

1. In a new Word document, start with a title for the Web page and then add at least two paragraphs of text.

2. Include at least two hyperlinks to Web sites that relate to your topic or to other blogs on your topic.

3. Include at least one picture or graphic that you copy from a Web site. The picture should link to the Web location on which you found it and should have a descriptive ScreenTip.

DID YOU KNOW?

The "blogo-sphere" (the world of blogs) is growing rapidly, with over 100,000 new blog sites a day. That's about 1.4 blogs created every second!

4. If the Welcome Center window appears, move the mouse pointer to the red Close button in the upper-right corner of the window. Click the left mouse button to close the window.

FIGURE G-1
Closing a window

WINDOWS TIP

When moving the mouse on the mouse pad, if you reach the edge of the pad, just pick up the mouse and put it in the center of the pad. This does not change the position of the pointer on the screen.

Use the Mouse Using Windows involves a *mouse,* a pointing device that is typically attached to your computer by a cable. You move the mouse on any flat surface or on a *mouse pad*, a smooth pad on which the mouse rests. A mouse typically has two buttons, one on the left and one on the right.

A *pointer* appears on the screen and lets you accomplish specific tasks by using the mouse. As you move the mouse, the on-screen pointer moves. When you move the mouse to your left, the on-screen pointer moves to the left. When you move the mouse to your right, the on-screen pointer moves to the right. Table G-1 lists and describes some of the basic things you can do using the mouse.

TABLE G-1 Mouse Terms

Term	Description
Point	Move the mouse until the tip of the pointer is touching the desired item on the computer screen.
Click	Quickly press and release the left mouse button.
Double-click	Quickly press and release the left mouse button twice.
Drag (or drag-and-drop)	Point to an object on-screen, hold down the left mouse button, and roll the mouse until the pointer is in position. Then release the mouse button.
Right-click	Quickly press and release the right mouse button.
Select	Hold down the left mouse button; move the mouse so the pointer moves from one side of an object to another. Then release the mouse button.

The pointer doesn't always look like an arrow. It can take other forms, depending on the action you are performing.

11. Save the Word document as *[your initials]***Practice17-3** using the same file type.

12. View the document in your browser. Check your blog links. Print the Web page in the browser.

13. Close your browser and close the Word document.

TEST YOURSELF 17-1

Rattlesnakes on the Web

It is not unusual to find Web pages on the Internet that are nothing more than a list of links to useful information. Evaluating and collecting quality links takes time and skill. You will create a document in Web page format that contains links about rattlesnakes.

1. Open the Word file **WP-Rattlesnakes**.

2. Start your browser and use a search engine to research rattlesnakes. Find at least four useful rattlesnake Web sites and list their Web addresses in your Word document.

3. Include a short description for each link.

4. Include in your list a link to a site that contains pictures of rattlesnakes. Copy one of the pictures into the document. Make the picture a hyperlink to the Web page it came from.

5. Apply a style to the picture. Below the picture, key a caption that describes the picture.

6. Make sure all the text in the document is consistently formatted, and make sure all the links are active (which means that you can click them to go to the Web address).

7. Apply a background page color to the document.

8. Save the document as *[your initials]***Test17-1** using the **Single File Web Page** file type.

9. Open the Web page in your browser to view it. Test the links and then close the browser.

10. Print the Word document; then close it.

TEST YOURSELF 17-2

World Music

Many styles of music exist throughout the world. People living in one part of the world often have no idea what styles are traditional in other parts of the world. You will create a document in Web page format that describes three styles of traditional world music. The document will include hyperlinks.

1. Open the Word file **WP-Music.** The document lists three styles of music you will research.

DID YOU KNOW?

Scientists estimate there are approximately 30 species of rattlesnake, with many sub-species.

DID YOU KNOW?

There were over 100 million Web sites in the world in 2007, compared to 18,000 in 1995.

TABLE G-2	Mouse Pointers	
Pointer	**Description**	
⌖ Pointer	Used to point to objects	
I I-beam	Used in keying, inserting, and selecting text	
↕ Two-headed Arrow	Used to change the size of objects or windows	
✛ Four-headed Arrow	Used to move objects	
🖑 Hand	Used in Window's Help system to display additional information	

Correct Keying Errors

As you key, you will make mistakes. Everyone does. Don't worry. It is easy to delete the error and key a correction.

To correct errors by using the Backspace key:

1. Move the I-beam I to the right of the incorrect character and click to position the insertion point there, if it is not there already.

2. Press the Backspace key to delete the character directly to the left of the insertion point. Press it again to delete the next character, and so on.

3. Key the correct character.

To correct errors by using the Delete key:

1. Move the I-beam I to the left of the incorrect character and click to position the insertion point there, if it is not there already.

2. Press the Delete key to delete the character directly to the right of the insertion point. Press it again to delete the next character, and so on.

3. Key the correct character.

To correct errors by selecting the incorrect text:

1. Select the incorrect text.

2. Key the correct characters.

Use the Arrow Keys

You can use the Arrow keys to move the insertion point in four different directions (up, down, left, and right). You can position the insertion point by using the Arrows keys instead of by clicking the mouse.

WINDOWS TIP

Refer to Table G-1 if you are not certain how to click the mouse.

WINDOWS TIP

Refer to Table G-1 if you are not certain how to select text by using the mouse.

5. In the Web site, at the top of the page, click the **Students** link. Under that, click **Programs**. You should see a list of continents. Copy the address for this page from the address bar of the browser.

6. In the most recent blog entry of your Word document, select the text "really cool places." Open the Insert Hyperlink dialog box. Paste the Web address in the **Address** text box. Click **OK**.

7. Start a new paragraph above the most recent blog entry. Key the day-after-tomorrow's date, followed by a colon and a space. Then key **If I were in this program, this would be my number 1 place to go.**

8. Go back to the Student Ambassador Web site in your browser. Locate a program that goes to a country you are interested in. Copy a picture from the Web page of that country.

9. Below your most recent blog entry, paste the picture you copied. Go back to the browser to copy the Web address for the page that contained the picture. In your document, create a hyperlink for the picture that links it to the Web address. Include a ScreenTip with the country name.

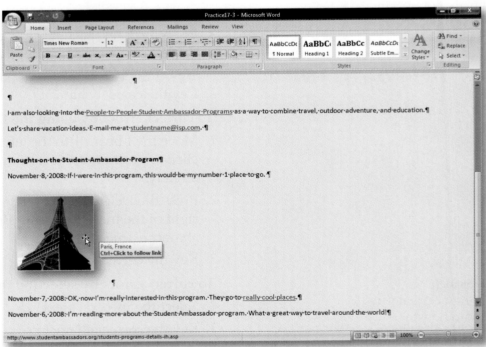

FIGURE 17-7
Web page with blog entries and hyperlinks

10. Size the picture and apply a picture style. Do not apply text wrapping—you want the picture positioned below the blog entry with no other text-wrapping around it. To left-align the picture, use the Align Text Left button ▤ on the Home tab.

ARROW KEYS

To move the insertion point by using the Arrow keys:

✦ Press → to move the insertion point one character to the right. Hold the key down to move the insertion point quickly past multiple characters to the right.

✦ Press ← to move the insertion point one character to the left. Hold the key down to move the insertion point quickly past multiple characters to the left.

✦ Press ↑ to move the insertion point one line up. Hold the key down to move the insertion point quickly up multiple lines.

✦ Press ↓ to move the insertion point one line down. Hold the key down to move the insertion point quickly down multiple lines.

Use the Windows Desktop

After you log on to Windows, the first thing you see is the *desktop*. Like the top of a desk, the Windows desktop is a work surface. Instead of having paper on it, the Windows desktop has icons on it. An *icon* is a picture that represents a feature or a program. A good example of an icon is the Recycle Bin on the desktop. This Windows feature contains files you have deleted from your computer.

FIGURE G-2
Windows desktop

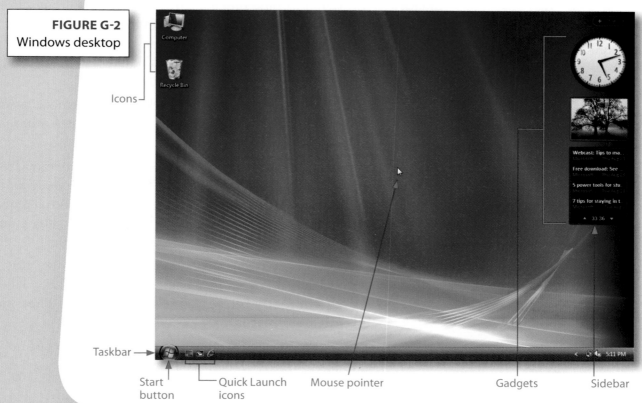

Icons

Taskbar →

Start button — Quick Launch icons — Mouse pointer — Gadgets — Sidebar

Creating a Blog (CONTINUED)

3. Below the title, key the blog entry. Use the **Blog Post** tab for formatting and styling. Use the **Insert** tab for inserting graphics and hyperlinks.

4. If you have a blog account, use the **Blog Post** tab to publish your blog post. If you don't have an account, save the blog post as a Word document and post it later.

To create blog posts on a Web page:

1. Designate a location on your Web page document for blog entries.

2. For your first blog entry, key the current date, followed by a colon and a space. Then key the thought or comment you want to post.

3. To key another blog entry, start a new paragraph above the first blog entry. Key the date, a colon, and the text you want to post. When adding a blog entry, always place the new entry above the previous entry.

4. Save the document and then open it in your browser for viewing.

BLOGGING TIP

A good idea is to have your blog on a large blogging site. These sites have many tools available to make blogging easier, and more people will see your postings.

PRACTICE 17-3

Create a Blog

You will add blog entries with hyperlinks to the bottom of the Word document used in the previous Practice. The first blog entry will have today's date, the second entry will be dated tomorrow, and the third entry is dated the day after that. This shows how daily entries are made.

1. At the end of your practice Web page document, press Enter and key the title **Thoughts on the Student Ambassador Program**. Make the title bold.

2. Below this title, turn off bold and key the current date, followed by a colon and a space. Then key **I'm reading more about the Student Ambassador program. What a great way to travel around the world!** (This is your first blog entry. See Figure 17-7 for what your entries will look like.)

3. Start a new paragraph above the first blog entry. Key tomorrow's date followed by a colon and a space. Then key **OK, now I'm really interested in this program. They go to really cool places.**

4. Click the Student Ambassador hyperlink in your document to open the Web site in your browser.

At the bottom of the desktop is the Windows *taskbar*. It contains the Start button 🪟, which opens a menu of options for starting programs and changing settings. The taskbar also shows Quick Launch icons of frequently used programs, and indicates programs that are running and files or folders that are open.

At the right of the screen is a new Windows feature called the *Sidebar.* It holds various *gadgets*, which are mini-programs that provide information at a glance. You can customize this feature or remove it from view.

To explore the Windows desktop:

1. Move the mouse pointer around the desktop without clicking a mouse button. Point to desktop icons to highlight them. Point to taskbar icons to identify them by name.

2. In the lower-right corner of the screen, click the time. Windows displays a clock and a calendar for the current month.

3. Click in a blank area of the desktop to close the display.

START WORD

Microsoft Word is a word processing program. You can start Word from the Windows taskbar.

To start Microsoft Word from the Windows taskbar:

1. Move the mouse to point to the Start button 🪟 in the lower-left corner of the screen. Whenever you point to a button or icon in Windows or any Microsoft program, a box appears with the button name and sometimes a description of the button's function.

2. Click the Start button 🪟. The Start menu appears.

3. Locate **Microsoft Office Word 2007** on the left side of the menu and click it to start Word. If Microsoft Word is not listed on the Start menu, click **All Programs** to display a list of all the programs on your computer. Click **Microsoft Office** (you might need to scroll down the list to locate it) and then click **Microsoft Office Word 2007**.

Start Microsoft Word

WINDOWS TIP

Desktop icons require double-clicking to open. Taskbar items need only one click.

Creating a Blog

A *blog post* is an entry you publish to a blog site. Blogs consist of a series of entries listed in reverse chronological order. This means the most recent entry is at the top of the page, with the second most recent entry under the first.

Word provides a special feature for creating a new blog post. You need to have a blog account to actually publish the blog post. Another way to create blog entries is to simply key them directly onto a Web page.

To use Word's New Blog Post feature:

1. Click the Office button 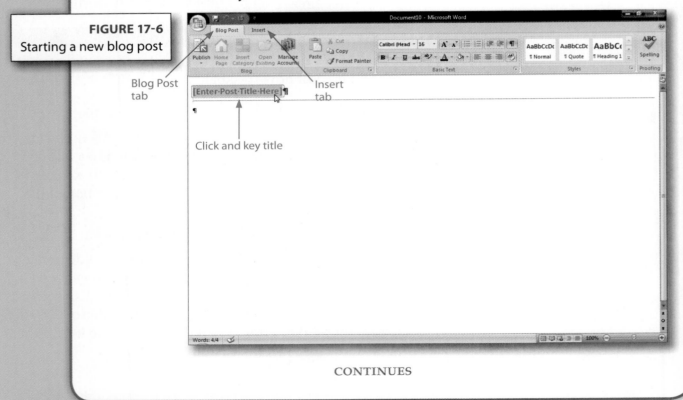 and choose **New**. In the New Document dialog box, double-click **New blog post**. A dialog box might appear, asking you to register your account. If you have an account, click **Register <u>N</u>ow**. If not, click **Register <u>L</u>ater**.

2. In the blog post window, click the placeholder **[Enter Post Title Here]** and key a title for the entry.

FIGURE 17-6
Starting a new blog post

Blog Post tab

Insert tab

Click and key title

CONTINUES

WINDOWS TIP

The left side of the Start menu lists the most recently used programs. Your menu may look different from the one in the figure.

UNDERSTAND THE WORD WINDOW

When Word starts, it appears as a window on the desktop. You can have more than one window open at a time. The *active window* is the window in which you are working. The *title bar* displays the name of the current document open in the active window. Word always starts with a blank document titled "Document1." At the bottom of the screen, the taskbar shows which programs or windows are currently open.

Resize the Word Window

When you work in Word, you can reduce the size of the window to reveal other items on the desktop or maximize the window to cover the desktop completely.

To resize the window by using Window buttons or the mouse:

1. Click the Minimize button ⊟ on the title bar to reduce the window to a button on the taskbar. The button is labeled with the name of the current window, "Document1 – Microsoft Word." See Figure G-4 on the next page.

2. Click the Word taskbar button to maximize the window.

3. Click the Restore Down button ⊡ on the title bar to reduce the size of the window. When a window is reduced, the Restore Down button ⊡ changes to a Maximize button ⊡.

11. Press the Spacebar or the Enter key at the end of the new paragraph to make the e-mail address a hyperlink.

12. Use your browser to search for an appropriate link you can attach to the picture in your document. Once you have located a good Web site, copy the Web address.

13. In your Word document, right-click the picture and choose **Hyperlink** from the shortcut menu. Paste the Web address in the **Address** text box.

14. Click **ScreenTip** and key a brief description of the Web site link. Click **OK**, and then click **OK** again.

15. Point to your document picture to test the ScreenTip. Press Ctrl and click the picture to test the hyperlink. Your browser displays the Web site.

16. Save the Word document as *[your initials]***Practice17-2** using the same file type.

17. Click the Start button 🪟 again and choose *[your initials]* **Practice17-2** from the **Recent Items** list. The revised document appears in a browser window. Check your links and the ScreenTip for your picture.

INTERNET EXPLORER TIP

If you are using Internet Explorer 7.0, the Web site linked to the picture appears in the browser on a new tab. You can display several Web sites at the same time with the tab feature.

FIGURE 17-5
Document in browser

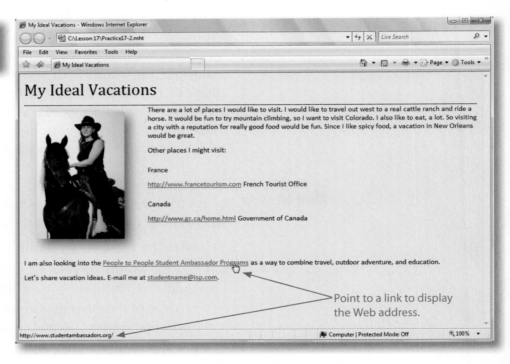

18. Close the browser windows. Leave the Word document open.

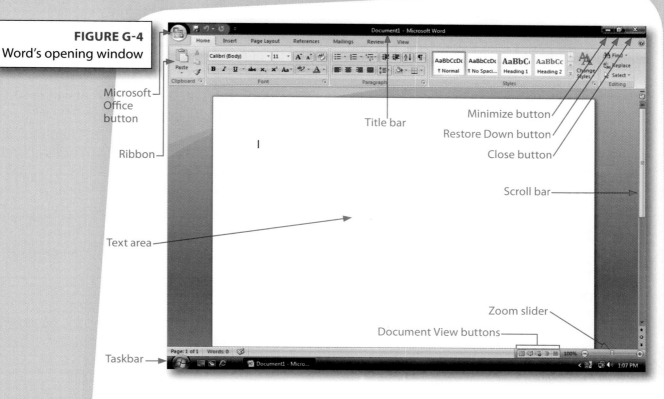

Microsoft Office button

Ribbon

Text area

Taskbar

Title bar

Minimize button
Restore Down button
Close button

Scroll bar

Zoom slider
Document View buttons

WINDOWS TIP

Refer to Table G-2 if you are not certain what the various mouse pointers look like.

4. Click the Maximize button 🔲 on the title bar to enlarge the window to fill the entire desktop again.

5. Click the Restore Down button 🔲 again to reduce the size of the window.

6. Move the pointer ☖ to the border of the window. When the pointer changes to a two-headed arrow ↕, hold down the mouse button and use the mouse to drag the border and change the window's size. See Figure G-5 on the next page. Then release the mouse button.

Move a Window

You can move an open window freely around the desktop by dragging it by its title bar.

To move a window that is not maximized:

1. Position the mouse pointer ☖ on the title bar and hold down the left mouse button.

2. Use the mouse to drag the window. Then release the mouse button.

Key Text

In a blank document window, you key text in the *text area*. The insertion point is located within the text area. The mouse pointer ☖ takes the shape of an I-beam ⌶ when it is in the text area, but it changes back to a pointer when you point to an element outside the text area.

PRACTICE 17-2

Insert and Edit Hyperlinks

1. With your Web page document still open in Word, start another paragraph and key **Other places I might visit:**

2. Think of two countries you want to visit. Start your browser and use a search engine to find an interesting Web site for each country. Copy each Web site address from the address bar of the browser and paste it into your Word document, below the last text you keyed. You might need to press the Spacebar after a Web address to make it appear as a hyperlink.

3. Include descriptions for the hyperlinks, such as the country name and/or Web site name.

4. Below your link information, key the following paragraph:

FIGURE 17-3

```
I am also looking into the People to People Student Ambassador
Programs as a way to combine travel, outdoor adventure, and
education.
```

5. Select the text "People to People Student Ambassador Programs." On the **Insert** tab, in the Links group, click **Hyperlink**.

6. In the Insert Hyperlink dialog box, key in the **Address** text box **www.studentambassadors.com** and click **OK**. The document text is now formatted as a hyperlink.

WORD TIP

When you key "www." in the Address text box of the Insert Hyperlink dialog box, Word automatically adds the prefix http:// for you.

7. Point to the new hyperlink text without clicking. A ScreenTip shows the Web address.

8. Right-click the hyperlink text you just created. Choose **Edit Hyperlink** from the shortcut menu. The Web address is incorrect. Change the suffix ".com" to **.org** and click **OK**.

9. Hold down the Ctrl key and click the hyperlink. Your browser starts, with the Web site displayed. (If your browser does not show the Web site, check the spelling of your Web address.)

10. In the Word document, start a new paragraph and key the following text, replacing "*[yourname]*" with your first name. This is a fake e-mail address. If you want, you can use a real e-mail address.

FIGURE 17-4

```
Let's share vacation ideas. E-mail me at [yourname]@isp.com.
```

FIGURE G-5
Using the two-headed
arrow to resize
a window

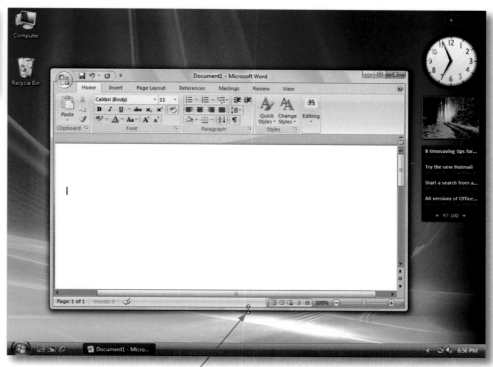

Two-headed arrow

You correct keying errors by using the Backspace key or the Delete key or by selecting the incorrect text and then using the Backspace key or the Delete key.

EXPLORE WORD'S COMMAND CENTERS

Word's opening window contains many features you'll use to perform various tasks. The first areas to explore are the Ribbon, the Office button, and the Quick Access toolbar. Once you learn how to use these features, you will be able to create a new document, key text, and save the document.

Explore the Ribbon

The portion of the Word window just below the title bar is called the *Ribbon*. It displays common Word features so you can find them quickly and easily. The Ribbon is organized by tabs, and each tab represents a major area of activity. Tabs contain groups of related items. These items are commands in the form of either a button, a menu, or a box for choosing or entering options.

To display and hide commands on the Ribbon:

1. Click the **Home** tab on the Ribbon, if it is not already selected. The **Home** tab displays groups of related commands. The names of the groups appear across the bottom of the Ribbon (for example, Clipboard, Font, Paragraph).

Inserting and Editing Hyperlinks (CONTINUED)

To key or copy a hyperlink, use one of the following methods:

◆ Key a Web address or e-mail address in the document. Press the Spacebar after the address to automatically format the address as a hyperlink.

◆ Select a Web address from the address bar of the browser or from a Web page. Copy the text and then paste it in the document. This ensures accuracy of the Web address.

◆ Right-click any other hyperlink (an image or text) on a Web page. Choose **Copy** from the shortcut menu, and paste the item into your document.

To create a custom hyperlink:

1. In your Word document, select the text or graphic that you want to make into a hyperlink.

2. On the **Insert** tab, in the Links group, click **Hyperlink**. In the Insert Hyperlink dialog box, under **Link to**, make sure **Existing File or Web Page** is selected. This is the option to link to a Web address.

3. Key the Web address in the **Address** text box.

<table>
<tr><td>

FIGURE 17-2
Insert Hyperlink dialog box

</td><td>

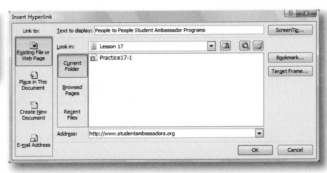

</td></tr>
</table>

4. To format the hyperlink with a ScreenTip (descriptive text that will appear when you point to the hyperlink), click **ScreenTip** and then key the text you want to appear. Click **OK**.

5. Click **OK** in the Hyperlink dialog box to apply the settings.

To edit and delete a hyperlink:

1. Right-click the hyperlink in your document. Choose **Edit Hyperlink** from the shortcut menu.

2. Make the necessary changes; you might want to add a ScreenTip or modify the Web address. Click **OK**.

3. To remove a hyperlink from text, right-click the hyperlink and choose **Remove Hyperlink** from the shortcut menu.

2. Move the pointer over some of the **Home** tab buttons. Pointing to a button reveals a box with the button's name and function.

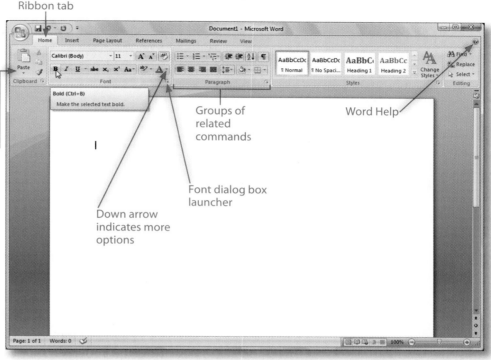

FIGURE G-6
Commands organized
on the Ribbon

Ribbon tab

Ribbon

Groups of
related
commands

Word Help

Font dialog box
launcher

Down arrow
indicates more
options

3. In the Font group of commands, locate the Font Color ⃞ button. Notice the small down arrow to the right of the button. The arrow indicates the availability of additional command options.

4. Click the down arrow to display a list of font color options. Click the arrow again to close the list.

5. In the same area of the Ribbon, click the arrow to the right of the word **Font**. This arrow is a dialog box launcher: it displays a dialog box of additional font commands. Close the dialog box.

6. Click another tab on the Ribbon to view the commands. Table G-3 lists a description of the types of commands on each tab.

7. Double-click the active Ribbon tab. The tab names remain, but the commands are hidden. This is a way of minimizing the Ribbon when you want more space for your document.

8. Double-click any tab name on the minimized Ribbon to restore the full Ribbon.

WORD TIP

You can click the Microsoft Office Word Help icon ⓦ on the right side of the Ribbon to activate a complete Help resource for all of Word's features.

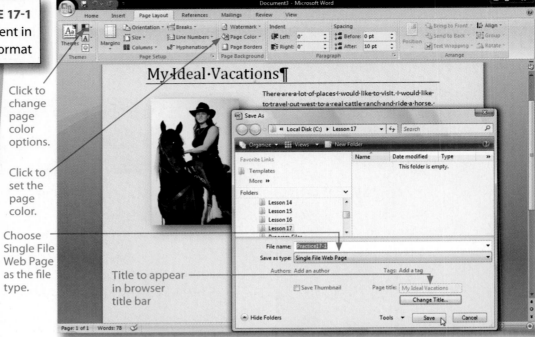

FIGURE 17-1
Saving a document in
Web page format

Click to change page color options.

Click to set the page color.

Choose Single File Web Page as the file type.

Title to appear in browser title bar

7. With your document still open in Word, click the Windows Start button 🪟. From the list at the right, click **Recent Items**. Choose your Web page file from the list. The file appears in your Internet browser. Notice your Web page title in the title bar of the browser.

8. Close the browser. Leave the document open in Word.

Microsoft Word

Inserting and Editing Hyperlinks

A Web site is only as useful as the information it contains. A carefully selected list of relevant hyperlinks often adds a great deal of value to the pages of a Web site. You can also use hyperlinks to navigate from page to page within a Web site.

There are several ways to insert a hyperlink in your Web page document. You can key a Web or e-mail address directly in the document, copy a hyperlink from a Web page and paste it in the document, or use the Insert Hyperlink dialog box to create customized hyperlinks for text or images.

CONTINUES

TABLE G-3	Tabs on the Ribbon
Tab	**Description**
Home	Contains commands used to edit and change the appearance of document text.
Insert	Contains commands used to insert elements in a document, such as a hyperlink or picture.
Page Layout	Contains commands used to change the overall design of a document and how document elements occupy space on the page.
References	Contains commands typically used for creating reports, such as adding a table of contents or footnotes.
Mailings	Contains commands used to create envelopes and labels, and to perform mass mailings.
Review	Contains commands used to check the spelling or grammar in a document, and to perform an online document review by adding comments or suggesting revisions.
View	Contains commands used to change the way documents appear on the screen, and to display certain screen items such as the ruler.

Explore the Office Button

The Microsoft Office button is the launching pad for basic Word functions. Click this button to open a menu with commands such as creating a new document; opening an existing document; saving, printing, and closing a document; and sending a document as an e-mail attachment.

To the immediate right of the Microsoft Office button is the Quick Access toolbar. It contains command buttons for frequently used functions, such as saving a document and undoing an action.

FIGURE G-7
Microsoft Office menu

Microsoft Office button

Menu options

List of recently opened documents

Quick Access toolbar with Save, Undo, and Redo commands

Developing a Simple Web Page (CONTINUED)

3. Click the Office button 🏢 and choose **Save As**. Locate the folder where you save your files. Key a filename in the **File name** text box.

4. Open the **Save as type** drop-down list and choose **Single File Web Page**. This Save option compresses all the Web page content, including images, into one file.

5. In the Save As dialog box, click **Change Title**. In the Set Page Title dialog box, key a title that will appear in the title bar of the browser. Click the **Save** button.

6. Preview the Web page in Web Layout view. (The document will automatically appear in Web Layout view after you save it in Web page format.)

7. View the page in your Internet browser by clicking the Windows Start button 🪟, choosing **Recent Items**, and clicking your Web page filename.

WORD TIP

If you don't like the default background colors, in the Themes group, click the Theme Colors 🔳▾ button and choose another group of colors.

WORD TIP

The filename extension for Single File Web Page is .mht. A file saved in Web page format can be read without using Microsoft Word.

PRACTICE 17-1

Develop a Simple Web Page

1. Open Word. In a new blank document, key **My Ideal Vacations** as the document heading.

2. Below the heading, key a three- to five-sentence paragraph that describes one or more places you would like to visit on vacation.

3. Format the text as desired. On the **Page Layout** tab, in the Page Background group, click **Page Color**. Choose a color to apply to the page.

4. Below your text, insert a clip that relates to your content. Style the image as desired.

5. Click the Office button 🏢 and choose **Save As**.

6. In the Save As dialog box, locate your document folder. Save the file with the filename *[your initials]*Practice17-1. Click the **Save as type** down arrow and choose **Single File Web Page**. Click **Change Title** and set the Web page title to **My Ideal Vacations**. Click **Save**. The document is saved in Web page format and now appears in Web Layout view (the location of your picture might have changed).

To open and close the Microsoft Office menu:

1. Click the Microsoft Office button 🔘. A menu appears with a list of commands. Each command is identified by an icon (see Table G-4). To the right of the menu is a list of recently opened documents.

2. Without clicking the mouse, move the pointer down the list of commands on the menu. Menu items with a right arrow have additional menu options.

3. Click the Microsoft Office button 🔘 again to close the menu. You can also press the Esc key to close a menu.

TABLE G-4	Microsoft Office Menu Items
Command	**Description**
📄 **New**	Starts a new blank document
📂 **Open**	Opens an existing document
💾 **Save**	Saves a document
🖫 **Save As**	Provides options to save a copy of a document
🖨 **Print**	Provides options to print and preview a document
📝 **Prepare**	Provides options to prepare a document for distribution
📧 **Send**	Provides options to send a copy of a document to other people
🖥 **Publish**	Provides options to distribute a document to others
📑 **Close**	Closes a document

CREATE A NEW DOCUMENT

You create a new document by opening the Microsoft Office menu and choosing the **New** command. Remember that you can have multiple documents open at the same time because they are each in a separate window within Word.

Develop a Web Page and a Blog

LEARN

A New Way to Publish

Everyone with something to say can now say it on the Web. If you want to communicate to the world, Web sites and blogging give you the power of publishing without relying on traditional print media.

A Web site is made of Web pages that organize information into small, manageable amounts. An individual's Web site can be as small as one page, while a large business or government Web site might have hundreds or thousands of pages.

A *blog* is a Web site that acts as a personal online journal. The word blog comes from the words "Web log." A blog is updated often and is usually devoted to a specific topic. Blogs may be written by one person or a group. Web sites and blogs exist on every imaginable subject.

Microsoft Word

Developing a Simple Web Page

Web designers typically use specific programs to develop Web sites. However, you can use Word to create a document and save it in Web page format. A document saved in this format can be published to the Internet, or it can be posted on a company's intranet. An *intranet* is a private computer network within a company, which uses Internet technology to provide information to employees.

When you create a document that is intended for online use, you can apply formatting not typically applied to printed documents, such as page background colors. After creating and formatting your document, you can preview it in Web Layout view, which shows how it would appear in a browser.

To develop a simple Web page:

1. Start Word. In a new blank document, key the information for your Web page. Or, open an existing document you want to save as a Web page.
2. Apply formatting and include images as desired. To apply a page background color, click the **Page Layout** tab. In the Page Background group, click **Page Color** and choose a color. Be sure to use a background color and font color that make your text easy to read.

CONTINUES

Create a New Document

To open a new blank document from the Microsoft Office menu:

1. Click the Microsoft Office button.
2. Choose **New** on the menu. The New Document dialog box appears.

FIGURE G-8
Creating a new document

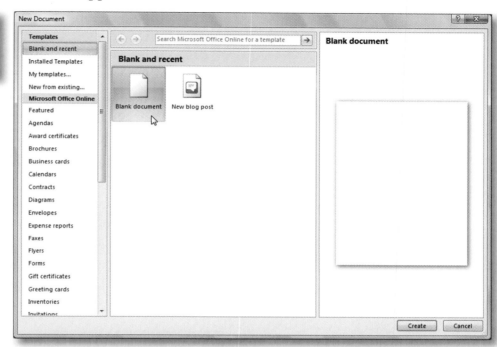

3. Double-click **Blank Document** (or click **Blank Document** once to select it and then click the **Create** button). Word opens a new blank document. If "Document1" was the label for the last document you had open, this document will be labeled "Document2."

Close a Document Without Saving

When you close a document without saving it, none of the work you have done in the document is saved.

To use a button to close a document without saving:

1. Click the Close button ☒ in the upper-right corner of the document window.

FIGURE G-9
Closing an open document by using the Close button

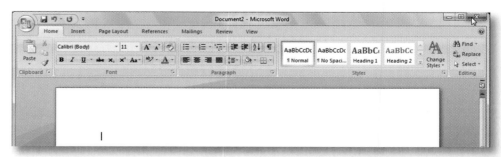

FIGURE 16-5
Dragonflies are the fastest insects on earth, capable of flying for short durations at speeds up to 30 mph.

DID YOU KNOW?

Medieval physicians placed a frog in the mouth of sufferers to cure a cough. Hence, the saying "frog in your throat."

WORD TIP

To avoid errors in keying the Web address for a source, copy the address from the browser address bar and paste it in your document.

TEST YOURSELF 16-2

Dragonfly Vision

You will use a search engine to write a multiple-page report on dragonfly vision and include an image.

1. Key **www.google.com** in your browser to initiate a search.

2. Search on any or all of the following sets of keywords:

   dragonflies +vision
   dragonflies +eyes
   dragonflies +visual ability
   dragonflies +visual sense

3. Scan the results. Gather information from at least three different Web sites.

4. Write a multiple-page report on dragonfly vision. Use the appropriate formatting and include a cover page and page numbering.

5. Search for an image of dragonfly eyes. Copy it into the body of your report and center it on the page.

6. Include a bibliography page for at least two Web sources. Include a source for the image.

7. Save the file as *[your initials]***Test16-2.** Print and close the document.

TEST YOURSELF 16-3

What's in a Saying?

We use them all the time, but do we know the origin of old sayings? In this project, you'll use search engines to research the meaning of the following old sayings: "none of your beeswax," "handwriting on the wall," "don't beat a dead horse," "love is blind," and "it's raining cats and dogs."

1. Create a multiple-page report that explains the origins of these old sayings. Use at least two different search engines for your research.

2. Format each saying attractively and key its origin below it.

3. Below each description, key the name of the search engine you used to find the information.

4. Key the Web site address for each description below the search engine name.

5. Format your report appropriately, including a cover page and page numbering.

6. Save the file as *[your initials]***Test16-3.** Print and close the document.

2. When Word asks if you want to save the changes to your document, click **No**.

To use a menu command to close a document without saving:
1. Click the Microsoft Office button 🗔.
2. Choose **Close** on the menu.
3. When Word asks if you want to save the changes to your document, click **No**.

OPEN AN EXISTING DOCUMENT

A document is saved as a *file*, which is a basic unit of storage on the computer. Files are stored in folders. A *folder* is a container for programs and files, and its icon looks like a manila folder. Folders are used to organize information on the computer. They can contain files, and they can also contain other folders. You can store folders and files on your computer's hard drive, on a CD in your CD drive, or on the hard drive of another computer that you can access. Sometimes you must search up or down several levels in a folder to locate a particular file.

Open an Existing Document You use the Microsoft Office menu to open an existing document. After you open an existing document, you can edit it or add new material to it.

To open an existing document:
1. Click the Microsoft Office button 🗔. Choose **Open** from the menu. The Open dialog box appears.

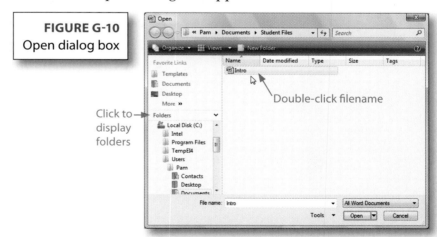

FIGURE G-10
Open dialog box

Click to display folders

Double-click filename

WINDOWS TIP

Another way to locate a file is to key the filename in the Search box of the dialog box.

2. If the folders on your computer are not displayed, click **Folders** (see Figure G-10). Go to the drive and folder where your student files are located. (If you don't know where your student files are located, ask your teacher.)

5. To the right of the search text box, click the button **Search the Web**. Google displays Web sites that have clip-art images of chocolate.

6. Find a clip you like from either the Web search or the image search. Right-click the clip and choose **Copy** from the short-cut menu.

7. Start Word and open the file **WP-Chocolate**.

8. Paste the clip in the document. Position, size, and style it attractively on the page.

9. Add your introductory information to the report (which should not exceed one page).

10. Save the file as *[your initials]***Practice16-3**. Print and close the document.

TEST YOURSELF 16-1

DID YOU KNOW?

In 1804, New York was the first state to require right-hand travel on all public highways. By the Civil War, the practice was followed in every state.

A Driving History Question

Settlers in Colonial America copied many things from their English ancestors. Why did Colonial Americans adopt the practice of driving on the right side of the road rather than the left? A search engine will help you find the answer.

1. Key **www.google.com** on the address bar of your browser and press Enter.

2. Key **driving history** +**right side of road** in the search text box and press Enter.

3. Scan the results and click the hyperlink text of a likely source. Look for an answer on the Web site. Select the text containing relevant information you wish to copy.

4. Right-click the selected text and choose **Copy**.

5. Start Word and open the document **WP-RightSide**.

6. Paste the copied text below "Answer:"

7. Edit the text you have copied to provide a brief answer to the question "Why did Colonial Americans adopt the practice of driving on the right side of the road rather than the left?" Format the text appropriately.

8. Insert a bibliography page with the Web source. Use the MLA style for online sources.

9. Insert a cover page with the appropriate information. Add page numbers to pages 2 and 3 of the document.

10. Save the file as *[your initials]***Test16-1.** Print and close the document.

3. Locate the file **Intro**.

4. Double-click the file to open it (or click the file once to select it and then click the **Open** button).

Change How You View a Document

Word gives you several ways to view a document, depending on the type of document you have open and your own working style. You might want to see an entire page in the document window or magnify a portion of the document.

There are also elements you might want to display while working in a document. For example, you can display the *rulers*, which show the size of the page and document formatting features such as margins and tabs. You can also display the space characters, tabs, and paragraph marks in your document.

FIGURE G-11
Document in
Print Layout view

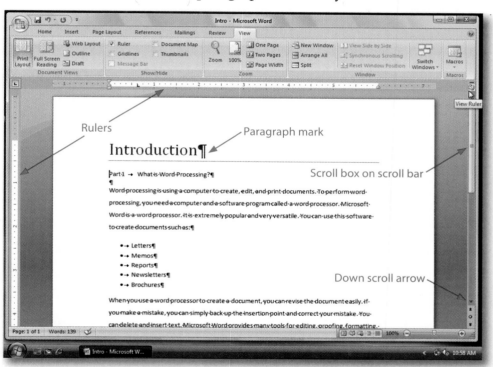

To change how you view a document:

1. Display the **View** tab on the Ribbon. In the Document Views group of commands, choose **Print Layout** if it is not already selected. Point to some of the other view options to display their descriptions.

2. Choose the view **Full Screen Reading**. This view shows the entire document and minimal command buttons. Click **Close** in the upper-right corner (or press the Esc key) to restore Print Layout view.

WORD TIP

You can also change how you view a document by using the Document View buttons at the lower-right of the window.

Windows Internet Explorer

Searching for Images

If you need clip art or a photograph for a document, you can use a search engine to search for images. You can then copy an image and paste it into Word.

To search for images:

1. Using Google as your search engine, click the link **Images** in the upper-left corner of the Google window.
2. Enter keywords in the search box for the type of image you need. Press Enter.
3. Browse the results. Right-click an image to copy it and then paste it into your document.

PRACTICE 16-3

Search for Images

1. If Google is not displayed, use the Back button ⬅ or the Recent Pages menu to go to the Google home page.
2. Click the link **Images** in the upper-left corner of the Google window.
3. Key **chocolate clip art** in the search text box and press Enter. Google performs the search and displays the results, which are pages of chocolate clip art.
4. Browse the image results (click **Next** at the bottom of the screen to view more pages of clips).

FIGURE 16-4
Searching for images

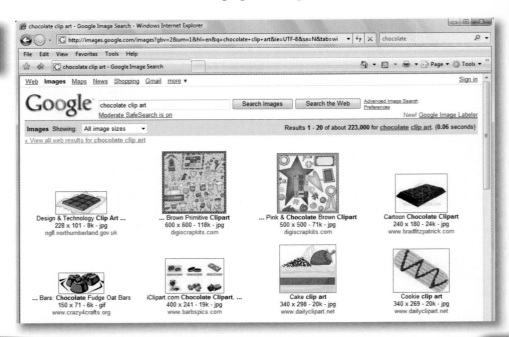

3. In the Show/Hide group of commands, click **Ruler**. Rulers appear along the top and left of the document.

4. Display the **Home** tab on the Ribbon. In the Paragraph group of commands, click the Show/Hide ¶ button ⬚. Now you can see the marks and symbols to indicate spaces between words, paragraph marks, and tabs in text. Showing these marks as you work is often helpful.

5. To the right of the top ruler, click the View Ruler button ⬚ to hide the ruler.

Use the Scroll Bars

Depending on the document view, you can use *scroll bars* to move right or left and up or down in a document to display text that doesn't fit on a single screen.

To scroll in a document:

1. With the document in Print Layout view, locate the scroll bar at the right side of the document window (see Figure G-11).

2. Click the down scroll arrow ⬚ to scroll down one line at a time until you see the end of the document. Then click the up scroll arrow ⬚ to scroll up one line at a time.

3. Drag the scroll box up or down to scroll in the document more quickly.

WINDOWS TIP

Refer to Table G-1 if you are not certain how to drag an object by using the mouse.

NAME AND SAVE A DOCUMENT

A document that has never been named or saved can be lost if you have a power failure or a computer hardware problem. The first step in saving a document is to give it a *filename*. A filename can have up to 260 characters, excluding the characters / \ > < * ? " : and |. You can include spaces and use uppercase or lowercase letters.

A filename also has a *filename extension*. This is a four-letter identifier that is automatically added to the end of a filename. The four letters help to identify the application in which a file was created. For example, Word adds the extension .docx to the end of its filenames. If you do not see file extensions at the end of filenames, your computer has been set to hide them.

You can use either the Save or Save As command to save a document. Use Save As when you name and save a document for the first time or save an existing document under a new name. Use Save to update an existing document.

SEARCH TIP

If you do not receive the number of hits you expected, check your spelling. Minor spelling errors can alter your results significantly.

4. Change the search text to **"dark chocolate" anti-cancer** and press Enter. Enclosing keywords in quotation marks tells the search engine to find only those matches that include the entire phrase "dark chocolate." Google narrows the search to about 18,000 hits.

5. Browse the list of hits. Notice the change in Web sites and that the hits are more closely related to your topic. Suppose you want to further refine the search results to include hits that contain specific information on antioxidants. (These are chemicals that help prevent cancer.)

6. Change the search text to **"dark chocolate" anti-cancer +antioxidants** and press Enter. (Make sure you include a space before the plus sign but not after it.) The plus sign tells the search engine that all hits must contain the word "anti-oxidants." Google narrows the search to fewer hits than the previous search.

7. Change the search text to **"dark chocolate" anti-cancer +antioxidants –.com** and press Enter. (Make sure you include a space before the minus sign.) The minus sign tells the search engine to exclude any hits from commercial (or business) sites that might have products to sell. Google now displays about 500 hits. You have refined your search to include only very relevant Web pages from more objective Web sites.

FIGURE 16-3
Using search operators

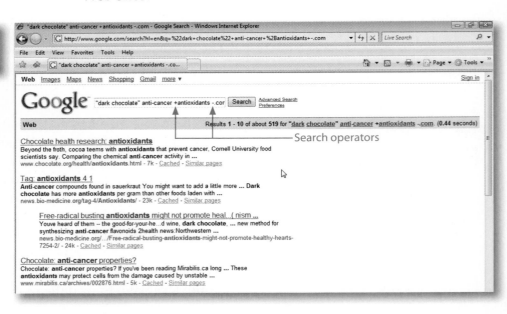

8. Leave the browser open.

Name and Save a Document

To name and save a new document or save an existing document with a new name:

1. Click the Microsoft Office button and click **Save <u>As</u>** (do not click the right arrow to choose another option).

2. In the Save As dialog box, display the folders list to locate the drive and folder into which you will be saving all your files. If you are not sure which drive and folder to use, ask your teacher.

3. Key a new document name in the **File name** text box.

WORD TIP

In this course, you typically save your files by using your initials and an assigned name. Together these make up the filename.

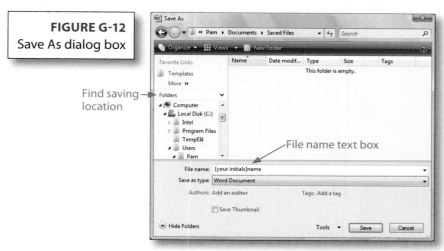

FIGURE G-12
Save As dialog box

Find saving location

File name text box

4. Click the **Save** button.

To update an existing document:

Click the Save button on the Quick Access toolbar at the top left of the document window or open the Microsoft Office menu and choose **Save.**

PRINT A DOCUMENT

After you create and save a document, printing it is easy. However, you should get in the habit of saving your document before you print it. That way, you will be less likely to forget to save it.

Your teacher will tell you when to print and what printer to use if more than one is available. Your teacher will also ask you to key your initials on your documents so you can identify them easily.

Print a Document

To print a document by using the default printer settings, open the Microsoft Office menu and choose **Print.**

To print a document with specific printer settings:

1. Open the Microsoft Office menu and choose **Print** (you can choose it from either the left or right side of the menu). See Figure G-13 on the next page.

Refining a Search by Using Search Operators

Search engines often create search results that include millions of Web pages. A good idea is to limit these results to the most useful ones. The most basic way to refine a search is to add more specific keywords. You can also use *search operators*. These are keyword punctuation marks that instruct the search engine to include, exclude, or specify the order of your keywords. Table 16-1 shows some common search operators.

TABLE 16-1	Common Search Operators
Search Operator	**Use and Function**
+word	Placing the plus sign before the search word requires the search word to be present in all search results.
–word	Placing the minus sign before the search word excludes the search word from all search results.
"multiword phrase"	Placing the search phrase in quotation marks limits the search to results that contain only this *exact* phrase.

PRACTICE 16-2

Refine a Search

1. Click the down arrow next to the Forward button ⊖. This displays the Recent Pages menu, which lists the Web pages you've just visited. Choose **Google** from the list.

2. In the search text box, delete just the keyword "health" and press Enter. Google searches for "dark chocolate" and displays the top matches from over 7,500,000 results. Browse through the first page of hits.

3. Change the search text to **dark chocolate anti-cancer** and press Enter. Google displays over 58,000 hits, much less than the 7,500,000 it found in the previous search. By simply adding another keyword ("anti-cancer"), you have narrowed your search results.

FIGURE G-13
Choosing the
Print command

2. In the Print dialog box, choose the settings you want.

3. Click **OK**.

CLOSE A DOCUMENT

When you have finished with a document, you can close it. Before Word will close the document, however, it may ask if you want to save the document.

To close an open document:

1. Open the Microsoft Office menu and choose **Close**.

2. If Word asks you to respond, click **Yes** to save and close the document. (You would click **No** to close the document without saving it or click **Cancel** to return to the document.)

CLOSE PROGRAMS

Your teacher will tell you what to do at the end of class. You may be asked to save your work and close your files, or close Word and return to Windows, or close all programs and shut down your computer.

Close Word and Return to Windows

To quit Word and return to the Windows desktop, click the Close button ❌ on the title bar, or open the Microsoft Office menu and choose **Exit Word**.

Shut Down Your Computer

Do not shut down your computer unless you are directed to by your teacher.

4. Review the first page of results. Some of these Web sites show information from books, some are articles, and some have products for sale. Now you'll compare Google's search results to those obtained by another search engine.

5. Key **www.dmoz.org** on the address bar and press Enter. The Open Directory Project home page appears. You will see search categories and a search text box.

FIGURE 16-2
Open Directory Project home page

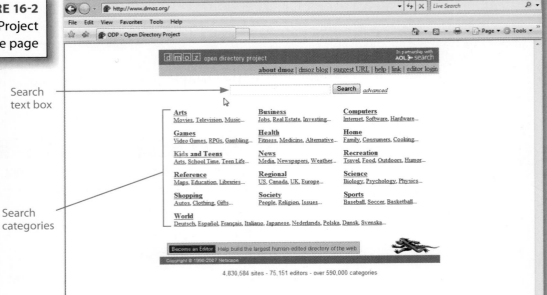

Search text box

Search categories

SEARCH TIP

The Open Directory Project search engine is the largest noncommercial human-edited search engine. It is compiled and maintained by volunteer editors and does not use spiders.

6. Key **dark chocolate health** in the search text box and press Enter. Open Directory returns just a few results. Note that there are few product-related sites in your results. Search engines produce results that vary in the quantity of sites and the quality of the information they contain.

7. Leave the browser open.

To close all programs and shut down your computer from the Windows desktop:

1. Click the Start button .

2. Click the right arrow at the lower-right of the Start menu and then choose **Shut Down**. This will close any open programs, shut down Windows, and turn off your computer.

FIGURE G-14
Closing Windows
and shutting down
your computer

Performing a Search (CONTINUED)

3. Key keywords into the search text box. Press Enter. The search engine creates one or more pages of results. The first page of these results appears in your browser.

4. Review the search results and click on any of the links. Your browser takes you to that Web site.

5. Click the Back button 🔙 to return to your search results and view more matches.

PRACTICE 16-1

SEARCH TIP

Search engines often use spiders to collect information from Web sites. A *spider* is a computer program that automatically collects information that is stored in a search engine.

Use Search Engines

You will use two search engines to research the positive health effects of dark chocolate and compare the results.

1. Connect to the Internet and start your Web browser.

2. Key **www.google.com** on the address bar and press Enter. The Google search engine home page appears.

3. Key **dark chocolate health** in the search text box and press Enter. Google performs the search and displays the top matches from over a million results. Notice that the keywords are highlighted in bold for each match. On the right side of the screen, Google displays sponsored links related to your search topic.

FIGURE 16-1
Performing a Google search

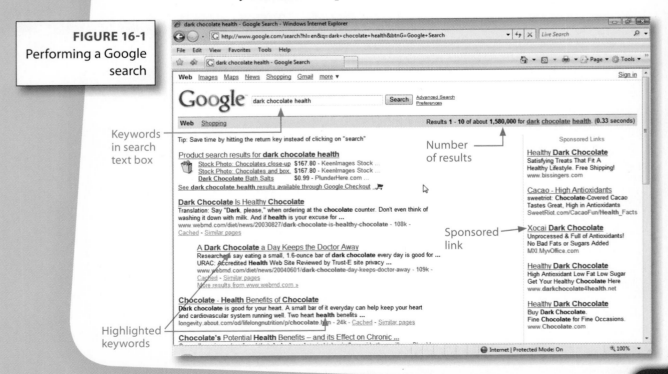

Keywords in search text box

Number of results

Sponsored link

Highlighted keywords

Keying Correctly

OBJECTIVES

After completing this portion of the Introduction, you will be able to:

☑ Explain how to choose appropriate equipment.

☑ Adjust a workstation for safety.

☑ Demonstrate correct keying posture, including positioning of the body, arms, and hands.

☑ Demonstrate how to avoid stress when keying.

☑ Explain the long-term benefits of keying correctly.

☑ Discuss bad keying habits and how to break them.

BREAKING BAD HABITS

If you have been keying before this class, you might also need to break bad habits you have developed.

The human body is not designed for long sessions of repetitive movement. You might even know someone who has strained their hands and fingers by playing video games. Keyboarding can present similar dangers. When you key, you repeat many small movements with your hands and fingers. You might be keying for a long time. If you position yourself correctly, however, you can avoid strain and fatigue.

Even if you do not practice healthy keying techniques, you might not experience any problems while you are young and flexible. However, over the years, if you don't begin to key correctly, you will repeat thousands of stressful movements. You risk painful long-lasting injury that can reduce the quality of your life and your ability to work. It pays to develop healthy keying habits now.

Keying correctly means:

✦ Choosing the appropriate equipment

✦ Adjusting the equipment to suit your needs

✦ Developing the correct posture

✦ Avoiding stressful positions

Search for Online Information

LEARN

Search Engine Basics

The Internet contains billions of pages of information. In fact, there are so many of them that no one really knows how many there are. Without search engines, finding specific information in this huge Web of data would be impossible. *Search engines* are indexes of information that you can search by topic. The search results contain hyperlinks so you can simply click on the Web sites that interest you.

How Search Engines Work

Most search engines *rank* or order the results of a search from the most relevant to the least relevant. The highest-ranking sites contain the most references to your search topic and appear first in your search results. Some sites appear because companies pay for high rankings. These are called *pay-for-placement sites*. Even though they might not be the most relevant sites, they appear at the top of your results. Search engines usually display the number of Web pages or hits found. *Hits* are Web site addresses and descriptions that contain references to your search topic.

Here are some of the more popular search engines:

- ◆ www.aol.org
- ◆ www.ask.com
- ◆ www.dmoz.org
- ◆ www.google.com
- ◆ www.live.com
- ◆ www.yahoo.com

Windows Internet Explorer

Performing a Search

You perform a search from your Internet browser. To begin the search, you enter one or more *keywords*, which are words or phrases that describes your search topic.

To perform a search:

1. Connect to the Internet and start your Web browser.
2. Key the Web address for the search engine in the address bar and press Enter. The search engine home page appears.

CONTINUES

CHOOSING EQUIPMENT

Ideally, all computer workstations would perfectly fit the needs of their users. Of course, this is rarely the case. Some workstations are used by people of different sizes. In a classroom, you will probably use whatever equipment is available.

If you have a choice in the equipment that you use at school or if you want to choose equipment for your personal use at home, here are some guidelines.

Monitor Stands and Workstands

Position your monitor so you can work at eye level. Most monitors can be tilted and swiveled. Ideally you shouldn't move your head a great deal or change focus as you key.

You can support a monitor with an adjustable stand or a fixed stand. Some monitors are placed directly on the computer. If you don't have a monitor stand, you can change the monitor height by using a box, a book, or a ream of paper. Just be sure that a heavy monitor is well supported.

Use a workstand or easel to hold your papers for easy reading. Some attach to the monitor; others stand on their own.

Chairs

A good chair is the foundation for good posture and comfort. Be sure the seat is large enough. Some experts recommend a chair without armrests so your arms are not trapped. Armrests, if you have them, should be short and padded. They won't bump the desk, and you can lean on them when you are resting (but not when you are keying). Key with your arms free. Never key with your arms resting on something.

An adjustable chair is ideal for a workstation that is used by people of different sizes. If you don't have an adjustable chair, find a chair that suits you. Different people might need different chairs at the workstation. Use a pillow or a book if you need to raise yourself.

Keyboard and Mouse Trays

Position your keyboard and pointing device (mouse or trackball) at the same height. Your keyboard support or mouse tray should be sturdy. Many mouse trays can be adjusted for height and angle. If you support your keyboard on a desk or table, be sure the height allows your elbows to bend at right angles while your hands hover over the keys.

EQUIPMENT TIP

Fancy or expensive equipment does not always mean it is better. You can often adjust your equipment to make it suit your needs.

FIGURE K-1
Some experts recommend a chair without armrests so your arms are not trapped.

---

3. Go to the next page and click the "David Hockney" link. Read the hypothesis.

4. Create a multiple-page report that explains how and why David Hockney and Charles Falco have concluded that some of the Old Master painters used optics. Include a cover page.

5. Include one or more images from the Web site in the report.

6. Include a bibliography page with the Web source. Use the MLA style for online sources.

7. Save the file as *[your initials]*Test15-3. Print the document.

ADJUSTING YOUR WORKSTATION

In a classroom you do not usually have much choice in the equipment you must use. However, flexible equipment and a little imagination can help you adjust your workstation.

Adjusting Your Keyboard and Mouse

You want your fingers to gently curve over the keys while your wrists are in a flat, neutral position.

✦ If wrist rests are available, place one in front of the keyboard as a guide. Never rest your arms, hands, or wrists while you are keying.

✦ Place your mouse or trackball at the same height as your keyboard, in easy reach of your preferred hand.

Adjusting the Slope of Your Keyboard

If your keyboard slants toward you, you need to adjust it so it is flat or slopes down away from you.

✦ Flatten the kickstand at the back of the keyboard.

✦ Alternatively, raise the front of the keyboard about ¾ inch by using door wedges, a wood strip, or a box.

Adjust at the Beginning of Each Class

Computers in most schools are used by many students. At the beginning of each class, take the time to adjust your individual workstation. The best procedure for adjusting your workstation is to adjust in stages:

1. Start with the angle of your keyboard and the position of your mouse or trackball.

2. Next, adjust the position of your chair and keyboard.

✦ Adjust the seat angle so your knees are slightly lower than your hips.

✦ Experiment with your seat height and keyboard height so your elbows bend at right angles when you hold your hands just above the keyboard. Your wrists should hover just over the wrist rest. Shorter people might need a footrest if their feet dangle.

✦ Be sure your feet are properly supported on a flat surface.

3. Now adjust the height of your monitor and work holder.

✦ Position the monitor so you can see the top of the screen while looking straight ahead.

✦ Position the work holder either in front of the monitor or to the side so you can see the work with little movement of your neck.

TECHNIQUE TIP

Never rest your arms, hands, or wrists on anything while you are keying.

FIGURE K-2
At the beginning of each class, adjust your workstation.

4. Copy a picture from the Web site and paste it into your report. Size, position, and style the picture attractively, keeping the report to one page.

5. Add a bibliography page. Include the name of the Web source. Use the MLA style for online sources.

6. Save the file as *[your initials]***Test15-2**. Print the document.

TEST YOURSELF 15-3

Lenses and the Old Masters

For hundreds of years, art historians have marveled at the artistic abilities of the Old Master painters. David Hockney, a contemporary artist, and his collaborator, Charles Falco, a physicist, have come up with a radical theory. They suggest that artists such as Lorenzo Lotto and Jan van Eyck created realistic masterpieces by painting images projected by lenses and concave mirrors. Write a report that explains their hypothesis.

FIGURE 15-6
Did Johannes Vermeer use lenses to paint "The Art of Painting" in 1666?

1. Use the following Web site:
   www.webexhibits.org/hockneyoptics
2. Read the Introduction page and print it.

CORRECT KEYING POSTURE

After you have adjusted your workstation, you need to maintain the correct keying posture.

CHECKLIST

Keying Correctly

☑ Center your body on the J key, about a hand's length from the keyboard and directly in front of the monitor.

☑ Hold your head straight over your shoulders, without straining forward or backward.

☑ Position the monitor at eye level about arm's length away so you look down about 10 degrees.

☑ Elongate and relax your neck.

☑ Keep your shoulders down.

☑ Tilt your keyboard slightly down toward the monitor. This helps you keep your wrists neutral and your fingers relaxed and curled.

☑ Adjust your chair and keyboard so your elbows bend at right angles.

☑ Keep your arms close to your sides but free to move slightly.

☑ Keep your wrists relaxed and straight in a "neutral" position.

☑ Keep your back upright or tilted slightly forward from the hips. Keep the slight natural curve of your lower back. Use a cushion or adjust the chair to support your lower back.

☑ Keep your knees slightly lower than your hips.

☑ Adjust your chair so your feet are well supported. Use a footrest, if needed.

AVOIDING STRESS WHEN KEYING

There are two ways to avoid stress when keying. First, you need to maintain the correct keying posture as you key. Second, you need to take a short break every 20 to 30 minutes and perform stretching exercises designed to help you avoid strain, fatigue, and injury.

Maintaining a Correct Keying Position

It's easy to start keying by using the correct keying position. As we key, however, many of us lose our focus, and bad habits begin to creep in. It's important to check your keying position to make sure you are still keying correctly.

DID YOU KNOW?

You can win scholarships and monetary awards with your National History Day entry.

TEST YOURSELF 15-1

National History Day

National History Day is a not-for-profit organization dedicated to improving history instruction and learning. Each year, the organization sponsors a National History Day Contest for sixth to twelfth graders. There are also state-level contests for National History Day. In this project, you will visit the national Web site and fill out an information sheet related to your state contest.

1. Connect to the Internet and start your Web browser.

2. Key **www.nationalhistoryday.org** on the address bar and press Enter. The National History Day Web site appears.

3. Click the "nat'l contest" link on the left side of the screen.

4. Click the hyperlink text "Project Examples" on the left side of the screen to get an idea of the kinds of history projects that have won in previous years.

5. Click the hyperlink text "State and District Contests" on the left side of the screen.

6. Click your state on the map to display reference information about your state's participation. Print this reference page. Leave the browser open.

7. Start Word and open the file **WP-HistoryDay**.

8. Key your state at the top. Key your name and the date. Enter the remaining information by using the reference page you printed.

9. Copy a picture or logo from the National History Day Web site or the state Web site and paste it into the document. Size, position, and style it attractively. Keep the document to one page.

10. Save the file as *[your initials]***Test15-1**. Print the document.

WORD TIP

Remember, to copy an image from a Web site, right-click the image and then choose the Copy command from the shortcut menu.

DID YOU KNOW?

It would take approximately 3,200 helium-filled birthday balloons to lift a 100-pound person.

TEST YOURSELF 15-2

Piloting Hot Air Balloons

The Internet is a great source of information for writing school reports. In this project, you will navigate through a Web site on "How Hot Air Balloons Work" and write a one-page report on piloting a hot air balloon.

1. With your browser open, go to the following Web address:
   www.howstuffworks.com/hot-air-balloon.htm

2. Click the hyperlink text "Piloting a Balloon" and read through the material.

3. Using Word, write a one-page report on "Piloting a Hot Air Balloon."

TABLE K-1:   Maintaining a Correct Keying Position

Maintain a Correct Position		Avoid Stressful Positions	
	**FIGURE K-3** Maintain a correct upright posture.		**FIGURE K-4** Avoid slouching, extending your elbows, or bending your wrists.
	**FIGURE K-5** Maintain a neutral position with your hands.		**FIGURE K-6** Avoid twisting your hands inward or outward.
	**FIGURE K-7** Maintain a neutral wrist position with gently curled fingers.		**FIGURE K-8** Avoid bending your wrists or using an upward-sloping keyboard.

Stretching and Resting

When you key for a long time, your muscles stiffen. You become fatigued and risk injury. You build tension in many parts of your body, including your neck, arms, and wrists. To relieve the tension and reduce the threat of injury, you should stretch before you start keying. You should also take short breaks from keying every 20 to 30 minutes and stretch.

Stretch 1: Neck Stretch
Sitting tall, bring your chin toward your chest, stretching the back of your neck. Slowly repeat two times. See the following page.

Microsoft Internet Explorer

Printing a Web Page (CONTINUED)

To print a Web page:

1. Display the Web page you want to print. On your browser toolbar, click the down arrow next to the Print button 🖶 and choose **Print**.
2. In the Print dialog box, choose an option under **Page Range**.
3. Click **Print**.

PRACTICE 15-3

Print Web Pages

1. At the career Web site, choose a career category that interests you, and then choose a career. For example, suppose you choose the category Music & Arts, and then choose Disc Jockey. A description of that job appears.
2. In the upper-right corner of the screen, click **HTML** to display a printer-friendly version of the Web page.
3. Click the down arrow next to the Print button 🖶 and choose **Print**.

FIGURE 15-5
Print dialog box

INTERNET TIP

Web pages may actually be many pages when printed. To check page length, click the Print button 🖶 down arrow and then click Print Preview. The number of pages will appear at the bottom of the screen.

4. Click **Print** in the dialog box to print your career page. Write Practice 15-3 and your name at the top of the printed page.
5. Click the Back button ⬅. Locate another job description from this category or another category that interests you. Print the description.

FIGURE K-9

Stretch 2: Head Turn

Begin with your head in a neutral position. Look all the way to the right without moving your chest or upper back. Then look to the left. Slowly repeat two times.

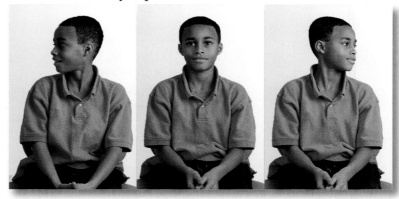

FIGURE K-10

Stretch 3: Head Tilt

Begin with your head in a neutral position. Bring your ear toward your shoulder without turning your head or lifting your shoulder. Hold for a count of five. Reverse directions.

FIGURE K-11

Creating Favorites (CONTINUED)

4. Click **Add** to save the page as a Favorite.

5. To view your Favorites, click the Favorites Center button ⭐. Click **Favorites** if they are not already displayed. Click a Favorite from the list to go to that Web site.

INTERNET TIP

If the menu bar of your browser is visible, you can use the Favorites command. You can also add a Web site to your Favorites list by using the keyboard shortcut Ctrl + **D**.

PRACTICE 15-2

Create Favorites

1. Display the Bureau of Labor Statistics Career Information Home Page, if it is not already displayed.

2. Click the Add to Favorites button ⭐ and choose **Add to Favorites**. In the **Add a Favorite** dialog box, "BLS Career Information Home Page" appears in the **Name** text box.

FIGURE 15-4
Add a Favorite
dialog box

3. Key or edit the text in the **Name** box to **BLS Career Info**. Click **Add** to save the page as a Favorite.

4. Click the Favorites Center button ⭐ to make sure the page description "BLS Career Info" was added to your Favorites list. (You might have to click **Favorites** in the drop-down list.)

5. Click anywhere on the screen to close the **Favorites** list.

6. Leave your browser open.

Printing a Web Page

You can print Web pages the same way you print in Word or other Office programs. Some Web sites provide a link to a printer-friendly version of the current page, which is usually a page without links and pictures.

CONTINUES

Stretch 4: Downward Wrist Stretch

With your left fingers pointing down and your palm in, place your right hand over your left knuckles. Extend your arms straight out. Gently press back with your right hand to a count of ten. Reverse hands. Repeat the stretches using a fist.

FIGURE K-12

Stretch 5: Upward Wrist Stretch

With your left fingers pointing up, place your right hand over your left palm. Extend your arms straight out. Gently press back with your right hand to a count of ten. Reverse hands. Repeat the stretches with fingers pointing down and the palm out.

FIGURE K-13

BENEFITS OF KEYING CORRECTLY

Training takes effort and time. If you already use a keyboard, you might have to re-teach your body to use correct techniques. You might ask yourself "Why make the effort? I'm already keying fast enough."

Just imagine you will probably be using a computer for the rest of your life. If you don't learn now, you will probably need to learn later. There's really no escaping it. Besides, if you learn to key correctly, you will:

+ Increase your speed.

+ Increase your efficiency, making fewer errors.

+ Increase your effectiveness because you can see the screen while your hands are free to work.

+ Stay healthy, avoid injury, and remain productive over your lifetime.

FIGURE 15-3
Career Information
home page

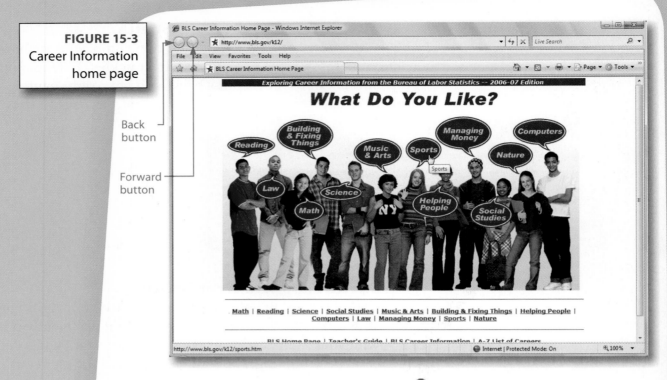

Back
button

Forward
button

6. Click the Forward button ⊕ to return to the Sports career page. Notice how the text on the address bar changes.

7. Click other links on the page. Click the Back button ⊕ until you return to the Career Information Home Page.

8. Leave your browser open.

Microsoft Internet Explorer

Creating Favorites

When you find Web sites you like, you can include them in your list of Favorites. Think of the Web as one big book where you can easily lose your place. *Favorites* are bookmarks to Web pages that help you find the pages easily in the future.

To create Favorites:

1. Use your browser to go to the Web address you want to save as a Favorite.

2. Click the Add to Favorites button 🌟 on the browser toolbar. Then choose **Add to Favorites**. The Add a Favorite dialog box appears. The **Name** text box displays the Web page name.

3. Key a more descriptive name into the **Name** text box or edit the current name if you want a different name for the Web page.

CONTINUES

FIGURE K-14
Many of us have developed bad habits that we need to break.

BREAKING BAD HABITS

Many of you might have been keying for years. However, without any formal training, you could easily have developed bad habits.

The best way to correct bad habits is to use natural breaks as checkpoints. For instance, look at your own habits at the end of each exercise, paragraph, or page you key. Consider your posture, sitting position, hand position, keying technique, and work habits.

To help you break your bad habits, here's a "Bad Habits Checklist." Check it when you start keying and when you take a break. If you know you have a particular bad habit, try to focus on the correction at the beginning of every keying session. Eventually the bad habit will be replaced by the good habit. It takes work, but it's worth it.

TABLE K-2:   Bad Habits Checklist

Bad Habits	Correction
Slouching	Sit up straight with your feet flat and well supported.
Reaching too far for the keyboard or the mouse	Sit one hand's length from the keyboard. Keep elbows at right angles.
Leaning your hand on the keyboard or the wrist support	Hover your hands over the keyboard; curl your fingers slightly.
Bending your wrists forward, back, left, or right	Keep your forearms and wrists straight and in the neutral position.
Pounding the keys	Strike keys lightly.
Looking at the keyboard	Position the workstand close to the monitor at eye level. Keep your eyes on your work.
Raising your elbows	Keep your arms close to your body.
Raising your shoulders	Keep your shoulders relaxed, with your chest open and wide.
Keying with the wrong fingers	Practice with correct fingers until you establish the right habit. Your speed will then improve.

Using Internet Addresses (CONTINUED)

You may have seen Internet addresses beginning with the letters http://. This part of an address indicates the protocol needed to access the information at that Internet address. A *protocol* is a set of rules or standards that allow computers to communicate with one another. Most Web browsers do not require you to key the protocol name.

To navigate the Internet and visit a Web address:

1. Connect to the Internet and start your Web browser.
2. Key the site address on the address bar.
3. Press Enter or click the Go button ➡. The browser takes you to the Web site. The Web site address is displayed on the address bar.

FIGURE 15-2
Keying a Web site address

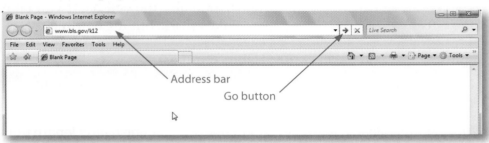

Address bar

Go button

4. Click any link you see on the Web page. The browser takes you to that location. The new Web site address is displayed on the address bar.
5. Click the Back button ⬅ to return to the initial Web site.

PRACTICE 15-1

Use Hyperlinks and Browser Buttons

You will use your browser to go to a Web site address with information on careers.

1. Connect to the Internet and start your Web browser.
2. Key **www.bls.gov/k12** on the address bar and press Enter or click on the Go button ➡. The Bureau of Labor Statistics Career Information Home Page appears. See Figure 15-3 on next page.
3. Under "What Do You Like?," move your pointer over the balloon text "Sports." The pointer changes to a hand, indicating that the item is an active link.
4. Click the Sports link. The link takes you to a page about possible careers in sports.
5. Click the Back button ⬅ to return to the Career Information Home Page.

Keyboarding

Navigating the Internet by Using a Web browser (CONTINUED)

TABLE 15-1	Frequently Used Buttons in the Browser
Button	**Result**
☒ Stop	Stops a page that is loading.
⟳ Refresh	Reloads the latest version of a page you are viewing.

Using Internet Addresses

Every Web site has a unique location or address on the Internet. An Internet address (also called URL for Uniform Resource Locator) tell you the location of the Web site, the name of the site, and the kind of site it is.

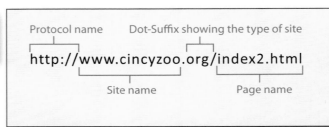

FIGURE 15-1
Web site address or URL

Table 15-2 lists some common types of sites. Web addresses are displayed on your browser's address bar. As you page through a Web site, you'll notice a slightly different address for each page.

TABLE 15-2	Common Types of Web Sites
Address Suffix	**Organization Type**
.com	Commercial organization
.org	Not-for-profit organization
.net	Networking organization
.edu	Educational organization
.gov	U.S. federal government

CONTINUES

Learn the Home Keys

HOME KEYS

A   Use the **A** finger.

S   Use the **S** finger.

D   Use the **D** finger.

F   Use the **F** finger.

J   Use the **J** finger.

K   Use the **K** finger.

L   Use the **L** finger.

;   Use the **;** finger.

The semicolon (;) is typically used between two independent clauses in a sentence. In a sentence, key one space after a semicolon.

KEYBOARDING TIP

On **;** only the semicolon is colored. This is because the key is used for two different characters. In this lesson, you learn how to key the semicolon. In a later lesson you will learn how to key a colon.

LEARN AND PRACTICE

Begin keying by placing your fingers on the eight keys—called the *home keys*—**A S D F J K L** and semicolon **;** as shown below.

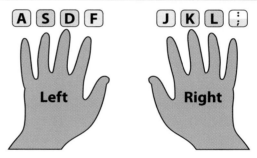

The index finger of your left hand should rest on **F**, your second and third fingers rest on **D** and **S**, and the little finger of your left hand rests on **A**. For your right hand, your index finger should rest on **J**, your second and third fingers rest on **K** and **L**, and your little finger rests on **;**.

From now on, the finger you use to press a key will be named for its home-key letter. For example, your left little finger is the **A** finger. Your right index finger is the **J** finger.

From the home keys, you can reach all the other keys on the keyboard. The keyboard diagram shows which home-key finger is used for each key. For example, you use the **D** finger to key all the keys in the band of green on the left. You use the **L** finger to key all the keys in the band of red on the right, and so on. When any finger is not actually pressing a key, you should keep it resting lightly on its home key.

The row of keys containing the home keys is called the *home row*. The row below the home row is the *first row*. The row above the home row is the *third row*.

Explore the Internet

LEARN

Using the Internet

A *computer network* is a group of two or more computers electronically linked together, using either special cables or wireless radio connections. The *Internet* is a massive network of millions of smaller networks, so it is sometimes called a "network of networks." It connects millions of computers located in countries around the world.

One of the ways to access information on the Internet is to use a Web browser. You use a *browser* to access *Web sites*, which are collections of computer files that may contain text, pictures, sounds, and video. A Web site may include *hyperlinks* (also called *links*). They look like colored or underlined text or can appear as pictures. Clicking on a link causes the browser to display another part of that Web site or some other Web site on the Internet.

In this lesson, you'll navigate the Internet by using a Web browser to locate and display Web sites. You'll also learn how to create a list of your favorite Web sites.

Microsoft Internet Explorer

Navigating the Internet by Using a Web Browser

A browser is computer software with which you can find, view, and save Internet documents for later use. These documents may contain text, sound, video clips, and pictures. All browsers have toolbar buttons at the top of the screen. You navigate the Internet by using the buttons on your browser toolbar. Table 15-1 shows some useful buttons on your browser toolbar.

TABLE 15-1	Frequently Used Buttons in the Browser
Button	**Result**
→ Go	Takes you to the Web address shown on the address bar.
← Back	Takes you back to the last page you viewed.
→ Forward	Takes you to the page you viewed before clicking the Back ← button.

CONTINUES

Spacebar — Use the thumb of your writing hand.

Enter — Use the [;] finger.

WORD PROCESSING TIP

Word capitalizes the first letter of each new line and adds a wavy underline to misspelled words. Your teacher can turn off these settings by clicking the Office button, and choosing Word Options, Proofing.

TECHNIQUE TIP

Begin with your fingers curled and lightly touching the home keys.

Learn and Practice the Spacebar

Notice that on the keyboard diagram, the keys you have learned are darker and tinted with their background color. Now locate the Spacebar on the diagram. You use the Spacebar to insert spaces between letters and words. You press it by using the thumb of your writing hand (that is, the hand you use for writing). You do not use the thumb of your other hand.

Key the home-key letters, inserting a space after each letter by pressing the Spacebar quickly and lightly. (Drill lines are numbered. Do not key the green numbers.)

```
1  a s d f j k l ;
```

Learn and Practice Enter

You do not have to wait for a text line to be "full" before starting a new line. Pressing the Enter key starts a new line of text whenever you need one. You press Enter by using the [;] finger. Try to keep the [J] finger on its home key when you press Enter.

Now press Enter (¶) to start a new line.

Key each of the lines below twice. Press Enter (¶) after each line.

```
2  asdf jkl; asdf jkl; asdf jkl;¶
3  ;lkj fdsa ;lkj fdsa ;lkj fdsa¶
4  fd jk sa l; fds jkl dsa kl;¶
5  dfsa l;kj ddss kkll ffaa ;;jj fjdk ls;a¶
```

Learn and Practice Double-Space

You can add a blank line between lines of text by pressing Enter twice. This is how you *double-space* text. (Two consecutive Enters are sometimes referred to as a *double line-space*.)

Key a line of text, press Enter, and then key it again. After you key a line the second time, press Enter twice before keying a new line. Using this method, key each line twice, and double-space after each pair of lines.

```
6  adfs jlk; aj sk dl f; aaa jjj sd kl ldsk¶
7  fjjf dkkd slsl da l; ks fj ;f sss lll dl¶
8  kkd dlk ds ddd ;f ff ;; fdl; sl f; ds kl¶
9  a as dad sad fads lads lass falls flasks¶
```

2. After your visit, create one of the following Word documents:

◆ A flier about one of the museum's current exhibits. Copy an image from the Web site to illustrate the flier.

◆ A one-page report about one of the museum's inventors. Include images and credit the Web addresses used.

◆ A one-page advertisement for an item from the USPTO Museum store. Include a picture of the item, a detailed description, the price, and how to order.

3. Save the Word document as *[your initials]*Test14-3. Print the document and close it.

4. Write an e-mail message describing your "visit" to the museum. Use an address provided by your teacher.

5. Attach the Word document you created to the e-mail message.

6. Include in your message a description of your attachment.

7. Print the message, and then send it.

8. Close Outlook and close your browser.

Improving Your Speed

The goal of this Keyboarding course is to increase your keyboarding speed. Every lesson helps you do that by using an "Improve Your Speed" speed drill.

Most of the speed drills are for one minute. The scale below the drill measures groups of five strokes (spaces and Enter count as strokes). Each group of five strokes is considered a "word." Your speed is measured by how many of these five-stroke words you can type in a minute. Your goal for the drill is indicated as the "Words per Minute" for you to key. ("Words per Minute" is abbreviated to "WPM.") So, for example, if you type ten five-stroke "words" in a minute, your WPM would be 10.

Your Starting Goal

Key the text below for one minute. If you reach the end before time is up, start again from the beginning. Your starting goal is to achieve a WPM of 8. Repeat this drill until you achieve a WPM of 8.

```
1 as a lass; as a lad¶
2 a sad lad; as a fad¶
```

Word count ──────────▶| 1 | 2 | 3 | 4   **WPM: 8**

KEYBOARDING TIP

Remember to press each key with approximately the same force, without hesitating over any key.

TEST YOURSELF

Key each line twice: first slowly and then faster. Press Enter after each line.

Home Keys

```
3 asdf jkl; ;lkj fdsa a;a;a slsl dkdk fjfj¶
4 aa dd ss ff jj ll kk ;; af ka; jdls kadl¶
5 fdj ld fa fsa kjk ksd jja ds laa alk ksd¶
6 kda dsa; lka jkd alls laf kajs kdjs sdsj¶
```

Words

```
7 a as la fa fad sad dad lad add adds fads¶
8 dad fad sad lad lass sass ads falls as a¶
9 lass falls; sad dad; lads sass; as a fad¶
```

TIME YOURSELF

```
10 lads fall; as a fad¶
11 lass adds; sad lads¶
```
| 1 | 2 | 3 | 4   **WPM: 8**

```
12 as a lass; all dads¶
13 alas as a lad falls¶
```
| 1 | 2 | 3 | 4   **WPM: 8**

Improve Your Speed

Each of these is a one-minute drill. Key the text in the drill for one minute. If you reach the end of the drill before time is up, start again from the beginning of the drill.

9. Use the Print button 🖶 on the Outlook toolbar to print your teacher's message.

10. Close Outlook.

DID YOU KNOW?

A television requires 35 different minerals. More than 30 minerals are needed to make a computer.

TEST YOURSELF 14-2

Mining the Internet

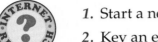

In this activity, you are part of a team writing a report on mining. You will use the Internet to research mining sites, and then include the sites in the e-mail message to your team member.

1. Start a new e-mail message.

2. Key an e-mail address in the **To** box, using an address provided by your teacher. Ideally, you should be sending the e-mail to a classmate you would be working with on the mining report.

3. Key a short description in the **Subject** box.

4. Key a short message explaining that you found Web sites about mining.

5. Use your Web browser to research mining. Find two or three Web sites and copy them into your e-mail message.

6. In your e-mail message, ask your team member if he/she thinks these sites will work for the report.

7. Check the spelling in your message.

8. Print the message, and then send it.

9. Close Outlook and close your browser.

TEST YOURSELF 14-3

DID YOU KNOW?

The inventor of VELCRO® reported that he thought of the invention while removing burrs from his pet's fur and his own pants after walking in the woods.

National Inventors Hall of Fame

The National Inventors Hall of Fame Museum recognizes the genius of over 200 inventors whose ideas have made a lasting contribution to the way we live our lives. Instead of going to the museum in person, you will explore the museum's Web site. You will write an e-mail and include an attachment about something you discovered at the museum.

1. Use your browser to find and explore the National Inventors Hall of Fame Museum. At the same site, explore the USPTO (United States Patent and Trademark Office) Museum and the museum store.

Review the Home Keys

REVIEW

The keyboard shows the keys you have learned so far. This lesson focuses on the keys highlighted in purple.

WARM UP

Key each line twice. Press Enter after each line.

```
1   asdf jkl; asdf jkl; asdf jk l; as df jkl¶
2   ;lkj fdsa ;lkj fdsa a;sl dkfj fdjk sa l;¶
3   fk dk sl a; fds jkl asd ;lkj k fd asf lj¶
4   sdl fdk kls ad; jfd salk klas dsf; flks;¶
```

PRACTICE

Key each line twice. Press Enter after each line.

Left-Hand Focus
```
5   fdsa asdf ff dd ss aa fd sa ds af asf fd¶
6   asdf df df sd sd as as fa af das fad saa¶
7   fads df as dfaa ddfs fada dada fafa sasa¶
```

Right-Hand Focus
```
8   jkl; ;lkj jj kk ll ;; jk l; kl j; jk; jk¶
9   jkl; l; l; kl kl jk jk ;j j; ;lk ;lk kjj¶
10  jlkj l; jk jll lkjj kkjl klk jkkl; kllj;¶
```

Home Keys
```
11  asdf jkl; fjdk l;sa fjk jfd dkl kds; all¶
12  jk df dk jf sl a; fjd kds; akl kdsl dkll¶
13  adkl dajk kads lfds; ljds jfds lks; jdlk¶
14  as a dad; all lads; all fads; as a lass;¶
15  lads; dads; as sad; lass; as all; a fad;¶
```

TECHNIQUE TIP

Concentrate on pressing the correct keys. Read silently letter-by-letter as you key. In this Warm Up do not focus on your speed.

BREAKING BAD HABITS

Do not hammer your fingers on the keyboard. Strike keys with a light tap.

TABLE 14-1   Popular Instant Messaging Abbreviations

Abbreviation	Meaning	Abbreviation	Meaning
2moro	Tomorrow	IOW	In other words
2nite	Tonight	IRL	In real life
AFK	Away from keyboard	JK	Just kidding
ATM	At the moment	L8R	Later
BRB	Be right back	LOL	Laughing out loud
BTW	By the way	NP	No problem
B4N	Bye for now	THX	Thanks
CUL	See you later	TMI	Too much information
FWIW	For what it's worth	TTYL	Talk to you later
GR8	Great	TYVM	Thank you very much
IMHO	In my humble opinion	VBG	Very big grin

DID YOU KNOW?

The Ancient Egyptians used symbols for decimals. They drew a single line for 1, a coil of rope for 100, a water lily for 1,000, a finger for 10,000, and a figure of a man with raised arms for 1,000,000.

MATHCOUNTS

TEST YOURSELF 14-1

MATHCOUNTS® is a competitive math enrichment program that promotes middle school math throughout the United States. In this activity, you will send an e-mail to your teacher asking about the requirements to participate.

1. Open Outlook. Click **New** on the Outlook toolbar.

2. Key the e-mail address provided by your teacher in the **To** box.

3. Key **MATHCOUNTS** in the **Subject** box.

4. Write a message to your teacher asking if you may participate in the MATHCOUNTS program (for information on the program, go to the Web site www.mathcounts.org). Include a salutation and a closing in your message.

5. Check the spelling in your message.

6. Click **Send**.

7. If you are able to receive a response, wait until your teacher tells you a response was sent to your e-mail address. Click **Send/Receive** on the Outlook toolbar. Click the **Inbox** folder.

8. Open the message from your teacher.

Word Wrap

You do not always need to press Enter at the end of a line. Most word processing programs have a feature called *word wrap*. This feature lets you keep keying, without pressing Enter, and the word processing program automatically moves to the next line. The text "wraps" to the next line.

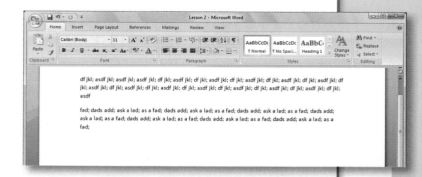

Using Word Wrap

Key the first line of text continuously until you wrap to the next line. Then continue keying until you wrap once more. Press Enter and then key Line 2 until you wrap to three lines as well. (See the Figure.)

```
1  df jkl; asdf jkl; as
2  fad; dads add; ask a lad; as a[space]
```

TECHNIQUE TIP

Make sure your back is straight or tilted slightly forward from the hips.

TEST YOURSELF

Key each line twice: first slowly and then faster. Double-space after each pair of lines. The "Home Keys" and "Words" drills are not word-wrap drills.

Home Keys
```
3  asdf jkl; fds af jkl klds dkjf a;ks skdf¶
4  fkd lds fd; jks klad kasl sakf lfds jafd¶
5  aff sadd lla dss jll add ffk ldd jjs fdd¶
6  dfs jks; sffd jkkl; fddk lssd; akkd dllf¶
```

Words
```
7  a as ad la fa fad sad lad all dad add as¶
8  add fads; dads lads; lass falls; add all¶
9  lads fall; dads add; as a fad; lass adds¶
10 flask; a lad; a lass; all ads falls alas¶
```

Word Wrap

This is a word-wrap drill. It uses the same procedure as was used for Lines 1 and 2. Key Line 11 until it wraps to three lines. Double-space and then key Line 12 until it wraps to three lines.

```
11 add fad; dad lad; lass sass;[space]
12 all fall; as a fad; sad lads;[space]
```

 ## TIME YOURSELF

```
13 as a sad lass; add a lad¶
14 lads fall; fads; add all¶
```
| 1 | 2 | 3 | 4 | 5   WPM: 10

Improve Your Speed

Key the text for one minute. Press Enter after each line. If you reach the end before time is up, start again from the beginning.

Using Instant Messaging

Instant messaging is a form of online chat that allows for quick communication. For instant messaging to work, both people must be online at the same time, and both must be signed up with an IM service, such as Windows Live Messenger, AIM, or Yahoo! Messenger. With some services, you can use audio and video with your chats and transfer files.

To send an instant message:

1. First choose, download, and install an instant messaging program.

2. Add contacts ("buddies") to your IM program. You will need to know your contact's user name or e-mail address. Your contact will need to accept you as a contact, too.

3. Click or double-click (depending on your program) a contact name to start an IM.

4. Key your message in the IM message window and click **Send**.

INSTANT MESSAGING TIP

Instant messaging is similar to texting on a cell phone, but you can spell out your message more fully in an IM by using your keyboard. Don't use abbreviations unless your IM contact understands your lingo.

CHECKLIST

Sending Instant Messages

Even though instant messaging is informal, it's a good idea to practice IM etiquette.

☑ In your first IM to a person, ask if they're available. Start with something like, "Hi, can you chat?"

☑ Keep your messages short.

☑ Be careful what you write. Save sensitive subjects for face-to-face communication.

☑ Use abbreviations (see Table 14-1 on next page) and emoticons only if they are appropriate for the person receiving the message.

☑ When you're too busy to receive messages, use your program's "busy" feature so people can see that you're not available.

WARM UP

Key each line twice. Press Enter after each line. Do not look at the keyboard when you are keying.

1 a dd aaa as asd sdf j jj jjj jk jkl jkl;¶
2 as ads ask; lass dada jask fads dads sad¶
3 lads dada daff; jajs ja salad dads; saks¶
4 jakk jall; jadd dajs ladd saddl aja had;¶

NEW KEYS

E Use the **D** finger.

H Use the **J** finger.

KEYBOARDING TIP

Press Enter at the end of every line unless you are told specifically to use word wrap. From this point on, the Enter symbol (¶) will not be shown unless there might be some confusion about whether to press it.

LEARN

Reach your **D** finger up and slightly left when you key **E**. Keep your **A** and **S** fingers anchored on their home keys. Reach your **J** finger directly left to key **H**. Keep the other right-hand fingers anchored on their home keys.

PRACTICE

Key each line twice. Press Enter after each line.

Practice e

5 d e d ddd eee de ede eed lee eel del eel
6 eee ddd lll eel led eee dell lee led lee
7 eee ddd elk elf sell eee ddd see lee fee

Practice h

8 j h jjj hhh jh hj jhj hjh jjj hhh jj hhh
9 aaa hhh ash sss ash hh ss aa has sa sash
10 ha had aha has heel she hee half hah has

Practice e and h

11 he he eh eh hhh eee she he eh she eh hee
12 hhh eee easel feed seed heed lead she he
13 jade desks head sake head lead seal jade
14 has heed; lad had; heel hale; seek sale;

Attaching a File to an E-Mail (CONTINUED)

To attach a file to an e-mail:

1. With your e-mail message window open, click the **Attach File** command on the **Message** tab in the Include group.

2. In the Attach File dialog box, locate the file you want to attach.

3. Click **Insert**. The attached file appears in the attachment box below the subject line of the e-mail.

PRACTICE 14-2

Send E-Mail with an Attachment

During this activity, you will create a Word document, attach it to the e-mail to your teacher, and send it.

1. Start a new blank document in Word. Create a simple flier for an announcement you would like to post on a school bulletin board. For example, you might want to announce the location of an event or that you're running for a school election. Or you might want to congratulate your team. The content is not important—this practice is to create a file to send as an attachment.

2. Format the flier attractively. Save it as *[your initials]* **Practice14-2**. Print the flier and close it.

3. In the e-mail message window, click **Attach File** on the **Message** tab in the Include group.

4. In the Attach File dialog box, locate the file you just created and click **Insert**.

5. Click **Send** to send your e-mail message and the attachment to your teacher.

6. When your teacher is able to respond to your e-mail, click **Send/Receive** on the Outlook toolbar. Click the **Inbox** folder.

7. Click the e-mail message from your teacher to read it.

8. Print your teacher's message by clicking the Print button 🖨 on the Outlook toolbar.

9. Close Outlook.

Special Types of Nouns

A *noun* is the name of a person, place, or thing. Most of the things you see, hear, or touch are *common nouns*. For example, "seal" (like the one shown on the right) is a common noun. Here is a list of three special types of nouns:

+ An *abstract noun* is the name of a quality or concept (for example, the *intelligence* of seals).

+ A *proper noun* is the official name of a particular person, place, or thing (for example, the seals in *Antarctica*).

+ A *collective noun* is the name given to a group of persons, places, or things (for example, a *herd* of seals).

Scrambled Nouns

Create two nouns out of each set of scrambled letters and then key the nouns. For example, the letters in "ealss" can be used to create the nouns "seals" and "sales." Hint: If you can't think of the nouns, try keying different combinations of the letters.

ealss   lafe   adel   alees   ehfsl   ahdess

TEST YOURSELF

Key each line twice: first slowly and then faster. Press Enter after each line.

Short Words

```
1   he she eh see eel lea sea ha has had hah
2   has sea as see she lead fee eel has held
3   feed fell fad fed has dad less leaf hall
4   she he sea eel sell fade feel he ale lad
```

Nouns

```
5   heel seed ladle jade head seal lake hall
6   lad flea head safe heel dale flash sheaf
7   ash sash hash shed sled deal kale saddle
8   lease seashell easel flake leaf hall ash
```

Longer Words

```
9    eased sashes deeded seeded heeded headed
10   shades dashes flashes false flakes asked
11   flasks jaded ladles leashes addle lashes
12   he heals; has deed; flash sale; had shed
```

TIME YOURSELF

```
13   he has a sled; she asked
14   she has a sash; he sells
```

| 1 | 2 | 3 | 4 | 5   **WPM: 10**

Improve Your Speed

Key the text for one minute. Remember to press Enter after each line. If you reach the end before time is up, start again from the beginning.

FIGURE 14-2

Dear [Teacher's Name]:

I have created a flier that I would like to post on our bulletin board. I am sending it to you as an attachment, for your approval.

Thanks for your help.

[Your Name]

FIGURE 14-3
E-mail composition window

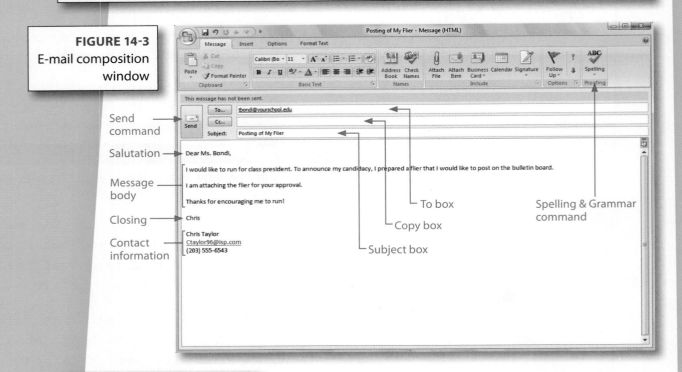

Send command

Salutation

Message body

Closing

Contact information

To box

Copy box

Subject box

Spelling & Grammar command

Microsoft Outlook

Attaching a File to an E-Mail

Along with your e-mail message, you can also send files over the Internet. To send a Word document, a picture, a PowerPoint presentation, or another type of computer file, you include it as an *attachment* to your e-mail message. You can send more than one attachment at a time.

CONTINUES

WARM UP

Key each line twice. Press Enter after each line. Concentrate on pressing the correct key each time.

1 ff fff ddd fd df jj jkj lkj fjk fdjk hhj
2 fed fej fek dek dell jade dale fake keel
3 lease lash lake ladle leak led leek feel
4 flea fled sea seal sell sleek shake heel

LEARN

NEW KEYS

[R] Use the [F] finger.

[I] Use the [K] finger.

Reach your [F] finger up and slightly left when you key [R]. Keep the other left-hand fingers anchored on their home keys. Reach your [K] finger up and slightly left to key [I]. Keep the other right-hand fingers anchored on their home keys.

TECHNIQUE TIP

Adjust your chair and keyboard so your elbows bend at right angles.

PRACTICE

Key each line twice. Press Enter after each line.

Practice r
5 fff frf frf fff rfr rffr fff rrr fff rrr
6 ra are far raf dare reef fear free freed
7 red jar lard reel dark darker hares rare

Practice i
8 k kk iii kik kkk ikki iki kk ii kkk kiki
9 ii ll jj kij sill jik ilk fill dill kids
10 if is silk kid hid kill ilk kiss hi hide

Practice r and i
11 ri ire ride sir rife fire dire sire rise
12 if ride hire hare hers rides fries dries
13 lair fair hair raid rid dill drill frill
14 riff sheared shire sear fire liars fried

PRACTICE 14-1

Write an E-Mail Message

You will prepare to send your teacher an e-mail. In the next Practice, you will send it with an attachment.

1. Open Outlook. In the Outlook Today window, click **New** on the toolbar.

FIGURE 14-1
Outlook Today window

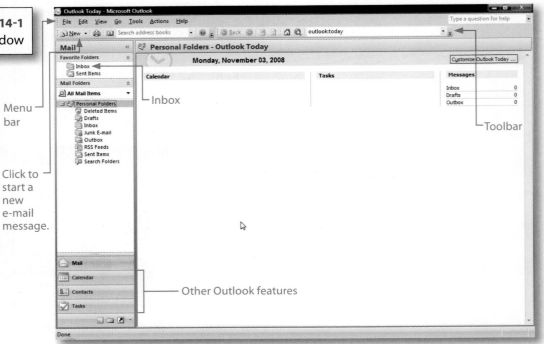

Menu bar

Click to start a new e-mail message.

Inbox

Toolbar

Other Outlook features

E-MAIL TIP

This lesson is based on Microsoft Outlook as the e-mail program. If you are using a different program, your screens will look different. All mail programs have basic command buttons to write, send, read, reply, and print mail and to attach a file.

E-MAIL TIP

You can have your name and contact information appear automatically at the end of your outgoing messages by creating an e-mail signature. A signature can also include graphics. Use the Signature command on the Message tab to create a new signature.

2. In the **To** box of the e-mail composition window, key the e-mail address provided by your teacher. Be sure to key the address correctly.

3. In the **Subject:** box, key **Posting of My Flier**

4. In the message pane, key the text shown in Figure 14-2 on the next page. Use your teacher's name and your name where indicated. Include a blank line between paragraphs.

5. On the **Message** tab, click **Spelling** to run a spelling and grammar check on your message text. Make corrections as needed.

6. Leave the message window open without sending the e-mail. You will send it in the next Practice.

Homophones

Homophones are words that sound the same but have different spellings.

Examples of homophones:

hall—a corridor   **bolder**—more daring
haul—to drag   **boulder**—a large rock

Backwards Homophones

All of the following pairs of words are homophones, but they are spelled backwards. To reveal the words, key each word from right to left. For example, for "der," key "red" and so on.

sale   sail

```
der      riaf      erah      reed
daer     eraf      riah      raed

eelf     laeh      reehs     rialf
aelf     leeh      raehs     eralf
```

TEST YOURSELF

Key each line twice: first slowly and then faster. Press Enter after each line.

Short Words
```
1  if hi is red rid fir her his ark hid ire
2  rid raid fear fire fish dish deer hi his
3  hers reed riff deer seer hired hard lard
4  ride like kid sill slid fresh share rail
```

Homophones
```
5  red read; reed read; real reel; sea see;
6  dear deer; led lead; ads adds; hear here
7  sale sail; hail hale; aid aide; air heir
```

Longer Words
```
8   dress dressier dreads drill hears kisses
9   shark shirred dried shreds redder raffle
10  erasers riddles relished driller fishers
11  frillier sillier raiders refried refresh
```

Improve Your Speed

Key the text for one minute. Press Enter after each line. If you reach the end before time is up, start again from the beginning.

TIME YOURSELF

```
12  she shares a fare; he is fair
13  her red dress has real frills
    | 1 | 2 | 3 | 4 | 5 | 6   WPM: 11
```

Writing E-Mail (CONTINUED)

9. Click the message you want to read.
10. To reply to a message, click **Reply** on the toolbar. Key your message and click **Send**.

CHECKLIST

Writing and Sending E-Mail

There are some basic guidelines to keep in mind for effective e-mail communication.

☑ Use the **To** box for the e-mail address of each recipient. Separate multiple addresses with a semicolon or comma.

☑ Use the **Cc** box for each person you want to receive a copy of the message.

☑ Use the **Subject** box to describe briefly and clearly what the message is about, typed in upper- and lowercase letters.

☑ For the message, use an organized structure with a salutation, body, and closing.

☑ Your salutation should be followed by a colon, such as *Hi, Sue:* or *Dear Sue*: or just *Sue:*

☑ For the body of the message, use short single-spaced paragraphs, with space between the paragraphs.

☑ Use standard spelling, grammar, and punctuation. Always use the spelling-check function.

☑ Never use ALL CAPS, which is considered shouting.

☑ At the end of the message, after your name, consider including contact information.

☑ Do not send sensitive information. Consider if you have written something that will embarrass or hurt you or someone else.

☑ Think before clicking the Send button. In most cases, you cannot change your mind and "unsend" an e-mail.

REVIEW

The keyboard shows the keys you have learned so far. This lesson focuses on the keys highlighted in purple.

BREAKING BAD HABITS

Do not look at the keyboard. Keep your eyes on the screen or on your work.

WARM UP

Key each line twice. Press Enter after each line.

1 all ale ad else sled sell sale lass less
2 sheer shear share ail air rile lair fair
3 hash flea his head lead lease deals dash
4 here hares hire hair jars jeer rear dear

PRACTICE

Key each line twice. Press Enter after each line.

Practice e and h

5 ddd dde ded dde eed ed deeds sea eel see
6 hhh hjh jhj jjj jjh hh ja had he has she
7 had shed he she jade lake head ease heed
8 deed heed seed heal seal fed easel lease

Practice r and i

9 rrr ffr frf rfr re are red her fair here
10 iii iki kik kki if ire dire kid lie like
11 rise iris frail rail err dear dire fires
12 sire fire liar lair rail hail jail riser

Practice e h r and i

13 heir hare hair heard hire here rare rear
14 lairs said share shire red her idea dare
15 jeers; sir fir hear; fare hare hair lair
16 sear shared; liars rails hired fired ire
17 hailed fresher fished rides herds shades

Use E-Mail and Instant Messaging

LEARN

E-Mail and Instant Messaging Basics

E-mail (or electronic mail) is a system for sending messages to one or more people over the Internet or over a private intranet. An *e-mail service provider* is a company that allows you to exchange messages with other e-mail users. Each user has an *e-mail account*, which is an electronic mailbox for sending and receiving messages. E-mail addresses are unique, so you are the only one who will receive messages sent to your e-mail account.

More immediate than e-mail is instant messaging, often shortened to simply "IM" or "IMing." *Instant messaging* is the exchange of text messages in real time. Instead of sending an e-mail and waiting for a reply, you can use IM software to see if someone is online, and then send an "instant" message. Both of you can then have a live, online chat session.

Microsoft Outlook

Writing E-Mail

An e-mail message includes three basic components: the recipient's address, the subject, and the message. No matter which service provider you use for e-mail, the steps you follow are about the same. This lesson demonstrates the steps with Microsoft Outlook.

To write, send, receive, and reply to an e-mail:

1. Open Outlook. The Outlook Today window opens. See Figure 14-1 on next page.
2. To send a message, click **New** on the Outlook toolbar. An e-mail composition window appears.
3. Key an e-mail address in the **To** box.
4. Key a short, descriptive subject in the **Subject** box.
5. Key a salutation, key your message, and then key your name as the closing.
6. To check the spelling and grammar of your message text, click **Spelling** in the Proofing part of the **Message** tab. Apply corrections as needed.
7. Click **Send**.
8. To read incoming e-mail, click **Send/Receive** on the Outlook toolbar and then click the **Inbox** folder.

CONTINUES

Proofreaders' Marks

Proofreaders' marks are handwritten corrections made to a page of text. The marks are a combination of symbols and short notations that are easy to understand.

Proofreaders' Mark	Marked Up Text	Final Text
⋏ Insert word/letter	notic͎able	noticeable
∿ Transpose	belelve	believe
⸓ Change or delete letter	assistḙnt	assistant
#⋏ Insert space	very⸓good	very good
⌣ Delete space	when⌣ever	whenever

Interpreting Proofreaders' Marks

The following line of text contains proofreaders' marks. Key the corrected text.

ladȩl   is⸓said   leẹse   re⸓al   sleded⋏

Key each line twice: first slowly and then faster. Press Enter after each line.

Corrected Text

1   hearȩ all; fire idae; reel trail; asis

2   re⌣lishs; fell free; seer fish; feilds

Left-Hand Focus

3   fee feed fear dad dear see sear read red

4   sass fad free safe radar deer sees reeds

5   reefs dear rare dares fares safer sadder

Right-Hand Focus

6   lie like hike; jail hill hiker silk kiss

7   kids ski skill jelled fill sill hike ill

8   hill hair like ill fill silkier silk ilk

Longer Words

9   feeder feelers jelled ladies reads riser

10 shires hikes shares drill saddle fiddles

11 header reader field ladles federal hides

⏰ TIME YOURSELF

Improve Your Speed

Key the text for one minute. Press Enter after each line. If you reach the end before time is up, start again from the beginning.

12 he fries fish; she feels fair

13 free idea; he likes fresh air

| 1 | 2 | 3 | 4 | 5 | 6 | WPM: 12 |

11. Replace "[Student Name]" with your name.

12. Save the document as *[your initials]*Test13-2. Print and close the document.

TEST YOURSELF 13-3

Weather Station Letterhead

You are the marketing supervisor for a new weather station. Create a letterhead that helps the station create a new company image.

In creating the letterhead, be sure to:

1. Create the letterhead in the header area of the document.

2. Use the following information in the letterhead:

   **The Weather Station
   55 Old Fort Street
   Austin, TX 78746
   (512) 555-3894
   www.weatherstation.com**

3. Be creative with fonts, font sizes, font effects, and other formatting.

4. Insert a graphic in the letterhead related to the weather you would expect to see in Texas.

5. Preview the document.

6. Save the document as *[your initials]*Test13-3.

7. Print and close the document.

FIGURE 13-6
A rainbow might make a good graphic for a weather station's letterhead.

WARM UP

Key each line twice. Press Enter after each line. Keep your fingers anchored on the home keys.

```
1  f ff fff fir fire fir fire fff ff fff ff
2  l ll lll lad lade lad lade lll ll lll ll
3  fall fell fill earl leaf field fife life
4  hall hall lire dire rare rash dash flash
```

NEW KEYS

T Use the **F** finger.

O Use the **L** finger.

LEARN

Reach your **F** finger up and right to key **T**. Keep your **A**, **S**, and **D** fingers anchored on their home keys. Reach your **L** finger up and slightly left to key **O**. Keep the other fingers of your right hand anchored on their home keys.

PRACTICE

Key each line twice. Press Enter after each line.

Practice t
```
5  f ff ttt ftf tft fftt the that this tree
6  this tall tree; tear it; lift the tires;
7  at all; third three first; at tea three;
```

Practice o
```
8  o ll o oo lol olo old lot soak sold told
9  ode doe rot dot lot lost slot joke joker
10 oars are solid; oats look food; a lot of
```

Practice o and t
```
11 ff tt trt ll oo lo ol ooo of to too toto
12 foot fool tools loot took jots lots soot
13 hoot; odes to; store; lots of lost tools
14 hold those; if told; he dotes; too short
```

BREAKING BAD HABITS

Do not rest your hands or arms on any support. Keep your hands over the keyboard as you key.

DESIGN TIP

Make sure the first line of the letterhead fits on one line.

5. Change the header position to 0.6 inch from the top of the page.

6. Apply a new font and font color to the entire letterhead. Format the first line of the letterhead in a larger font size.

7. Select the entire letterhead and apply shading and a border.

8. Apply a font effect to the first line in the letterhead.

9. Change the margins of the document to a 2-inch top margin and 1.25-inch left and right margins. Insert a blank line above the date to space it further from the letterhead.

10. Replace "Diane Hill" at the bottom of the letter with your name.

11. Replace the date in the date line with the current date.

12. Save the document as *[your initials]*Test13-1. Then print and close it.

DID YOU KNOW?

The personal computer was first developed over 30 years ago.

TEST YOURSELF 13-2

Software Training Course Certificate

1. Open the file **WP-Course**. This document contains text for a certificate for the completion of a software training course.

2. Apply the following Quick Styles to the five paragraphs (the last paragraph contains two lines): **Heading 1**, **Subtitle**, **Heading 1**, **Heading 2**, **Heading 3**.

3. Change the page orientation to landscape.

4. Change the style set to **Formal**.

5. Select all the text and use the Grow Font button A to make the text as large as possible to fit on one page.

6. Add a page border that coordinates with the borders used in the document.

7. Insert a star shape. Size the star about 7 inches high and wide. Send the shape behind the text. Add a light fill color and remove the shape outline. Drag to position the shape in the center of the page (or use the Arrow keys to position it).

8. Apply a shadow effect to the star. Use the **Shadow Color** command at the bottom of the **Shadow Effects** list to make the shadow color a lighter shade.

9. Add a shadow text effect to the first and third paragraphs.

10. Make any other changes to the document as desired. For example, use the **Change Styles** command to change the font or colors.

Science Connection

Cryptology

Cryptology is the science that deals with coded messages. In a coded message, words, phrases, or sentences are replaced by letters or numbers. Cryptology has often been used for secret messages. Today it is used to protect storage of data and transactions between computers on the Internet. Data that is coded is referred to as *encrypted data*.

Decipher a Coded Message

One simple way to create a coded message is to substitute each letter of the message with the next letter of the alphabet. You would change "a" to "b" and "c" to "d." For example, "dog" would be changed to "eph." See if you can decipher the following message. (Hint: The first letter is "t.") Then key the deciphered message.

```
uif ebub jt tbgf
```

TEST YOURSELF

Key each line twice: first slowly and then faster. Press Enter after each line.

Third-Row Focus

```
1  tie toe rot to too tot err ire tier trio
2  rot riot rioter rotor trite terror error
3  tree rite rote root toot retort retie it
4  trot retire roe tort or torte hot hi hit
5  stole soil; fit a tire; to look so solid
```

All Keys Learned

```
6  shirt for her; are those the three dolls
7  he took hot toast; she ordered the roast
8  she takes tea at her resort at the shore
9  tooth or teeth; asks for a jar of treats
10 she likes to eat the fried food; to talk
```

Coded Messages

Type each line twice. The first time, type the line as it appears. The second time, substitute the letter "t" for every "o." Press Enter after each line.

```
11 oake ohe firso orail
12 seo io ao ohe ohird oree
13 oear ohese leooers
14 lifo ohe hao; soeer lefo
```

Improve Your Speed

Key the text for one minute. Press Enter after each line. If you reach the end before time is up, start again from the beginning.

 TIME YOURSELF

```
15 those tools are foolish; these too
16 jets dot the air; lift off so fast
```

| 1 | 2 | 3 | 4 | 5 | 6 | 7 | WPM: 13

12. On the **Page Layout** tab, click **Themes**. Move the pointer down the gallery of themes. Notice the changes in font, color, and fill effects. Click a theme you like or click outside the theme gallery to keep the formatting you have.

FIGURE 13-5
Choosing a theme

Theme Colors

Theme Fonts

Theme Effects

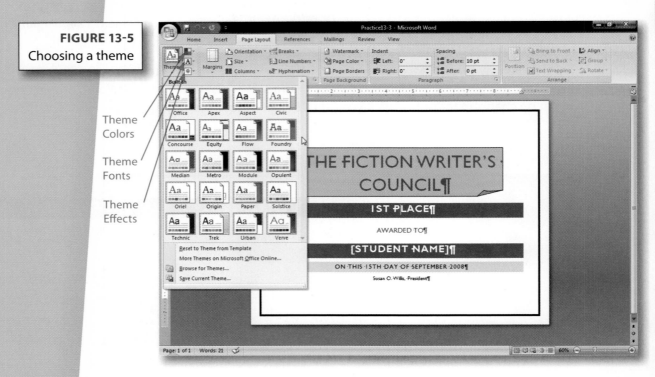

FIGURE 13-5
Choosing a theme

13. Make any other changes to the certificate you desire.

14. Replace "[Student Name]" with your name. Update the fifth line with the current date.

15. Save the document as *[your initials]***Practice13-3**. Print and close the document.

TEST YOURSELF 13-1

DID YOU KNOW?

Training a dog creates a bond between the dog and the owner.

Animal Behavior Institute Letterhead

1. Open the file **WP-Animals**. You will create a letterhead for this letter.

2. Key the following letterhead information in the header area.

   The Animal Behavior Institute
   870 W. Angler Road
   Boise, ID 83709
   (208) 555-0009 www.abi.com

3. Insert a symbol between the phone number and the Web address.

4. Center-align the letterhead text.

LESSON 7   Learn G and N

NEW KEYS

G Use the F finger.

N Use the J finger.

TECHNIQUE TIP

When keying, hold
your head straight,
without tilting it
forward or backward.

WARM UP

Key each line twice. Press Enter after each line. Keep your wrists and
fingers relaxed.

```
1  f ff fff fit file fail fir fr ftr ftt tf
2  j jj jjj jar jail has hill jhj jj hhj jj
3  feel foil life half heal this that those
4  joke hers rake fast haste hoist lash lid
```

LEARN

Reach your F finger directly right to key G. Keep the other fingers
of your left hand anchored on their home keys. Reach your J finger
down and left to key N. Keep the other fingers of your right hand
anchored on their home keys.

PRACTICE

Key each line twice. Press Enter after each line.

Practice g

```
5  g gg ggg fgf fgtg tgf go gal got get lag
6  sag sage stag stage gas rag egg edge leg
7  dog ledge keg grog get tiger grade grail
```

Practice n

```
8  n nn nnn jnj jnhn hnjn no on in kin none
9  rind seen lane train lane lean nine lion
10 tan ten ton tin tones none nasal tinnier
```

**Practice
n and g**

```
11 ff gg gg jj nn nn gn ng ing ing nag ring
12 nag anger gnarl range longer green grind
13 ring grand glean grin gone gentle ginger
14 tangle dangle strange slings and strings
```

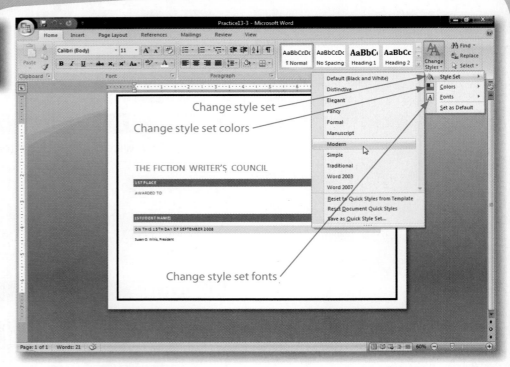

FIGURE 13-4
Choosing another
style set

Change style set

Change style set colors

Change style set fonts

5. To modify the styles to suit the certificate, select all the text and center-align it. With all the text still selected, on the **Home** tab in the Font group, click the Grow Font button [A'] three times, until the title text is 48 points.

6. Increase the font size for the two lines that use Heading 1 style to 26 points.

7. Change the paragraph spacing for "Awarded to" to 24 points before and 24 points after (**Page Layou**t tab, **Spacing Before** and **Spacing After** settings).

8. Return to the **Home** tab. Click **Change Styles** and choose **Fonts**. Scroll the list, moving the pointer over the font combinations. Some use the same font for headings and body text; some use two different fonts. Click a font combination you like to apply it.

9. Insert the Folded Corner shape in the document (second row, fourth shape in the Basic Shapes group). Draw the shape to cover the title text. Send the shape behind the text.

10. Adjust the size of the shape until it fits snugly around the title text. Then apply a fill color to the shape.

11. On the **Home** tab, click **Change Styles**, and choose **Colors**. Move the pointer down the list of color combinations. Click a combination you like or click outside the color list to keep the colors you have.

Verbs

A *verb* is a word that expresses action (for example, "run") or a state of being (for example, "is"). The letters "ing" are often added to verbs to create a *present participle* (for example, "running"). Present participles can be used as:

✦ Part of a verb (example, "She was running").

✦ The subject of a sentence (example, "Running is good exercise").

✦ An adjective (example, "the sound of running water").

Present Participle Challenge

Using only the letters you have learned so far (a, d, e, f, g, h, i, j, k, l, n, o, r, s, and t), key as many participles as you can. Key three participles per line. Include one space between words.

TEST YOURSELF

Key each line twice: first slowly and then faster. Press Enter after each line.

Left-Hand Emphasis

1 are sad seed deeds free of late fee daft
2 gaffe fades fake gets jelled gates frets
3 sees signs sends seat fear that are seen
4 great stars these rates seed their anger
5 red strings stranger than these she said

Verbs

6 sing ring ding fling tell talk read sail
7 sled like look ail lose lag sag ski rise
8 hike grin train listen finish dress gain
9 fight fish glide hide ride tear log hold
10 go light greet slide toil nail kneel get

Right-Hand Emphasis

11 oil in lake; loose nails; to not join in
12 fallen in; like a loon; no noodles jokes
13 still solid; loin of; shinier shone nine
14 jingle; hills; ilk; in jokes; kind; hone
15 noon; folk; join in; look in inn on hill;

⏰ TIME YOURSELF

16 sitting in this light; long nights
17 golden raisins and grains are good

| 1 | 2 | 3 | 4 | 5 | 6 | 7 | WPM: 14

Improve Your Speed

Key the text for one minute. Press Enter after each line. If you reach the end before time is up, start again from the beginning.

Working with Style Sets and Themes (CONTINUED)

Applying a theme is another way to change the look of a document. A *theme* is a set of coordinated formatting choices that includes theme colors, fonts for headings and body text, and fill effects.

To change the style set for Quick Styles:

1. On the **Home** tab, in the Styles group, click **Change Styles**. Choose **Style Set** from the drop-down list.

2. Point to different style sets in the list to observe the changes in the document. Click a style set to apply it.

3. To customize the fonts used in a style set, click **Change Styles**, click **Fonts**, and then choose a font combination.

4. To customize the colors used in a style set, click **Change Styles**, click **Colors**, and then choose a color combination.

To apply a theme:

1. On the **Page Layout** tab, in the Themes group, click **Themes**.

2. Point to different themes in the gallery to observe the changes in the document. Click a theme to apply it.

3. To customize the fonts used in a theme, click the Theme Fonts button A⏷ and choose a font combination.

4. To customize the colors used in a theme, click the Theme Colors button ⏷ and choose a color combination.

PRACTICE 13-3

Apply Style Sets and Themes

1. In the current document, apply the following Quick Styles:

The Fiction Writer's Council	Title
1st Place	Heading 1
Awarded to	Subtitle
[Student Name]	Heading 1
On this 15th day of September 2008	Heading 2

2. Leave the last line as Normal.

3. On the **Home** tab, click **Change Styles**, and choose **Style Set**.

4. Move the pointer down the list of style sets without clicking. Notice the changes in the styled document. Click the style set **Modern** to apply it.

Learn Left Shift and Period

NEW KEYS

Shift Use the **A** finger.

Use Left Shift for right-hand capital letters (and for all other shifted right-hand characters).

 Use the **L** finger.

A period is used in abbreviations and to mark the end of a sentence. Typically, one space follows a period.

BREAKING BAD HABITS

Do not look at the keyboard. Keep your eyes on the screen or on your work.

WARM UP

Key each line twice. Press Enter after each line. Keep your fingers curved.

```
1  a aa aaa j jj jjj; a aa aaa j kk lll jkl
2  l ll lll lag lags land doll dill toil in
3  all lie like kite kin of ode or ore idea
4  lashes slides knell soil sails rill roil
```

LEARN

Reach your **A** finger down and left to press the Left Shift key. With Left Shift pressed, you can strike any right-hand key. Then release Left Shift. Reach your **L** finger down and slightly right to key . Keep your **J** finger on its home key.

PRACTICE

Key each line twice. Press Enter after each line.

Practice Left Shift
```
5   jJ Jj Jd kK Kk Kf lL Ll Ls JdJ fKKf sLLs
6   hH Hj Ha aHHa; Jill Hill Lee; Hall Iris;
7   Hi there Hello; Here he is; Leo the lion
```

Practice Period
```
8   a. l. s. k. d. j. f. e. r. t. i. o. n. a
9   adj. alt. art. e.g. gal. i.e. inf. sing.
10  in. ft. kil. gr. lit. orig. transl. del.
```

Practice Left Shift and Period
```
11  Kan. La. OH OK HI N.H. N.J. Jos. I. Kant
12  Long. Lat. N.H.L. Joe and Jed; King Lear
13  I see. I said. I sit. I sat. I do. I do.
14  Ode to Leo. Oh. His is. No. One. Listen.
```

FIGURE 13-3
Changing a portrait
document to landscape

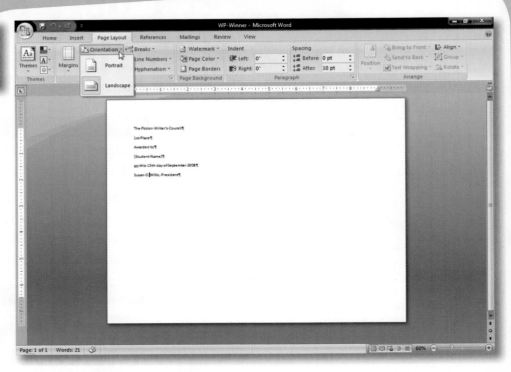

3. On the **Page Layout** tab, click the Page Setup dialog box launcher 🔲 .

4. In the Page Setup dialog box, click the **Margins** tab. Notice that you can change orientation here too.

5. In the Page Setup dialog box, click the **Layout** tab. Change the **Vertical alignment** to **Center**.

6. Click the **Borders** button in the Page Setup dialog box. In the Borders and Shading dialog box, choose a **Box** border and set the width to **6 pt**. Click **OK**.

7. Leave the document open. Next, you'll format the text with styles.

Microsoft Word

Working with Style Sets and Themes

You have already worked with Quick Styles, the predesigned formats for titles, headings, body text, and other document text. Quick Styles are available in a variety of style sets. A *style set* is a coordinated group of styles that are designed to work together to produce a professional document. After applying Quick Styles, you can change the style set to produce a completely different-looking document.

CONTINUES

Haiku

Haiku (hī´kōo) is the shortest literature form in the world. The Japanese word "haiku" translates as "short verse." It has been a traditional poetic form in Japan for 400 years. A haiku consists of 3 lines which together contain 17 syllables— approximately a single breath. The first line has 5 syllables; the second, 7; and the third, 5. Haiku usually focuses on some subject in nature.

俳句

fresh frost on the grass

a single golden leaf falls

too soon; seasons end

Create Haiku

This haiku example uses the letters you have learned so far. Key the example and then write a haiku of your own. You can use sentence fragments. You might find the "Haiku Fragments" section, below, helpful in creating your poem.

TEST YOURSELF

Key each line twice: first slowly and then faster. Press Enter after each line.

Left-Shift Focus

1 jJ kK lL; hH iI oO; He; Hi; Ho; Lo; Ind.
2 Has He Had His Hat Hid Her On Off Intro.
3 Hesse; Jones; Keats; Kafka; Helen Keller
4 Lois Lane Kate Hal Noel Len Jeff Jed Jr.
5 Kent; J. Olson; Jones Ltd.; Land of Nod;

Haiku Fragments

6 Long nights. Little kitten. Hard stone.
7 Night fall. Halfhearted. Lithe snake.
8 No tears. Hearts of gold. Large firs.
9 Halo of light. Jagged edge. High tide.
10 Lost friends. Life lesson. Old trees.

Phrases and Short Sentences

11 Oh no. Not that again. Here Joe. He did.
12 He goes to Ireland. Kids go on. Not one.
13 If she has one. It is far. His dog Otto.
14 Kin of all kinds. Hills like tall sails.
15 One Irish lad. On to Leeds. Jane and Ike

TIME YOURSELF

16 Ken likes Jen. He said John is in.
17 Hold on. OK. I see. No one has it.

| 1 | 2 | 3 | 4 | 5 | 6 | 7 | **WPM: 14**

Improve Your Speed

Key the text for one minute. Press Enter after each line. If you reach the end before time is up, start again from the beginning.

10. Apply square text-wrapping to the star clip and change the height to 1 inch.

11. Drag the clip to the left of the indented text, as shown in Figure 13-2 on the previous page.

12. Apply a picture style to the clip.

13. Use the clip art task pane to search for "lines." Insert a simple line in the header area. Apply square text-wrapping to the line, make it 6.5 inches wide, and drag it until it is centered below the header, as shown in Figure 13-2.

14. Double-click below the header area. Replace the date placeholder with the current date. Add a blank line space before the date. Replace "Georgia Atkins" with your name at the bottom of the letter.

15. Preview the document.

16. Save the document as *[your initials]*Practice13-1.

17. Print and close the document.

Microsoft Word

Changing Page Orientation

Page orientation is the direction in which a page prints or appears on-screen. You can choose between two page orientations: *portrait*, which is taller than it is wide, or *landscape*, which is wider than it is tall. The default page orientation when you open a document is portrait.

To change page orientation:

1. On the **Page Layout** tab, in the Page Setup group, click **Orientation**.

2. Click **Landscape** to change a portrait document to landscape.

3. To can change the document back to portrait orientation, click **Orientation** and choose **Portrait**.

PRACTICE 13-2

Changing
Page
Orientation

1. Open the file **WP-Winner**. You will design a certificate using this text.

2. On the **Page Layout** tab, display the **Orientation** drop-down list and choose **Landscape**.

Review T O G N Left Shift and Period

REVIEW

The keyboard shows the keys you have learned so far. This lesson focuses on the keys highlighted in purple.

WARM UP

Key each line twice. Press Enter after each line. Concentrate on pressing the correct key each time.

1   t to to tot toe not note got gotten tote
2   jJ kK lL hH iI oO. Joke; Kids like Jake.
3   Joanne is terse. Nora nods. Kane is kin.
4   Kirk tends to the garden. Lana looks on.

TECHNIQUE TIP

Center your body on **J**, about a hand's length from the keyboard, directly in front of your monitor.

PRACTICE

Key each line twice. Press Enter after each line.

Practice t and o

5   ttt ooo fff lll to too toot tot toe tote
6   to tone toner foot oat lot jot rote goat
7   toast knots trots lost stones toes ghost

Practice g and n

8   ggg nnn ggg nnn no go; gone; genes; sign
9   long longer longest longing song singing
10   no nod node; note done; gig agog; gotten

Practice Left Shift and Period

11   JKL; IO. KNOLL. Jr. Kg. Lg. Kg. Jds. Hd.
12   Kin are kind. Logan Hotel. Otis loiters.
13   L. L. H. H. K. K. J. J. I. I. I. Hi. No.

Practice t o g n Left Shift and Period

14   to go to. Nine tons. No one going. Ogden
15   green gnarl great gross gnats grain gilt
16   N.J.L. L.J.K. J.I.N.; Old Ohio. Old Hat.

WORD TIP

Remember: To change the top margin, choose Margins, Custom Margins, and then change the Top margin setting in the Page Setup dialog box.

3. On the **Header & Footer Tools Design** tab, in the Position group, click the up arrow next to **Header from Top** until the default header position of 0.5 inch changes to 0.7 inch.

4. Switch to the **Page Layout** tab and change the top margin to 2 inches. Remember, this places the date in a letter 2 inches from the top of the page.

5. On the ruler, delete the center tab in the header. Remember, to delete a tab marker, point to it and drag it off the ruler. Keep the default right tab.

6. Key the following text on separate lines in the header area. Press Tab and Enter where indicated.

Stars Observatory[Enter]
123 Stars Boulevard[Tab](512) 555-0090[Enter]
Austin, TX 78747[Tab]www.starsforeveryone.org

7. Select the header text. On the **Page Layout** tab, increase the **Left** indent to 1.2.

8. Format the company name "Stars Observatory" as 28 points and choose an attractive font. Apply the Shadow font effect.

9. To the left of the company name, insert a piece of clip art that has to do with stars. (If you search for "stars," you will find the clip used in Figure 13-2.) Leave the clip art task pane open after inserting the clip.

FIGURE 13-2
Customized header as letterhead

World Cities

A *city* is a densely populated urban center whose inhabitants are engaged primarily in commerce and industry. A city is larger than a town, which is larger than a village. A *metropolis* is a large or important city, such as the capital of a country or state.

Locate Cities

See how many names of cities you can key by using the letters you have learned (a d e f g h i j k l n o r s t). Begin with cities in your state, and then branch out to include cities in the United States. Remember that with the Left Shift key, you can key only cities that begin with capital I, O, H, J, K, L, or N.

Shanghai

TEST YOURSELF

Key each line twice: first slowly and then faster. Press Enter after each line.

Simple Sentences

1 He has it. Karen does not. John is here.
2 Oren is in Leeds. He is. Hallie is fine.
3 Keith leads. He trails dogs. Hide those.
4 Kids like hot dogs. Lane eats his fries.
5 Keiko filled ladles. Not all are hiring.
6 Lisa Jo joins John Jr. Jill tells jokes.

World City Names

7 London Oslo Hong Kong Osaka Kigali Lagos
8 Lieding Helsinki Harare Koln Jinan Haifa
9 Lilas Lahore Jakarta Hanoi Nanjing Jinan
10 Nagasaki Kingston Kinshasa Haifa Odessa

Left Shift

11 Jose Jan His He Nell Neil Not Look Holds
12 Knife King Keen Lakes Loaded Liken Longs
13 Into London. La. Ltd. Latino lang. Lorna
14 Jed Join Hoist Hark Hole Hone Head Herds
15 Onions Oars Odd Old Offer Offset Offsite
16 If Ideas Indigo Indian Illinois Irrigate

TIME YOURSELF

17 Nikki greets Lara. I told Ossie a joke.
18 He kids Les. Nan is Irish. Lea led Nat.

| 1 | 2 | 3 | 4 | 5 | 6 | 7 | 8 | WPM: 16

Improve Your Speed

Key the text for one minute. Press Enter after each line. If you reach the end before time is up, start again from the beginning.

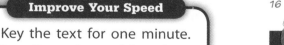

Creating Customized Headers (CONTINUED)

To activate the header area:

1. Start a new blank document or open an existing document. Display the rulers.

2. Place the pointer in the blank top inch of the document and double-click. The insertion point is now in the blank header area. (You can also display the **Insert** tab and choose **Header**, **Edit Header**.)

To adjust the position of the header:

1. With the header area activated, make sure the **Header & Footer Tools Design** tab is displayed.

2. In the Position group, change the setting for **Header from Top**. Increasing the setting positions the header text further from the top of the page; decreasing the setting positions the header text closer to the top edge of the page.

FIGURE 13-1
Activated header area

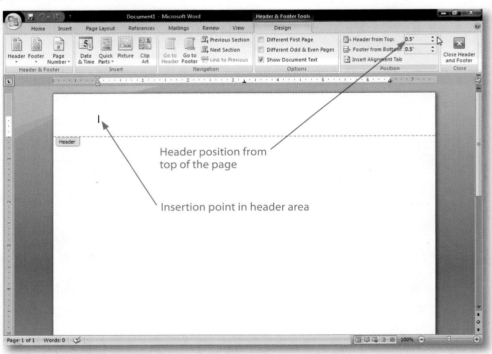

Header position from top of the page

Insertion point in header area

PRACTICE 13-1

Customize Headers and Create Letterhead

1. Start Word and open the file **WP-Stars**. In this letter you will create a letterhead in the header area.

2. Working in Print Layout view, double-click in the top inch of the page, which is the location of the header. The header area is activated.

NEW KEYS

C Use the D finger.

U Use the J finger.

TECHNIQUE TIP

Hold your head up and relax your neck.

WARM UP

Key each line twice. Press Enter after each line. Strike the keys with a light tap.

1 d dd ddd sad sat dot dog done dotes adds
2 j jj jjj Jill Join hill her his hat hits
3 Lili held on. Jade is green. Jess holds.
4 does he dial one or three; drifted east;

LEARN

Reach down and slightly right with your D finger to key C. Keep the A and S fingers anchored on their home keys. Reach up and slightly left with your J finger to key U. Keep the K, L, and ; fingers anchored on their home keys.

PRACTICE

Key each line twice. Press Enter after each line.

Practice c

5 d dd c cc dc dc dcd cad cat cater decade
6 lacks class clicks coins; Nick can cook.
7 lace cask flock shock Jack likes cheese.

Practice u

8 j jj u uu ju ju juj ujuj us use sue uses
9 due hue hurt huge urge; He is Uncle Kurt.
10 Used lutes and flutes; noun run nuts hut

Practice c and u

11 cur cue cut cud curt cute cuff cure curd
12 cull could cough couch accuse occur ouch
13 curls cushion curious cluck scour ruckus
14 such count culture course cruel function

Design Projects

LEARN

Design Documents

With the skills you learned in the previous lessons, you can now design your own documents. In this lesson, you will use your design skills to create attractive letterheads and certificates.

You were introduced to letterheads in Lesson 1 when you created business letters. One way to create a letterhead in Word is to place text in the document header. This way, when you key your letter, you don't have to worry about accidentally changing the letterhead.

CHECKLIST

Creating a Letterhead

☑ Activate the header area of the document.

☑ Key the content of the letterhead (the company name, address, phone number, fax number, Internet address, e-mail address).

☑ Apply any desired formatting to the letterhead text, such as tabs, font effects, font color, WordArt, borders and shading, or Quick Styles.

☑ Insert any desired clip art, photos, or symbols.

☑ When you are satisfied with the appearance of the letterhead, save it. You can easily reuse it for future correspondence and update it as needed.

Microsoft Word

Creating Customized Headers

You can create a customized header by setting tabs, inserting symbols, formatting text, and inserting and manipulating images. You make these changes to the header the same way you would make them to the document itself. The first step is to activate the header area. You can also adjust the position of the header from the top of the page to accommodate your header content.

CONTINUES

Language Arts Connection

Foreign-Language Words

English words translated into other languages can be spelled very similarly in the other language or they can look completely different. Look at the example below.

English	Spanish	French
line	linea	ligne

Translate Words

Key each English word on a new line. After each English word, key the Spanish word and then the French word, inserting a space between words.

English	Spanish	French
if	?	?
cat	?	?
three	?	?

TEST YOURSELF

Key each line twice: first slowly and then faster. Press Enter after each line.

J Finger Focus

1 Hun nun null nuance juice judo huge hula
2 nuclear unclear Union Jack unison unkind
3 units unknot unlock until junk Jude Juno
4 hound nouns under thunder hinder nothing
5 Juliet Julius junction junior Hugo hunks

Foreign-Language Words

Languages shown: English, Spanish, French, Italian, German

6 one uno un uno eins
7 coffee cafe cafe caffe kaffee
8 night noche nuit notte nacht
9 laugh risa rire risata lachen

F Finger Focus

10 race reach tug gust true fun feuds trust
11 tog raft rift rough tough through frugal
12 fact grace future furrier tearful fugues
13 fuss frog fret frat serf surf turf fruit

TIME YOURSELF

14 Julia hugs her cousin Lucie once again.
15 Urge Louis to accrue one hundred coins.
   | 1 | 2 | 3 | 4 | 5 | 6 | 7 | 8   WPM: 16

Improve Your Speed

Key the text for one minute. Press Enter after each line. If you reach the end before time is up, start again from the beginning.

11. Use the **SmartArt Tools Format** tab to change the height of the SmartArt chart to 6 inches. Move the chart as needed to place it attractively on the page.

12. Apply a SmartArt style to the chart. Make sure your text is legible.

13. Use the **Change Colors** command and apply one of the **Colorful** styles that coordinates with the text box title.

14. Select the Mr. Graves box and use the **SmartArt Tools Format** tab to apply a different shape fill color.

15. Draw a small text box at the lower-right of the page with the text **Prepared by** *[your name]*. Format the text box with a coordinating fill color, no outline, and a drop shadow.

16. Draw a **Rectangle** shape (from the Basic Shapes group of shapes) that covers the entire organization chart.

17. Send the rectangle shape to the back, behind the chart. Drag to position the rectangle as needed. Apply one of the gradient styles to the rectangle, using a coordinating color.

18. Save the file as *[your initials]***Test12-2**. Print and close it.

TEST YOURSELF 12-3

Teach How to Use Drawing Tools

DID YOU KNOW?

The best way to learn is to teach.

Create a two- or three-page report about how to use Word's drawing tools.

In writing your report, be sure to:

1. Include a title in a shape or text box.

2. On the first page, describe the benefits of using Word's drawing tools. Also explain the skills required. Describe how to draw, customize, and add text to shapes. Include an example.

3. On page two, include a SmartArt radial diagram from the Cycle group. Label the center object either "Why use diagrams" or "Skills you need." Include at least four surrounding objects for the diagram.

4. Insert a document footer with your full name and the page number.

5. Save the document as *[your initials]***Test12-3**. Print and close it.

LESSON 11

Learn W and Right Shift

WARM UP

Key each line twice. Press Enter after each line. Keep your arms close to your sides but free to move.

1 s ss sss sash ski skits sour sell sister
2 so; does; sun; stars; sass; losses; dust
3 Hugh shares his fish. He leads us south.
4 sack; cast; usage; soccer; lesson; sense

NEW KEYS

W   Use the S finger.

Shift   Use the ; finger.

Use Right Shift for left-hand capital letters (and for all other shifted left-hand characters).

LEARN

Reach up and slightly left with your S finger to key W. Keep your F and D fingers anchored on their home keys. Reach your ; finger down and right to press the Right Shift key. (Keep your J and K fingers anchored on their home keys.) With Right Shift pressed, you can strike any left-hand key. Then release Right Shift.

TECHNIQUE TIP

Remember to use the Right Shift key for left-hand capital letters and the Left Shift key for right-hand capital letters.

PRACTICE

Key each line twice. Press Enter after each line.

Practice w

5 s w ss ww sss ws sws wsw sss www sws wsw
6 saw awe dew draw jaw law wall well wills
7 sag wad owe we wan wall week wear wealth

Practice Right Shift

8 S; St; SA; W.A.G. F Fa Go Ta Da Ed We Fr
9 Fast Far Face Dad Dash Deal Sad Sash Add
10 AHA; Cold Drinks; Fine Sand; Grills Fish

Practice w and Right Shift

11 The Fresh Air Fund; The Far East; C.O.D.
12 WAAF Go slowly. Walt thinks; Tess walks;
13 Glow Aware Flaw Waist Rower Ewe Chew Few
14 Raw Flow Worn Waif Grown Stew Stow Worth

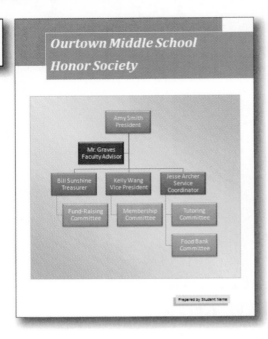

FIGURE 12-11
Final organization chart

3. Below the text box, insert the SmartArt design called **Organization Chart**. It is the first design in the Hierarchy category.

4. Use the **Arrange** command on the **SmartArt Tools Format** tab to apply **S**quare text-wrapping to the chart. Drag the chart down by its outside frame (make sure you use the four-headed arrow pointer) toward the middle of the page.

5. In the top box of the organization chart, key **Amy Smith**. Press Shift + Enter to insert a manual line break and then key **President**. Use this method for starting a new line after each person's name in the chart.

6. In the box below Amy Smith, key **Mr. Graves** and **Faculty Advisor** on separate lines.

7. In the three bottom boxes, key the following text:

Bill Sunshine	**Kelly Wang**	**Jesse Archer**
Treasurer	**Vice President**	**Service Coordinator**

8. Select the Bill Sunshine box and add a shape below it with the text **Fund-Raising Committee** (you don't need a manual line break for the remaining boxes).

9. Add a box below Kelly Wang with the text **Membership Committee**.

10. Add two boxes below Jess Archer. In one box, key **Tutoring Committee**; in the other, key **Food Bank Committee**.

Inventions

When inventors invent something, the first thing they typically do is apply for a patent to protect their rights. A *patent* is a property right granted by the United States to an inventor. The patent keeps "others from making, using, offering for sale, or selling the invention throughout the United States or importing the invention into the United States." Not all ideas can be patented: for example, a patentable idea must be novel, useful, "nonobvious," and cannot be about an abstract concept.

Alexander Graham Bell invented and patented the telephone in 1876.

Inventors and Their Inventions

Find the inventors of the following inventions. Key the invention, key a semicolon and a space, and then key the inventor. Start each new invention on a new line.

Radio	Gasoline tractor	Dishwasher	Escalator

INTERNET RESEARCH ?

TEST YOURSELF

Key each line twice: first slowly and then faster. Press Enter after each line.

Shift Keys
1 Washington WA; Delaware DE; Iowa IA; USA
2 Who What Where When Wade Owen Wei Edward
3 Theo Tuwa Edwin Walt Gwen Rhona Ewan Lew
4 D. Goodwin; J. Watt, T. Woods; A. Walker

Inventors
5 Edward Goodrich Acheson; Gertrude Elion
6 An Wang; Randi Altschul; Charles R. Drew
7 Jack Johnson; Walter Hunt; Helen Free
8 Elisha Otis; E. H. Land; Jean Foucault

S Finger Focus
9 South West SW SE Swiss swan stars sasses
10 She sews saddles. His sweater has flaws.
11 Stew dresses in Western wear. Sweet Sue.
12 Cassie is Swedish. Swans flew southwest.

 ## TIME YOURSELF

13 Shawn wanted to write. Rowan went west.
14 Dan is a D.A. in D.C. He was a witness.

| 1 | 2 | 3 | 4 | 5 | 6 | 7 | 8 | **WPM: 16**

Improve Your Speed

Key the text for one minute. Press Enter after each line. If you reach the end before time is up, start again from the beginning.

2. Double-click an outside border of the rocket to select it and to display the **Drawing Tools Format** tab. The rocket is a drawing made from grouped shapes. Resize the rocket to 4.5 inches high and use the **Position** command to place it at the bottom left of the page.

3. At the top of the document, insert the shape **Explosion 2** from the **Stars and Banners** group of shapes. Begin drawing the shape in the upper-left corner and drag down and to the right. Size the shape to be 3 inches high by 6 inches wide. Position it at the top center of the page.

4. Right-click the explosion shape and add the text **Rocketry Club**. Select the text and format it as 36-point Showcard Gothic italic, center-aligned. Adjust the height of the shape to fit the text. (If this font is not available, choose another font.)

5. Draw a text box that is 3.5 inches high and 2.75 inches wide. Key on separate lines **Join Us!**, **Tuesday**, **September 29**, **3:00 PM**, and **Room 155**. Format the text as 28-point Calibri bold, center-aligned. Position the text box as shown in Figure 12-10 on the previous page.

6. At the lower-right corner of the page, insert a small text box with the text **Prepared by** *[your name]*. Format the text box to have no line color and no fill color.

7. Add a 1/2-point shadow page border to the entire document (use the **Page Layout** tab). Make sure your drawing objects are within the border.

8. Select both the explosion shape and the Join Us text box and group them. Apply the same style to both objects.

9. Apply a different style to the rocket drawing. Adjust the position of your objects, if necessary.

10. Save your document as *[your initials]***Test12-1**. Print and close it.

TEST YOURSELF 12-2

Organization Chart

DID YOU KNOW?

Organization charts show control and responsibilities within a formal group.

1. Start Word and open a new blank document. You will create an organization chart that looks like Figure 12-11 on the next page.

2. At the top of the page, insert the predesigned text box called **Tiles Sidebar**. In the text box, key **Ourtown Middle School** and **Honor Society** on separate lines. Format the text as 36-point bold italic (change the font if desired).

NEW KEYS

X   Use the S finger.

M   Use the J finger.

TECHNIQUE TIP

Keep your shoulders down.

WARM UP

Key each line twice. Press Enter after each line. Keep your wrists relaxed.

1   s ss sss w ww www sw wsw sw saw sew swat
2   j jj u uu jiujitsu Julio jingle just jaw
3   Chris Wes Wendi sacks socks clock roasts
4   as is was SST Sid idle snack snake straw

LEARN

Reach down and slightly right with your S finger to key X. As you make the reach, keep your F finger anchored on its home key. Reach down and slightly right with your J finger to key M. Keep your K, L, and ; fingers anchored on their home keys.

PRACTICE

Key each line twice. Press Enter after each line.

Practice x

5   s ss x xx sx xsx xs xss S X XSX six axis
6   ax axe axel ox oxen fox flex sax sox FAX
7   Rex hoax nix next index annex Saxons XXI

Practice m

8   j jj jm mj jmmj mmjm mm mmm JM MJ me mom
9   Milk makes more might. gamma mailman mum
10   mammoth makes mole mire magma Mark merge

Practice x and m

11   wax tax lax gum gem exam remix minx coax
12   mold mile mere more magic marred maximum
13   Tom Mix; Max; Mr. Maxwell; Ms. M. Maxine
14   maxim mixture axiom Manx matrix exclaims

FIGURE 12-9
SmartArt radial design

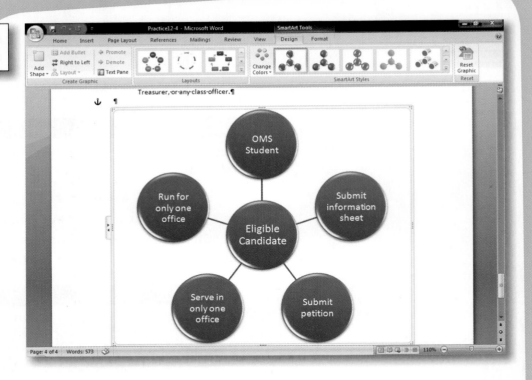

DID YOU KNOW?

There are national rocketry clubs, with competitions, exhibits, and conferences through the year.

TEST YOURSELF 12-1

Rocketry Club Flier

1. Start Word and open the file **WP-Rocket**. This document contains a drawing of a rocket. You will use it to create a flier for a school rocketry club. See Figure 12-10 for the layout of the flier.

FIGURE 12-10
Final layout of flier

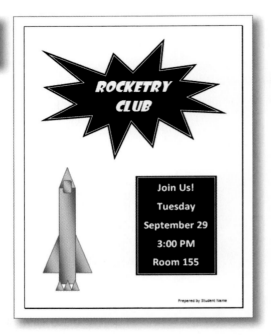

Mythology

Ancient Greek and Roman mythology have strongly influenced our language and culture. For instance, do you know what it means when we say that a person has the Midas touch? (In Greek mythology, King Midas was granted the wish to change all he touched into gold, a wish that became a curse when he could no longer eat.) Or do you know why Cupid is a symbol for sweethearts? Cupid, the Roman god of love, is usually depicted as a winged child with bow and arrow. Those shot by his arrow would fall in love.

Cupid, Roman god of love

Identify Mythological Figures

Complete the following sentences by identifying the mythological figure. Key each sentence twice.

```
The Greek goddess of agriculture is          .
The Greek goddess of wisdom is          .
The Roman god of war is          .
```

TEST YOURSELF

Key each line twice: first slowly and then faster. Press Enter after each line.

U.S. Cities
1 Des Moines; Durham; Madison; Miami; Nome
2 Madison; Alamosa; Camden; Richmond; Ames
3 Salem; Milford; Medford; Amarillo; Macon
4 Omaha; Selma; Tacoma; Stamford; Monroe

Mythological Figures
5 Minos Midas Hermes Orion Artemis Adonis
6 Medusa Nike Atlas Medea Minotaur Theseus
7 Ajax Nemesis Andromeda Heracles Achilles

Alternate-Hand Focus
8 hum wax knoll exact milk Texas hulk card
9 junk exert kohl taxes mink text kiln axe
10 join axed moon Dexter him traces hill Xe

TIME YOURSELF

11 Mr. Marx meets Xena in March.
12 Tim fixes machines in Mexico.
13 Matt Solomon mined metal ore.

| 1 | 2 | 3 | 4 | 5 | 6 WPM: 17

Improve Your Speed

Key the text for one minute. Press Enter after each line. If you reach the end before time is up, start again from the beginning.

9. Apply a SmartArt Style and use the **Change Colors** command to apply new colors.

10. Display the **SmartArt Tools Format** tab. Use the **Arrange** command to position the SmartArt object at the bottom center of the page, with square text wrapping.

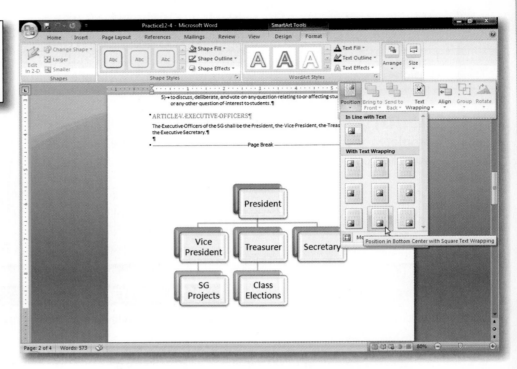

FIGURE 12-8
Customizing and positioning the SmartArt design

11. Use the **Size** command to increase the height of the graphic as desired.

12. At the end of page 4 of the document, insert a Smart-Art graphic using the **Basic Radial** design from the Cycle category (second design in the third row).

13. Click one of the outer circles and use the **Add Shape** command so you have five circles. (You can add the shape before or after the selected shape.)

14. Key the text shown in Figure 12-9 on the next page. Apply a style and change color, as desired. Position the graphic in the middle center of the page. Increase the height of the graphic, as desired.

15. Add page numbers to the bottom of the page and include your name. Do not number the first page.

16. Save the file as *[your initials]***Practice12-5**, print it, and close it.

Review C U W X M and Right Shift

REVIEW

The keyboard shows the keys you have learned so far. This lesson focuses on the keys highlighted in purple.

WARM UP

Key each line twice. Press Enter after each line.

1 Dd Ss Cc Jj Uu Ww Xx Mm cue cruel tuxedo
2 sugar smudge mail male malls urges under
3 Ursa Essex Tom mow met metric metal axle
4 Caitlin wash wish wells waxes masc. fem.

TECHNIQUE TIP

Key by using the correct reach; other fingers should remain in their home positions.

PRACTICE

Key each line twice. Press Enter after each line.

Practice c and u
5 muck duck duct tuck luck lucid cull cuss
6 cute could crush crust touch truck scull
7 deuce stuck stack sticks success custard

Practice w and Right Shift
8 William Washi Wen Winslow Woodrow Wilson
9 Wolfgang Winona Wade Wheeler Wilma Wendi
10 Willow Wallace Wanda Ward Wes Walt Willa

Practice x and m
11 mix Mexican maximum maximal Maddox moxie
12 mixer Alex examined axmen taxman Maxwell
13 mass exits extremes exhumes sixth summer

Practice c u w Right Shift x and m
14 Cellist Cancels a Concert. Felix meowed.
15 Dexter Wexler Chuck chum chew chow exits
16 Sammie worries that few hear much music.

PRACTICE 12-5

Use SmartArt

1. At the end of page 2 of your document, position the insertion point in the blank paragraph before the page break.

2. On the **Insert** tab, click **SmartArt**. From the Hierarchy category, choose the second design, called **Hierarchy**. Click **OK**.

FIGURE 12-7
Choosing a SmartArt design

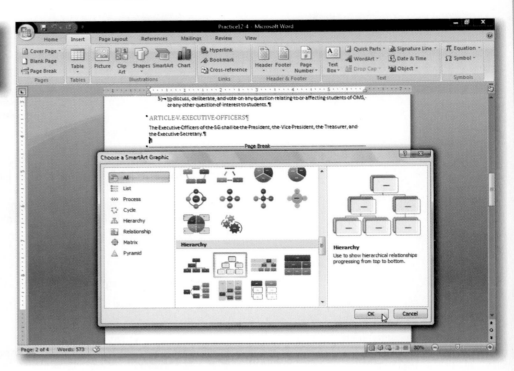

3. With the top box selected, key **President**. Click in the first box reporting to the president and key **Vice President**. Key **Treasurer** in the second box.

4. To add another box reporting directly to the president, click the President box to select it. On the **SmartArt Tools Design** tab, click the first command, **Add Shape**. Choose **Add Shape Below** from the drop-down list.

5. In the new box, key **Secretary**

6. In the first box under the Vice President, key **SG Project**

7. In the box under the Treasurer, key **Class Elections**

8. Delete the extra box under Vice President by clicking the blue outline border of the box and pressing Delete.

Celebrating Native Americans

The first "American Indian Day" was celebrated in 1916 in New York. Some states now celebrate Native Americans on the fourth Friday in September; others have designated Columbus Day as "Native American Day." Since 1990, November has been proclaimed "National American Indian and Alaska Native Heritage Month."

Notable Native American Leaders

Match the Native American leader to his or her tribe. Key the leader's name, a space, and the tribe's name. Start each leader on a new line.

Leader	Tribe
Sacajawea	Shawnee
Tecumseh	Shoshone
Charles Curtis	Kiowa
Lone Wolf	Kansa

TEST YOURSELF

Key each line twice: first slowly and then faster. Press Enter after each line.

Academy Award Winners

1 Hamlet; Crash; Titanic; Chariots of Fire
2 Annie Hall; Letters from Iwo Jima; Reds
3 The Sound of Music; Out of Africa; Gigi
4 On the Waterfront; The Sting; Gladiator
5 Gandhi; Gone with the Wind; The Exorcist
6 Amadeus; Rain Man; The Lord of the Rings

Native Americans

7 James Logan; Little Turtle; Samson Occom
8 Mangas Coloradas; Uncas; Maria Tallchief
9 William Weatherford; Canonicus; Hiawatha

Abbreviations

10 Ms. Mrs. Mme. Mr. Messrs. Dr. Jr. Sr. MD
11 DDE JFK FDR Dem. Sen. USDA UNICEF UNESCO
12 L.A. CA MD WI TX UT; GMAT CAT ATM I.O.U.
13 .html .xls .com MIDI chem. Ext. misc. IT

Improve Your Speed

Key the text for one minute. Press Enter after each line. If you reach the end before time is up, start again from the beginning.

TIME YOURSELF

14 Michi locates the crux of it.
15 Dr. Dux makes music on a sax.
16 Her hat is crushed in a rush.

| 1 | 2 | 3 | 4 | 5 | 6 | **WPM: 18**

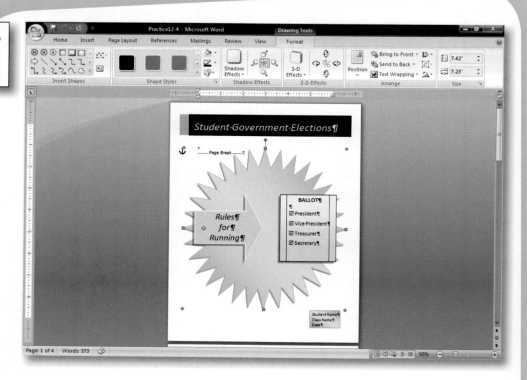

FIGURE 12-6
Grouping and ordering drawing objects

9. Apply a shape style to the selected star.

10. Save the file as *[your initials]***Practice12-4** and leave it open.

Microsoft Word

Using SmartArt

You've worked with tables and shapes to display information in a document. Word provides yet another tool: SmartArt. *SmartArt* is a collection of diagrams composed of shapes for organizing information and communicating ideas. A common use of SmartArt is creating an organization chart.

Like other Word graphics, you can customize SmartArt by applying styles and effects, changing colors, resizing, and so on.

To insert SmartArt:

1. On the **Insert** tab, in the Illustrations group, click **SmartArt**.

2. Select a design and click **OK**.

3. Click in a shape to enter text.

4. Use the **SmartArt Tools Design** tab and the **SmartArt Tools Format** tab to customize the graphic.

LESSON 14 Learn B and Y

WARM UP

Key each line twice. Press Enter after each line. Do not look at the keyboard.

1 if elf fast fill fun effort effect faded
2 end hen den jail Julie hale hinge jogger
3 gas sash fish half fresh joshes freshman
4 Edward jest heft cleft gash grass jagged

LEARN

Reach your **F** finger down and right to key **B**. Keep your **A** finger anchored on its home key. Reach your **J** finger up and left to key **Y**. Keep the other right-hand fingers anchored on their home keys.

PRACTICE

Key each line twice. Press Enter after each line.

Practice b
5 fff fbf bfb bbb fbf bbb fb bf baa be fib
6 bee bib bat bar rub dub cub club tub but
7 been bias bunt tuba stub beef bark about
8 cable rabbit cabbie ribbon rubber bubble

Practice y
9 jjj jyj yyj jjy jyj yyy jy yj yd jay hay
10 you yet yes say sty dry day aye fly away
11 joy jay jury ray rely yolk yen nosy body
12 Young York Yak yam yummy tiny teeny tidy

Practice b and y
13 Bryce buys a bulb to brighten the lobby.
14 Buddy the bulldog labors to bury a bone.
15 Brody yearns for a yacht; bye bye money.

NEW KEYS

B Use the **F** finger.

Y Use the **J** finger.

BREAKING BAD HABITS

Do not reach far for the keyboard. Keep elbows at right angles but free to move slightly.

Grouping and Ordering Drawing Objects (CONTINUED)

To change the order of overlapping drawing objects:

1. Select a drawing object.

2. On either the **Text Box Tools** or **Drawing Tools Format** tab, in the Arrange group, click **Bring to Front** or **Send to Back**. You can also display the drop-down lists for these commands and choose **Bring Forward** or **Send Backward**. The object is moved forward or backward relative to others on the page.

PRACTICE 12-4

Group and Order Objects

1. Click the arrow object to select it. Hold down Shift and click the flowchart object. Both objects are now selected.

2. Display the **Format** tab. Notice that these shapes are now both considered text boxes, because you added text to them.

3. Display the **Group** drop-down list and choose **Group**. The two objects are now a single object with one set of sizing handles.

4. Display the **Format** tab again. Click the Shape Fill 🎨 down arrow and choose another fill color. The color is applied to both objects.

5. Change the page view to **One Page**. Move the grouped objects to the center of the page (point to a border of either shape and drag with the four-headed arrow pointer).

6. On the **Insert** tab, choose the shape called **32-Point Star** from the Stars and Banners category. To draw the star, position the crosshairs below the lower-left corner of the "Student Government Elections" text box. Drag down and to the right, creating a large star that almost covers the grouped objects. See Figure 12-6 on the next page to get an idea of the size.

7. With the new shape still selected, click **Send to Back** on the **Drawing Tools Format** tab. The star moves behind the grouped objects.

8. Adjust the position of the star with the Arrow keys, as needed.

Hurricanes

A *hurricane* is a tropical storm with winds of over 74 miles per hour (mph). The term "hurricane" most often relates to storms that occur over the North Atlantic Ocean. The same type of storm occurring over the Western Pacific Ocean is called a typhoon; over the Indian Ocean, it is a tropical cyclone.

Hurricanes are ranked in strength on the Saffir/Simpson Scale. A Category One hurricane has winds from 74 to 95 mph, while a Category Five hurricane has sustained winds greater than 155 mph.

Satellite view of Hurricane Linda

Famous Hurricanes

Match the hurricane name with its category. Key the name and its category, starting each name on a new line.

Hurricane Charley	Category Two
Hurricane Isabel	Category Three
Hurricane Bonnie	Category Four

TEST YOURSELF

Key each line twice: first slowly and then faster. Press Enter after each line.

Dogs
1 Beagle Bloodhound Greyhound Basset Hound
2 St. Bernard Border Collie Siberian Husky
3 Samoyed Rhodesian Ridgeback Bichon Frise

Famous Hurricanes
4 Katrina Linda Betsy Beulah Bob Ernesto
5 Frederic Bonnie Frances Allison Gilbert
6 Hugo Andrew Gordon Luis Bertha Michael
7 Georges Mitch Floyd Dennis Jeanne Agnes

Sentences
8 Brittany truly belongs to a younger set.
9 Bella says trendy styles suit Abby best.
10 Beryl lobbed the ball; Toby hit it back.
11 Jay dabbled a bit in the study of birds.
12 The boa had beady eyes and a blunt tail.

Improve Your Speed

Key the text for one minute. Press Enter after each line. If you reach the end before time is up, start again from the beginning.

TIME YOURSELF

13 Moby brings Ben a toy rabbit.
14 Becky enjoyed yoga yesterday.
15 Rob blabbed about your story.

| 1 | 2 | 3 | 4 | 5 | 6 | WPM: 18

3. Format the text as 28-point italic, center-aligned.

4. Add the text to the flowchart shape as shown in Figure 12-5 (on the previous page). Format "BALLOT" as 20-point bold, center-aligned. Include a blank line after "BALLOT."

5. Format the text below "BALLOT" as 18-point with 1.5 line spacing.

6. Before the word "President," insert the check-box symbol ☑. This symbol is part of the Wingdings font, in the last row of Wingding characters. (Remember, symbols are on the **Insert** tab.) If this symbol is not available, choose another one.

7. Add a space character after the symbol and before "President." Copy the symbol and space and paste it before the next three titles on the ballot.

8. Leave the document open.

WORD TIP

Another way to format text in shapes is to apply Quick Styles.

Microsoft Word

Grouping and Ordering Drawing Objects

You can group multiple drawing objects in a document, including text boxes, shapes, or lines. Grouping makes them into one object that you can then move and format as a single unit.

Inserting more than one shape in a document can cause shapes to overlap. Shapes are inserted in layers on a page. The last object inserted is higher than the ones inserted before it. The order of these layers determines which object appears on top when they overlap. You can change the order of objects to create a new effect.

To group drawing objects:

1. Choose the objects to group. Click one object to select it. Then hold down Shift and click another object to add it to the selection. (This is referred to as a Shift + click.) Sizing handles appear on each selected object.

2. On either the **Text Box Tools** or **Drawing Tools Format** tab, in the Arrange group, click the **Group** command 🔳. The grouped object appears, with one set of sizing handles.

3. To separate a grouped object, select the object and choose the **Ungroup** command.

CONTINUES

WARM UP

Key each line twice. Press Enter after each line. Key by using the correct reach.

1 ff gg bb fbf fans feels Biff baffles bye
2 j; Jill; lo; hi; his; hers; their; lake;
3 good friend; forge ahead; lost messages;
4 ironclad; tea for two; title match; I.D.

LEARN

Reach your **F** finger down and slightly right to key **V**. Keep your **A** and **S** fingers anchored on their home keys. Reach your **;** finger up and slightly left to key **P**. Keep the other right-hand fingers anchored on their home keys.

PRACTICE

Key each line twice. Press Enter after each line.

Practice v

5 fff fv fv vf fvv vfv vgf fvf fvv vet eve
6 vow van vat vex vote vast vase vest vary
7 ivy ever even envy eave avid alive above

Practice p

8 ;; ;p; pp; ;pp p; pp; ;p ppp pat pad ape
9 pep papa pass pond pane pick paste price
10 sap clap tape press supper paddle puddle

Practice v and p

11 pave peeve prove privy vamp VIP provider
12 vapors viper verve pivot private prevail
13 evil powers oval pools develop viewpoint
14 vampire approve overlap overpaid popover

NEW KEYS

V   Use the **F** finger.

P   Use the **;** finger.

TECHNIQUE TIP

When using your **;** finger to reach for **P**, keep your right elbow close to your side.

WORD TIP

Use conservative style and effect options when working with multiple shapes in a business document.

9. Apply a style to each shape. Then modify the style by changing the Shape Fill color 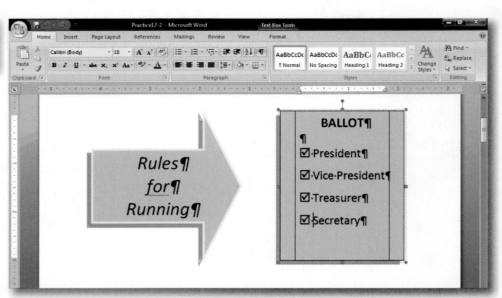, changing the Shape Outline color, or adding a simple shadow effect. You can format each shape the same or use different options that complement each other.

10. Save the document as *[your initials]***Practice12-2** and leave it open.

Microsoft Word

Add Text to Shapes

A shape, like a text box, can also contain text. Some shapes, such as banners and callouts, are more suitable for text than other shapes. You add text to a shape by using the shortcut menu.

To add text to a shape:

1. Right-click the shape.
2. From the shortcut menu, choose **Add Text**.
3. Key text. Format the text and resize the shape as desired.

PRACTICE 12-3

Add Text to Shapes

1. Right-click the arrow shape and choose **Add Text** from the shortcut menu. The insertion point is now in the shape.

2. Key the three lines of text as shown in the arrow shape in Figure 12-5. Use Enter to start a new line.

FIGURE 12-5
Adding text to shapes

Butterflies

A butterfly is an insect. It goes through four developmental stages in its life: egg, larva, pupa, and adult. Butterflies live for only about three months.

Butterflies and moths belong to the same group of insects. However, most moths are active at night, and butterflies are active during the day. Most moths rest with open wings; butterflies rest with closed wings.

North American Butterflies

Match the English name for each butterfly below with its formal Latin name. Key the English name, key a comma and a space, and then key the Latin name. Start each English butterfly name on a new line.

Black Swallowtail butterfly

Black Swallowtail	Plebejus neurona
Cranberry Blue	Glaucopsyche lygdamus
Silvery Blue	Vacciniina optilete
Veined Blue	Papilio polyxenes

TEST YOURSELF

Key each line twice: first slowly and then faster. Press Enter after each line.

Women Senators

1 Carol Moseley Braun; Eva Kelly Bowring
2 Rebecca Latimer Felton; Dianne Feinstein
3 Kay Bailey Hutchison; Dixie Bibb Graves
4 Hillary Rodham Clinton; Debbie Stabenow

North American Butterflies

5 Apricot Sulphur; Harvester; Cassius Blue
6 Miami Blue; Small Blue; Regal Fritillary
7 Swamp Metalmark; Pipevine Swallowtail

Double-Letter Words

8 upper hippo puppies savvy ripple wrapped
9 hippest snippets supposed revved trapped
10 apple copper upped divvy skipper clipper
11 topples supple wrapped millions approved

TIME YOURSELF

Improve Your Speed

Key the text for one minute. Press Enter after each line. If you reach the end before time is up, start again from the beginning.

12 Vince has one pet peeve.
13 Liv appeared very peppy.
14 View Venus and the moon.
15 Buy very purple violets.

| 1 | 2 | 3 | 4 | 5   WPM: 19

Draw Shapes

1. Reduce the magnification of the document to 50% or **One Page** view. Make sure rulers are displayed.

2. Display the **Insert** tab. In the Illustrations group, click **Shapes**.

3. In the Block Arrows group of shapes, choose the first shape, called **Right Arrow**.

4. At the middle left of the page, drag to draw the arrow. Make the arrow shape about 3 inches tall by 3 inches wide.

5. To size the arrow more precisely, set the Shape Height and Shape Width boxes on the **Drawing Tools Format** tab to 3 inches. See Figure 12-4.

> **WORD TIP**
>
> To key a new value in a Size text box, select the existing number, key the new number, and press Enter.

FIGURE 12-4
Drawing shapes

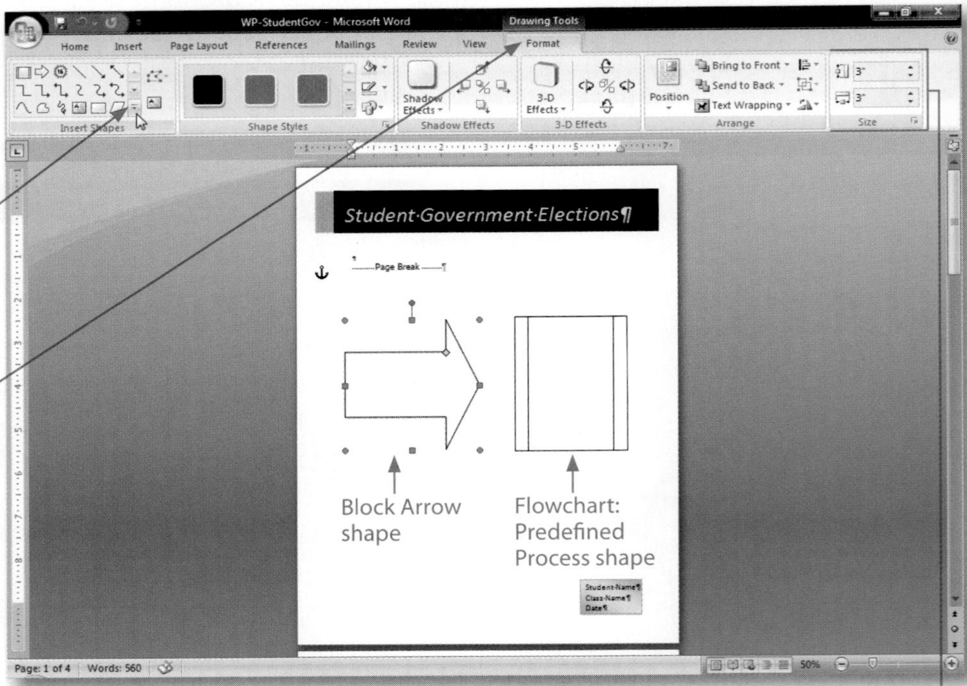

Click the More button to display shapes

Drawing Tools Format tab

Student·Government·Elections¶

Block Arrow shape

Flowchart: Predefined Process shape

Shape size commands

6. On the **Drawing Tools Format** tab, click the Insert Shapes More button ⬇ to reopen the shapes gallery.

7. In the Flowchart group of shapes, choose the fifth shape in the first row, called **Flowchart: Predefined Process** (see the right shape in Figure 12-4).

8. Draw and position the shape as shown in the figure. The shape should be 3 inches high by 2.5 inches wide.

WARM UP

Key each line twice. Press Enter after each line. Strike each key with the correct finger.

1. as aim aide avid aster ashes adapt adept
2. key kid king kit kiss kiln milks kippers
3. okay lanes lake like lamb Luke live long
4. all alarm call rail raffle river Alabama

NEW KEYS

Q Use the **A** finger.

, Use the **K** finger.

The comma is used to separate words and phrases for clearness.

LEARN

Reach your **A** finger up and slightly left to key **Q**. Keep your **D** and **F** fingers anchored on their home keys. Reach your **K** finger down and slightly right to key the comma **,**. Keep your **L** and **;** fingers anchored to their home keys.

PRACTICE

Key each line twice. Press Enter after each line.

Practice q
5. aa aq aqqa qqaa aqa qqa qa qua aqua quad
6. quit quay quite quick quill quilt quaint
7. equip equal squid squad quest quack Que.

Practice ,
8. k, kk, ki, jk, A, B, C, D, E, F, G, H, I
9. one, two, three, four; red, white, blue,
10. Joaquin owned a cat, a dog, and a mouse.

Practice q and ,
11. quiet, quota, quote, squat, squaw, squib
12. Raquel, quail, squirrel, sequel, conquer
13. equate, equator, Quincy, squares, squirt
14. Queen, quake, quasi, qualm, quirk, quash

BREAK ING
BAD HABITS

Do not bend your wrists forward, back, left, or right. Keep them relaxed and straight.

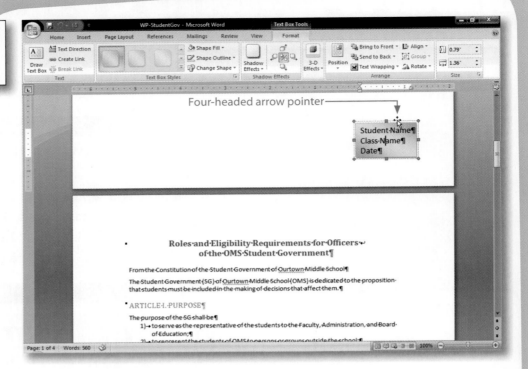

FIGURE 12-3
Dragging selected text box by its border

Four-headed arrow pointer

Student·Name¶
Class·Name¶
Date¶

Roles·and·Eligibility·Requirements·for·Officers↩
of·the·OMS·Student·Government¶

From·the·Constitution·of·the·Student·Government·of·Ourtown·Middle·School¶

The·Student·Government·(SG)·of·Ourtown·Middle·School·(OMS)·is·dedicated·to·the·proposition·
that·students·must·be·included·in·the·making·of·decisions·that·affect·them.¶

ARTICLE·I.·PURPOSE¶

The·purpose·of·the·SG·shall·be¶
1)→to·serve·as·the·representative·of·the·students·to·the·Faculty,·Administration,·and·Board·
of·Education;¶
2)→to·represent·the·students·of·OMS·to·persons·or·groups·outside·the·school;¶

Microsoft Word

Drawing Shapes

Word provides a group of ready-made shapes to add to your documents. These shapes include lines, circles, arrows, callouts, flowchart symbols, stars, and banners. You can move, size, and format a shape. You can also add text to a shape.

To draw a shape:

1. Display the **Insert** tab. In the Illustrations group, click **Shapes**.
2. Click a shape and then drag the crosshairs pointer to draw the shape in the document.

To resize, position, and format a shape:

1. Click the shape to select it.
2. To resize the selected shape, drag one of the corner or side sizing handles. Or, use the Size commands on the **Drawing Tools Format** tab.
3. To position a shape, point to the shape and drag to another location. Or, use the Position commands on the **Drawing Tools Format** tab.
4. To format a shape, apply a style or effect on the **Drawing Tools Format** tab.

Adjectives

An *adjective* modifies a noun or pronoun, providing more detail. In the example "tall building," the adjective "tall" modifies the noun "building."

A *comparative adjective* ends in "er" (taller, nicer) or is preceded by the word "more" (more attractive). A *superlative adjective* ends in "est" (tallest, nicest) or is preceded by the word "most" (most attractive). When an adjective ends in a "y," the "y" is changed to an "i" before adding "er" or "est" (happy, happier, happiest).

Comparative and Superlative Adjectives

Key the following adjectives and their corresponding comparative and superlative adjectives, separating the adjectives with a comma.

Adjective	Comparative	Superlative
long	?	?
sunny	?	?
formal	?	?
soft	?	?

TEST YOURSELF

Key each line twice: first slowly and then faster. Press Enter after each line.

King Arthur and Camelot

1 Queen Igraine, Sir Bors, Sir Lancelot
2 Uther Pendragon, Queen Guinevere, Merlin
3 Sir Galahad, Sir Gawaine, Sir Mordred

Adjectives Modifying Nouns

4 bad news, better idea, quickest route
5 most qualified buyer, quirkiest habit
6 funny quote, long queue, simple query
7 quiet times, more damaging earthquake

Ⓛ Finger Focus

8 love lore loft lull Lola labors operates
9 Oct. Nov. vol. pop. Col. Lt. Corp. long.
10 Slower lion. Only one. Most lovely. Old.

TIME YOURSELF

Improve Your Speed

Key the text for one minute. Press Enter after each line. If you reach the end before time is up, start again from the beginning.

11 Quentin quips about age.
12 Buy quarts, not gallons.
13 She asks for equal time.
14 Do not quibble with him.

| 1 | 2 | 3 | 4 | 5 | **WPM: 19**

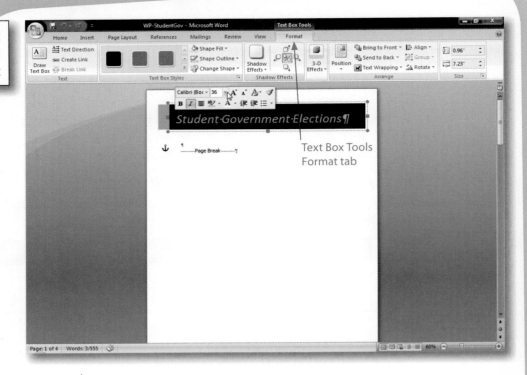

FIGURE 12-2
Keying and formatting
text in the text box

Text Box Tools
Format tab

7. Click outside the text box to deselect it.

8. Click the **Text Box** command again and choose **Draw Text Box**. The pointer looks like a plus sign.

9. Place the pointer in the middle of the page and drag to draw a small rectangle; it should be roughly large enough for the title word "Elections" to fit into it (about 1-inch high and 2-inches wide).

10. In the text box, key your name, your class name, and the date, on three separate lines.

11. Select the text and increase the font size to 14 points.

12. Resize the text box to fit the text by dragging a corner or side sizing handle. Drag to make the box as wide as the longest line and high enough to fit the three lines.

13. With the text box still selected, scroll the Text Box Styles on the **Text Box Tools Format** tab. (You can click the More button ⊡ to display all styles.) Click a style to apply it.

14. Point to a border of the selected text box. When you see the four-headed arrow pointer (as shown in Figure 12-3 on the next page), drag the text box to the lower-right corner of the page.

WORD TIP

Dragging a corner sizing handle allows you to change the width and height at the same time.

REVIEW

The keyboard shows the keys you have learned so far. This lesson focuses on the keys highlighted in purple.

WARM UP

Key each line twice. Press Enter after each line.

1 fad frail Frank Alfred bug bud bush vast
2 hen Hanna vary very your young yell yelp
3 bevy; pamper; prove; pixie; posh; gladly
4 year, ache, acre, squish, piquant, quint

TECHNIQUE TIP

Make sure your back is straight or tilted slightly forward from the hips.

PRACTICE

Key each line twice. Press Enter after each line.

Practice b and y
5 byte ruby abyss shabby tabby bygone days
6 bay birthday yellow belly bully boundary
7 gabby cubby abbey bubbly burly hobby buy

Practice v and p
8 vapor vapid pensive pave preview prevent
9 Vice President V.I.P. overpaid passivity
10 Pablo plays the vibraphone very happily.

Practice q and ,
11 Quite, squab, quickens, quibble, quantum
12 Queens, quits, toque, quarrels, quantity
13 Quinn squashed it quickly and then quit.

Practice b y v p q and ,
14 pay pry bypass bumpy pebbly pygmy opaque
15 brave, vinyl, brevity, behave very badly
16 Bowery Boys, Marquis, Beverly, Quasimodo

Working with Text Boxes (CONTINUED)

To draw a text box:

1. Display the **Insert** tab. In the Text group, click **Text Box**.
2. Below the gallery of text boxes, click **Draw Text Box**.
3. Drag the crosshairs pointer to create a box. Release the mouse button when you have the size and shape you want.

To resize, position, and format a text box:

1. Click within the text box to select it.
2. To resize the selected text box, drag one of the corner or side sizing handles. Or, use the Size commands on the **Text Box Tools Format** tab.
3. To position the text box, point to an outside border of the text box and drag the box to another location. Or, use the Position commands on the **Text Box Tools Format** tab.
4. To format the text box, apply a style or effect on the **Text Box Tools Format** tab.

PRACTICE 12-1

Insert Text Boxes

1. Open the document **WP-StudentGov**. The document already has a blank first page on which you will place drawing objects.
2. Display nonprinting characters. With the insertion point on the first page, display the **Insert** tab and click **Text Box**.
3. Scroll the gallery of text boxes. Notice the styles for quotes and sidebars.
4. Click the last text box, called **Transcend Sidebar**. The text box is inserted in the document and the **Text Box Tools Format** tab appears. You will use this preformatted text box for a title.
5. With the placeholder text in the text box already selected, key **Student Government Elections**
6. Select the text you just keyed and use the Mini toolbar to increase the font size to 36 points.

Roller Coasters

Many people enjoy the thrill of riding roller coasters at amusement parks, but do you know how a roller coaster works?

Though the typical roller coaster speeds along at over 60 miles per hour, it has no engine. The roller coaster cars are pulled to the top of the first hill and then released to run the course. This converts potential energy to kinetic energy. All of the kinetic energy needed to complete the course is available when the train falls down that first hill.

The Cyclone
Astroland Park
Coney Island, NY

Great Roller Coasters

Match the roller coaster names below to the amusement park in which the ride is found. Key the coaster name, a comma, a space, and the park.

```
Mean Streak          Six Flags Over Texas
Titan                Hersheypark
Roller Soaker        Cedar Point
```

TEST YOURSELF

Key each line twice: first slowly and then faster. Press Enter after each line.

NCAA Athletic Conferences
1 Atlantic Coast, Southeastern, PAC Ten
2 Mountain West, Ohio Valley, Northeast
3 Metro Atlantic Athletic, Atlantic Ten
4 Gateway Football, Independent, Ivy Group

Roller Coasters
5 The Villain, Quantum Loop, Poltergeist
6 Yankee Cannonball, Little Dipper, Nitro
7 Cyclone, Vortex, Wild Mouse, Sidewinder

D Finger Focus
8 fed, deck, deed, decent, deceive, decree
9 creed, chanced, needed, decided, fleeced
10 Eddie and Cedric dared to do good deeds.
11 precede, deduce, recede, succeed, deemed

TIME YOURSELF

12 Maya bought a new Viper.
13 I provided yellow paper.
14 Pave your patio, please.
15 Quit playing that piano.

| 1 | 2 | 3 | 4 | 5   **WPM: 20**

Improve Your Speed

Key the text for one minute. Press Enter after each line. If you reach the end before time is up, start again from the beginning.

Use Drawing Tools

LEARN

Drawing in Word Another way to illustrate ideas in your document is to create your own graphics with drawing tools. You can draw lines, arrows, text boxes and other shapes and apply styles and special effects to these objects. You can also use the SmartArt feature and create predesigned diagrams, such as organization charts, to display information clearly and attractively.

Microsoft Word

Working with Text Boxes

A *text box* is a free-floating rectangle that contains text. Word provides several predesigned text boxes to enhance your documents. You can also draw your own textboxes and then change their position, size, and format.

To insert a predesigned text box:

1. Display the **Insert** tab. In the Text group, click **Text Box**.
2. Click one of the text box styles to insert it in the document.
3. Key text in the text box.

FIGURE 12-1
Inserting a text box

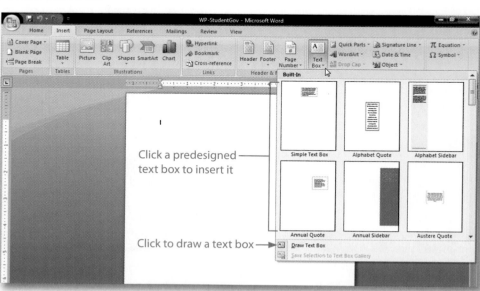

Click a predesigned text box to insert it

Click to draw a text box

CONTINUES

WARM UP

Key each line twice. Press Enter after each line. Keep your wrists relaxed and straight.

1   debut past perk park chances dares tries
2   flurry hurry scurry enjoy delays happens
3   salve settles vessel vassal caste create
4   Frasier will pursue a career in finance.

NEW KEYS

Z   Use the **A** finger.

:   Use Left Shift and the **;** finger.

The colon (:) is used in numerical expressions and to direct attention to information that follows (as in "For example:").

LEARN

Reach your **A** finger down and slightly right when you key **Z**. Keep the left-hand fingers anchored on their home keys. Keying the colon is like keying a capital letter. Hold down the Left Shift key and strike **:**. Then release Left Shift.

SPACING TIP

In a sentence, you use one space after a colon.

PRACTICE

Key each line twice. Press Enter after each line.

Practice z

5   a az aza zza zaz aqza za azq zza zap zoo
6   zoom zest zeal Zen zinc zone cozy zipper
7   Zuni fizz fuzz zigzag zebra zero pizzazz
8   zip quiz lazy mezzo muzzle zenith frozen

Practice :

9   ; ;: :: ;: :; ::: Sirs: Ext: As follows:
10   Memo To: From: Date: Subj: RE: CC: ATTN:
11   To Whom It May Concern: Dear Madam: Ref:

Practice z and :

12   Dear Elizabeth: To: Mrs. Dezanne Ziegler
13   Puzzle answer: ZIP Code: Zone: Size: NZ:
14   Zoe: Zora: Oz: Ziggy: Ezra: Zelda: Buzz:

FIGURE 11-10
Chinese astrology uses 12 animals to represent the character of people born in different years. Which animal represents your birth year?

The Chinese Zodiac

Create a one- or two-page report on the signs of the Chinese zodiac.

In writing your report, be sure to:

1. Include a title formatted as WordArt.

2. Insert a document header or footer with your name. If the document is longer than a page, also include the page number.

3. Use at least two illustrations. Use clip art, files in **Lesson11clips/Chinese astrology**, or illustrations you find on the Internet.

4. Set text wrapping for your illustrations so you can position them anywhere on the page.

5. Place illustrations so they are visually balanced on the page.

6. Size the illustrations so they are right for your subject.

7. Apply appropriate picture styles and/or special effects that enhance the images and the document.

8. Save the document as *[your initials]***Test11-3**. Print it, and then close all open documents.

Exploring the Americas

For about 1,000 years—from Leif Ericsson's arrival in Newfoundland to the founding of the United States—British, Spanish, French, Portuguese, and Dutch explorers crisscrossed the oceans of the world in search of knowledge and treasure. Their discoveries and interactions with the people already living in the "New World" are an important part of human history.

Exploration Terms

Define each of the following exploration terms. Key the term, a colon, a space, and the definition. Start each term on a new line.

Cartographer	Astrolabe
Chronometer	Sextant
Quadrant	Caravel
Compass rose	Flotsam

TEST YOURSELF

Key each line twice: first slowly and then faster. Press Enter after each line.

Scientific Terms

1 Hz, quartz, analyze, fossilize, iodized,
2 neutralize, ionization, ozone, polarize,
3 optimize, hybridization, polymerization,
4 hypothesize, enzyme, fertilize, rhizoid,

Explorers and Exploration

5 cape, sextant, caravel, quadrant, fathom
6 equator, North Star, Aztec, Maya, Cortez
7 Magellan, Champlain, Vespucci, Verrazano
8 Montezuma, chronometer, compass, flotsam
9 Henry Hudson, Balboa, Vikings, Vancouver

(A) Finger Focus

10 aqua daze lazy plaza graze ablaze amazed
11 piazza bazaar quad quizzes dazzle Brazil
12 haze raze zany snazzy jazz hazard quasar
13 AZ Arizona Amazon Anasazi Zaire Zanzibar

 ## TIME YOURSELF

14 A piazza is a public square in a town in
15 Italy. It functions as both a meeting
16 place and a market place.

| 1 | 2 | 3 | 4 | 5 | 6 | 7 | 8 | **WPM: 21**

Improve Your Speed

Key the paragraph for one minute. Use word wrap. If you reach the end before time is up, start again from the beginning.

DID YOU KNOW?

Coins were essential to ancient Greek trade and helped spread Greek culture.

Ancient Greek Coins

1. Start Word and open **WP-CorinthCoins**. You will add clip art and WordArt to illustrate this document. The document contains text in square brackets to indicate the placement for art: [Map], [Pegasus], [Dolphin], and [Demeter].

2. Select all the text except the last line and change the font size to 14 points. Format the selected text with justified alignment.

3. Delete [Map] and, in its place, insert either the file **corinthmap** or the file **greece-corinth** from the */Lesson11Clips* folder.

4. Apply square text wrapping to the map. Change the height to 1.3 inches. Apply a picture style to the map.

5. Drag the map below the first line of text in the first paragraph (which begins "The ancient Greek city-state").

6. Delete [Pegasus]. Insert the file **Pegasus** in its place. Apply square text wrapping and size the clip to 1-inch high. Apply a picture style to the clip.

7. Drag the Pegasus clip to the right of the second paragraph, aligned with the right margin. After dragging the picture into place, you can use the Arrow keys to fine-tune the position of the picture, if desired.

8. Delete [Dolphin]. Insert the file **Dolphin** in its place. Format the size, text wrapping, and picture style the same as **Pegasus**. **Dolphin** should align at the left margin. The top of the picture should align with the top of the third paragraph (which begins "From about 415 B.C.").

9. Delete [Demeter]. Insert the file **Demeter** in its place. Format the size, text wrapping, and style as you did the previous two images. Drag the clip to the right of the last paragraph (which begins "Some figures"), aligned with the right margin.

10. Delete [WordArt]. Select the title and convert it to WordArt. Select a style and size that allows the document to print on one page.

11. Add a document footer with your name.

12. Save the file as *[your initials]***Test11-2**. Print and then close the document.

LESSON 19 Learn

NEW KEYS

 Use the ⌨ finger.

The apostrophe (') has many purposes. Use it to form contractions (don't) and possessives (John's).

 Use Left Shift and the ⌨ finger.

Use quotation marks (" ") to enclose direct quotations, to emphasize words, and to display certain titles.

BREAKING BAD HABITS

Do not hammer your fingers on the keyboard. Strike keys with a light tap.

WARM UP

Key each line twice. Press Enter after each line. Keep your eyes on the page and not on the keyboard.

1 fizz fuzz dizzy gaze buzzer prized gizmo
2 Abbot alley fast has lasts dash flag lab
3 play; pram; pads; my pals; swamps; pique
4 Name: Address: FAX: cars, planes, trains

LEARN

Reach your ⌨ finger right to key an apostrophe . Keep the J, K, and L fingers anchored on their home keys. To key a quotation mark, hold down Left Shift, reach your ⌨ finger right, and strike .

PRACTICE

Key each line twice. Press Enter after each line.

Practice '
5 ;' ;';' ';'; 's s' it's I'm isn't aren't
6 Jill's Dave's Omar's didn't don't aren't
7 isn't hadn't should've would've could've

Practice "
8 ;" ";"; "x" "y" "A" "B" "My Way" "Okay."
9 "Not me." "Maybe soon." "See you later."
10 "Just enough," she said. "Oh, we agree."

Practice ' and "
11 "It's Magic" "Let's Dance" "That's Life"
12 "Don't hang up." "I'll call." "I'm Sue."
13 "Malcolm's moved the boxes," Rubin said.
14 It's the book "Emma" for Mr. Hu's class.
15 "Lillie won't travel on New Year's Eve."

7. Add a document header with your name.

8. Save your document as *[your initials]***Practice11-5**. Print it and close all open documents.

TEST YOURSELF 11-1

DID YOU KNOW?

Decorative art can add interest to mathematical material.

Add Interest to Calculations

1. Start Word and open **WP-Percent of Change**. Edit the document header to include your name. You will add decorative clip art and WordArt to this document.

2. Position the insertion point at the beginning of the paragraph that begins "Look at the farm production data." You will insert clip art at this location.

3. Display the Clip Art task pane and search for clips using the keyword **corn**. If you get no suitable results, search for **crops**. Click the clip you want to insert. As an alternative, open the document **WP-Corn Clipart**. Copy one of the clips and paste it into your document.

4. Position the insertion point at the beginning of the first paragraph (which begins "Percents show"). You will insert a picture from a file at this location.

5. Display the Insert Picture dialog box and navigate to the folder **Lesson11clips**.

6. View the files in the dialog box as large icons, and then select either **sales1** or **sales2** to insert.

7. Apply square text wrapping to the sales clip.

8. Size the picture to 1.4 inches in height.

9. Select the corn clip. Use the **Position** command to place the picture in the middle right of the page.

10. Size the corn clip to 1.7 inches in height.

11. Apply a picture style to both clips.

12. Select the title "Percent of Change" (exclude the paragraph mark). Use it to create WordArt. In the Edit WordArt Text dialog box, change the font size to 28 points.

13. After inserting the WordArt title, center-align it (use the Align Text button in the Text group on the **WordArt Tools Format** tab). You might first have to move the sales picture down slightly to make room for the title.

14. If the document exceeds one page, make adjustments to the size of the art.

15. Save the file as *[your initials]***Test11-1**. Print it. Close all open documents.

Adverbs

Adverbs, like adjectives, are modifiers. Adverbs can modify:

- ✦ A verb (He typed quickly. "Quickly" modifies the verb "type.")
- ✦ An adjective (He's a fairly fast typist. "Fairly" modifies the adjective "fast.")
- ✦ Another adverb (He typed quite quickly. "Quite" modifies the adverb "quickly."

Adverbs are often used to emphasize or downplay something:

    I absolutely enjoy going.   I somewhat enjoy going.

ADVERBS OFTEN DESCRIBE:
When?
Why?
Where?
How?
How much?

Using Adverbs

Key the following sentences, inserting an adverb for emphasis in each of the blanks.

```
"I am            aware of the situation," Zola assured them.
The teacher is          satisfied with the class's good grades.
Joel told the audience, "I am          happy to win."
After getting his car tuned up, it ran          well.
```

TEST YOURSELF

Key each line twice: first slowly and then faster. Press Enter after each line.

Clichés
1. "No guts, no glory." "Time will tell."
2. "I'm so glad to be able to contribute."
3. "You've got to walk before you can run."
4. "It's always darkest before the dawn."

Adverbs
5. absolutely certainly heartily completely
6. literally attractively highly intensely
7. He said the pizza tasted amazingly good.
8. "Eric dresses extremely well," said Lea.

Contractions and Quotations
9. Jayden said, "I'm sure they've gone in."
10. "My brother's car didn't budge," I said.
11. "Mary's thinking we're in Roz's office."

Improve Your Speed

Key the paragraph for one minute. Use word wrap. If you reach the end before time is up, start again from the beginning.

TIME YOURSELF

12. When a teacher gives good grades to a
13. class, it shows that both the class and
14. the teacher have done their work.

| 1 | 2 | 3 | 4 | 5 | 6 | 7 | 8 | **WPM: 22**

Creating WordArt

WordArt is a tool for converting text into a decorative image. You can shadow, mirror, or stretch WordArt text and fit it to a specific shape.

To create WordArt:

1. Select the text you are converting to WordArt.

2. Display the **Insert** tab. From the Text group, click **WordArt**. Click a WordArt style from the gallery.

3. If you are using WordArt with new text (or you need to edit existing text), key or edit the text in the Edit WordArt Text dialog box. You may change the font and size. Then click **OK**.

4. To modify the WordArt image, use the tools on the **WordArt Tools Format** tab (if the tab is not visible, double-click the WordArt image).

FIGURE 11-9
WordArt Tools
Format tab

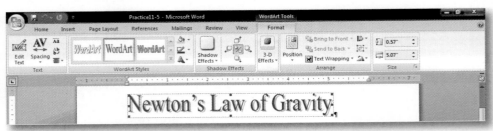

PRACTICE 11-5

Creating WordArt

1. Select the title "Newton's Law of Gravity." Do not select the paragraph mark.

2. On the **Insert** tab, click **WordArt** to display the WordArt gallery.

3. Click a style in the gallery. The Edit WordArt Text dialog box appears.

4. Click **OK**. The selected text is now a WordArt image in your document. The image is an inline graphic that you can move and size as you would any graphic.

5. On the **WordArt Tools Format** tab, in the Size group, increase the width 🔲 of the WordArt image to 6 inches so it extends from the left to the right margin.

6. If the WordArt makes your document go to two pages, reduce the height of the WordArt or choose another style on the **WordArt Tools Format** tab. You can also reduce the size of your other images, as needed.

NEW KEYS

 Use the 🔑 finger.

A hyphen (-) is used to divide words between lines. It is also used for compound words.

❓ Use the 🔑 finger.

A diagonal (/), often called a forward slash, is used in abbreviations, in fractions, and to express alternatives or relationships.

SPACING TIP

In normal use, do not space before or after the diagonal.

WARM UP

Key each line twice. Press Enter after each line. Hold your head straight, without leaning it forward or backward.

1 "Let's go pick apples," Sophie proposed.
2 Paco's parrot piped up, "I'm not Polly."
3 Shipped to: Paul Lopez; PS: Please RSVP.
4 Piper liked papaya; Piper's aunt didn't.

LEARN

To key a hyphen, reach your 🔑 finger up and slightly right and strike . Keep the Ⓙ finger anchored on its home key. To key a diagonal, reach your 🔑 finger down and slightly right and strike ❓. Keep the other right-hand fingers anchored on their home keys.

PRACTICE

Key each line twice. Press Enter after each line.

Practice -
5 ;p; ;p-p; ;-; ;-; -er one-on-one T-shirt
6 side-by-side, after-effects, part-timers
7 toll-free, good-humored, close-captioned

Practice /
8 ;/; ;//; ;//;/ a/b I/we he/she East/West
9 true/false, owner/manager, and/or, AM/FM
10 his/her, on/off, either/or, input/output

Practice - and /
11 best-case/worst-case, high-rise/low-rise
12 left-hand/right-hand, mid-week/mid-month
13 paper-thin/see-through, ice-cold/red-hot
14 tax-exempt/tax-sheltered one-way/two-way

WORD TIP

If the Picture Tools Format tab is visible, you only need to click a picture to select it for formatting. If the Picture Tools Format tab is not visible, double-clicking the picture selects the picture and displays the tab.

PRACTICE 11-4

Styling Images

1. Double-click the image of Newton. In the Picture Styles group, click the More button ⊡ to see all the styles.

2. Move the pointer over each style without clicking. The style name appears when you point to it, and the image displays the style formatting.

3. Choose the framed style in the second row, called **Simple Frame, Black**.

4. Click the apple image. Apply the third picture style in the fourth row, called **Perspective Shadow, White**.

FIGURE 11-8
Applying picture styles

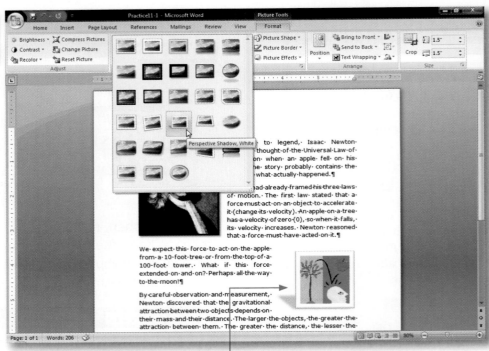

Perspective shadow: white

5. Click the moon image. Apply the second picture style in the fourth row, called **Rotated, White**.

6. With the moon still selected, display the **Picture Effects** drop-down list. Click **Glow**. Apply any color from the second row of glow variations. The glow effect is added to the already styled picture.

Morse Code

In 1835, Samuel Morse, a professor of arts and design at New York University, proved that electrical wires could be used to transmit signals. Using the telegraph, Morse created a communication system of dot and dash signals that was named the Morse Code.

MORSE CODE							
a	.–	h	....	o	– – –	v	...–
b	–...	i	..	p	.– –.	w	.– –
c	–.–.	j	.– – –	q	– –.–	x	–..–
d	–..	k	–.–	r	.–.	y	–.– –
e	.	l	.–..	s	...	z	– –..
f	..–.	m	– –	t	–	period	.–.–.–
g	– –.	n	–.	u	..–	comma	– –..– –

Message Decoding

The following Morse Code messages are made up of dots (periods) and dashes (hyphens). Each forward slash marks the end of a word or sentence. Key each line of code, followed by its English translation.

```
.– – .– .–.. –.–/– .... ./–.. – – – – –/.–.–.–/
.– – ./–.–. .– –../– .– .–.. –.–/.–.–.–/
```

TEST YOURSELF

Key each line twice: first slowly and then faster. Press Enter after each line.

Hyphenated Names

1 Rudolf-Heinz, Samantha-Lynn, Gray-Abbott
2 Ada-Marie, Vinh-Loc, Paul-David, Mei-Lin
3 Xiao-Li, Guo-Hong, Jan-Pieter, Ellie-Mae
4 Jackie Johnston-Smith, Pat Rodman-Greene

Morse Coded Messages

Key each line of code, followed by its English translation.

5 ../.– – –/.... .– .– –. .– – – .––.–/.–.–.–/
6 .–.. . – –/..– ...–/– –. – – –/– – – –.. /.–.–.–/
7 .. – /.. ... /..–. .– –. –. – – –/.–.–.–/

Punctuation Review

8 She labeled it "c/o Mrs. A. James-Wynn."
9 "It's probably win-or-lose/hit-or-miss."
10 "Yes," she said, "it's open year-round."
11 Their washer/dryer was included "as is."

SPACING TIP

Do not space before or after a hyphen.

SPACING TIP

Space before the first quotation mark in a pair. Space after the second quotation mark in a pair.

Improve Your Speed

Key the paragraph for one minute. Use word wrap. If you reach the end before time is up, start again from the beginning.

⏰ TIME YOURSELF

12 It's fun to pick apples in the fall. If
13 you pick a bushel, get ready to eat a
14 lot of apples or bake some pies.

| 1 | 2 | 3 | 4 | 5 | 6 | 7 | 8 | WPM: 22

7. Select the apple image. Click **Position**. Choose Middle Right with Square Text Wrapping. See Figure 11-7.

FIGURE 11-7
Position options

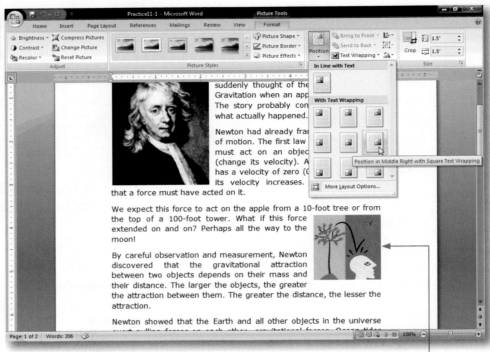

Art is positioned in the middle right of the page with square text wrapping.

8. Select the moon image. Choose the position Bottom Left with Square Text Wrapping.

9. Leave the document open.

Microsoft Word

Styling Images

Word provides many tools for enhancing your inserted images. You can apply prede-signed styles and special effects, which include shadows, frames, reflections, soft edges, 3-D effects, and much more.

To style an image:

1. Double-click the image to select it and display the **Picture Tools Format** tab.

2. In the Picture Styles group, choose a style. (Click the More button ⬛ to see all the styles.) Click a style to apply it.

3. To see more options, click **Picture Effects**. From the drop-down list, choose an effect category and then click an effect variation to apply it.

Review Z ; " — and ?/

REVIEW

The keyboard shows the keys you have learned so far. This lesson focuses on the keys highlighted in purple.

WARM UP

Key each line twice. Press Enter after each line. Begin with your fingers curled and lightly touching the home keys.

1 brazen shilly-shally sizzle crazy quartz
2 Don's fez, Via: tilt-a-whirl willy-nilly
3 mightn't hadn't "Don't say such things."
4 http://www.si.edu "wall-to-wall" mi./hr.

PRACTICE

Key each line twice. Press Enter after each line.

Practice z and :

5 Price per dozen: Prize: Size: Zookeeper:
6 Zone: Bronze medal: Tarzan: Waltz: Czar:

Practice ' and "

7 "Neither a borrower nor a lender be." S.
8 "Don't just say 'Don't' like that's it."

Practice - and /

9 street-smart/quick-witted/sharp-sighted;
10 He/she must give a blow-by-blow account.
11 She provides on-site support for E-mail.

Practice z : ' " - and /

12 "door-to-door" 'self-employed' in-house:
13 log-jam low-flying "Long-Range" two-term
14 Zig Lenz: Writer/Producer; life-or-death
15 A day of dappled sea-born clouds. -Joyce

SPACING TIPS

Remember: Do not key a space before or after a hyphen in a hyphenated word. Do not key a space before or after a diagonal.

Text Wrapping and Positioning Images (CONTINUED)

FIGURE 11-6
Text Wrapping options

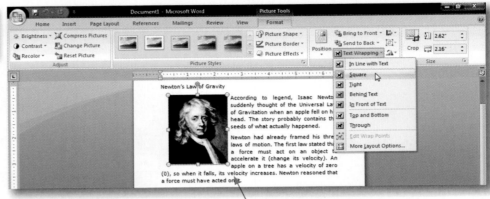

Text wraps around picture

3. Point within the image and hold down the mouse button.

4. Drag the image to a new location, and release the mouse button.

To choose a specific position for an image:

1. Double-click the image to select it and display the **Picture Tools Format** tab.

2. In the Arrange group of commands, click **Position**. Choose an option from the drop-down list. The Text Wrapping options will position the image in a specific location on the page and wrap text around the image.

PRACTICE 11-3

Positioning Images

1. Click the image of Newton. Then point within the image and hold down the mouse button.

2. Drag down until the mouse pointer moves the insertion point to the beginning of the second paragraph. Release the mouse button.

3. Undo the move.

4. Select Newton again. Make sure the commands on the **Picture Tools Format** tab are visible; if they are not, double-click the Newton picture.

5. In the Arrange group, click **Text Wrapping** and choose the **Square** option. The text wraps around the right side of the image.

6. If the document title is not aligned with the left margin, drag the picture down very slightly.

WORD TIP

You can also move a selected image by using the Arrow keys.

The Romantic Period

The Romantic Period in British literature lasted from about 1785 to about 1830. In art and literature, this was a time when emotion and the striving for self-expression were central to artists and writers. Some of the well-known poets of this period are John Keats, William Blake, and Lord Byron (George Gordon).

Lord Byron

Romantic Poetry

Key the following opening lines from Lord Byron's poem "She Walks in Beauty." Press Enter at the end of each line.

```
She walks in beauty like the night
Of cloudless climes and starry skies,
And all that's best of dark and bright
Meet in her aspect and her eyes;
Thus mellowed to the tender light
Which heaven to gaudy day denies.
```

TEST YOURSELF

Key each line twice: first slowly and then faster. Press Enter after each line. Concentrate on each letter.

Volcanoes
1 In New Mexico: Zuni-Bandera, Carrizozo
2 In Caribbean: Qualibou, Kick-'em-Jenny
3 In Japan: Iwo-jima, Kozu-shima, Unzen
4 In Russia: Zavaritzki, Ozernoy, Zaozerny

Romantic Poems
5 "The Tyger" "Tintern Abbey" "Christabel"
6 "The Haunted Beach" "Eternity of Nature"
7 "To a Sky-Lark" "Adonais" "Rose Aylmer"
8 "Ode to a Nightingale" "Abou Ben Adhem"

Food
9 Italian Food: baked ziti, pizza, calzone
10 mozzarella cheese, panzanella, orzo soup
11 Snacks/dessert: glazed donuts, pretzels
12 crepes suzettes, hazelnuts, Brazil nuts

Improve Your Speed

Key the paragraph for one minute. Use word wrap. If you reach the end before time is up, start again from the beginning.

TIME YOURSELF

13 Poets often write about the stars and
14 clouds they see in the skies, and about
15 what they see in a loved one's eyes.

| 1 | 2 | 3 | 4 | 5 | 6 | 7 | 8 | WPM: 23

Resizing Images

1. Click the picture of Newton to select it. Point to the sizing handle in the upper-right corner. Drag the handle toward the center of the picture until the picture is about half as tall.

2. Double-click the apple image. On the **Picture Tools Format** tab, click the down arrow next to the Shape Height ↕ box until the setting is **1.5**.

FIGURE 11-5
Sizing commands on the Picture Tools Format tab

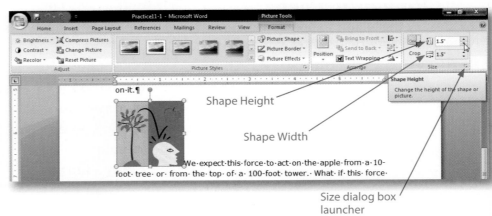

3. Click the moon image. Click the Size dialog box launcher ⬛.

4. In the Size dialog box, under **Scale**, key **25%** in the **Height** box. Click **Close**.

5. Leave the document open.

Microsoft Word

Text Wrapping and Positioning Images

Text wrapping is a property of an image that determines how text flows around it. By default, an image is inserted as an *inline graphic*. It aligns with the paragraph and is treated as a character.

By changing an image's text-wrapping property, you can make it a *floating graphic*. You can move a floating graphic freely in a Word document. You can control how text flows around a floating graphic.

To change text wrapping and position an image by dragging:

1. Double-click the image to select it and display the **Picture Tools Format** tab.

2. In the Arrange group of commands, click **Text Wrapping**. Choose an option from the drop-down list.

CONTINUES

Learn Caps Lock and

WARM UP

Key each line twice. Press Enter after each line. Focus on your technique, not on speed.

1 AR append alternate Aswan Dallas daisies
2 Q.E.D. client-server peer-to-peer hi-res
3 Pass/Fail E/G/B/D/F play-by-play on-site
4 La Paz quizzical A-OK on-again/off-again

NEW KEYS

Caps Lock Use the **A** finger.

Use Caps Lock to key capital letters without pressing Right Shift or Left Shift.

Use Left Shift and the ; finger.

Use a question mark (?) at the end of a sentence that asks a question.

LEARN

Reach your **A** finger left to press Caps Lock. Keep all other fingers on their home keys. (Once you press Caps Lock, it stays on until you press it again.) The question mark is a shifted diagonal. Press Left Shift, reach your ; finger down and slightly right, and strike ?.

PRACTICE

Key each line twice. Press Enter after each line.

Practice Caps Lock

5 NBA, NFL, AND NCAA ANNOUNCE RULE CHANGES
6 ASPCA FINDS LOST DOG; ROVER RETURNS HOME
7 IMAGINE: MEN WALK ON MOON; READ ABOUT IT

Practice ?

8 ;/; ;?; :?? ?:? ?;? ?/?/? Who? How? Why?
9 Me? When? Soon? What day? Are you going?
10 Can you? Would you? Could you? Call me?

Practice Caps Lock and ?

11 VISITOR FROM SPACE? AN ECONOMIC SETBACK?
12 PRESIDENT'S TRIP ON HOLD? TWO TEE TIMES?
13 VIKINGS IN THE NEW WORLD? KENNEWICK MAN?
14 MASSIVE CALCULATION ERRORS TO BLAME? US?

TECHNIQUE TIP

The Caps Lock key works only on letter keys. You still have to press Left Shift to key punctuation such as a question mark, a colon, or a quotation mark.

Resizing Images (CONTINUED)

To resize an image by hand:

1. Click the image to select it. Sizing handles appear on the corners and sides of the selected image.

2. Drag a corner sizing handle toward the center of the image to make the image smaller, or away from the center to make the image larger. A corner handle resizes the image proportionally. (Dragging a center handle distorts the image.)

FIGURE 11-3
Resizing an image

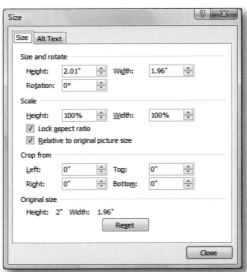

Rotation handle

Use corner handle to resize the image proportionally.

Sizing handles

To resize an image to an exact measure:

1. Double-click the image to select it and display the **Picture Tools Format** tab on the Ribbon.

2. In the Size group (at the right side of the Ribbon), adjust the settings for shape height 🔲 or shape width 🔲. Changing one setting automatically changes the other to maintain the proportions of the image.

3. For more sizing controls, click the dialog box launcher 🔲 in the Size group to display the Size dialog box. You can use this dialog box to size, rotate, scale, and crop an image, or to reset an image to its original size.

FIGURE 11-4
Size dialog box

State Names

Since the first state, Delaware, entered the union in 1787, each new state has chosen a name. A state's name was often a link to the origins of its people or to European ancestry. For example, the name "Kentucky" comes from an Iroquoian word "Ken-tah-ten" meaning "land of tomorrow."

Meanings of State Names

The following states were all named after Native American words. Match the state with its meaning. On a separate line for each state, key the state, a colon, a space, and the correct meaning in quotes.

State	Meaning
Connecticut	"People of the south wind"
Michigan	"Beside the long tidal river"
Kansas	"Great or long lake"
Mississippi	"Father of Waters"

Texas is named after a Native American word meaning "friends."

TEST YOURSELF

Key each line twice: first slowly and then faster. Press Enter after each line.

Painters
1. CEZANNE CHAGALL DUCHAMP ESCHER TITIAN
2. GOYA VAN GOGH KAHLO KANDINSKY KIRCHNER
3. KLEE PICASSO O'KEEFFE REMBRANDT RENOIR
4. LEONARDO MAGRITTE MATISSE MICHELANGELO

State Names
5. Idaho: An invented name, unknown meaning
6. North Dakota: Sioux word for "allies"
7. Louisiana: Named for Louis XIV of France
8. Pennsylvania: Named for Sir William Penn

Alternate Hand Letters
9. DID AL PAY FOR THE RUG HE GOT FOR GLENA?
10. MRS. QUAID, DID THE BIG TURKEY PAN FIT?
11. THE DOG I DO WISH FOR IS THE SHELTIE.

Improve Your Speed

Key the paragraph for one minute. Use word wrap. If you reach the end before time is up, start again from the beginning.

TIME YOURSELF

12. Idaho is a state with a name of unknown
13. origin. The name cannot be traced back
14. to a native word or to an early settler.

| 1 | 2 | 3 | 4 | 5 | 6 | 7 | 8 | WPM: 24

5. Scroll through the results to find an apple. Then click the apple you find to insert it at the insertion point. (If no apple images appear in your search, you can insert one as a picture as in steps 7 and 8.)

6. Position the insertion point at the beginning of the first paragraph (beginning with "According to legend").

7. On the **Insert** tab, choose **Picture**.

8. In the Insert Picture dialog box, browse the Lesson11 clips folder, select **Newton**, and click **Insert**. (You can also double-click a picture to insert it.)

WORD TIP

To preview pictures before you select them, click the Views down arrow in the Insert Picture dialog box and choose Medium or Large Icons.

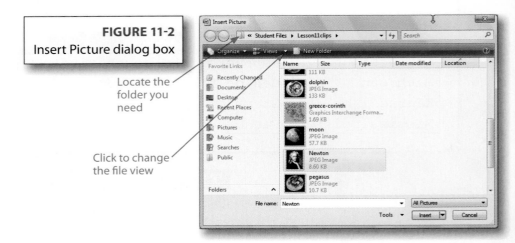

FIGURE 11-2
Insert Picture dialog box

Locate the folder you need

Click to change the file view

9. Open the file **WP-Moon**. Click the image to select it. A selected image has sizing handles around the outside. See Figure 11-3 on the next page. Copy the image.

10. Position the insertion point in the Newton document at the end of the last paragraph. Paste the image.

11. Close the Clip Art task pane.

12. Save the document as *[your initials]*Practice11-1, and leave it open. You will be resizing and positioning the inserted images.

Microsoft Word

Resizing Images

You can resize an image by hand or to an exact measurement. You can also *scale* an image, resizing it in proportion to its current or original size.

CONTINUES

Learn Tab

WARM UP

Key each line twice. Press Enter after each line.

1 adamant ACADEMIA adzuki AARDVARK amalgam
2 Alabama Havana Agra Qatar Panama Jamaica
3 La Salle, La Mancha, La Plata, La Spezia
4 aquatic AQUARIUS aqueous AQUILA aqueduct

NEW KEYS

Tab Use the **A** finger.

Press Tab to align items into columns or to indent text for paragraphs. Tabs are automatically set every half-inch.

LEARN

Reach up and left with your **A** finger to key Tab. Keep the **F** finger on its home key. Keep your elbows close to your sides.

PRACTICE

Key each line twice. Press Tab where you see an arrow. Press Enter after each line.

WORD PROCESSING TIP

On the Home tab, click Show/Hide ¶ ¶ so you can see the tab characters you key. Do not key a space before or after pressing Tab.

Practice Letters and Tab
5 aba→ bcc→ cdd→ dee→ efe→ ghh→ hii→ ijj
6 jkk→ llm→ mnn→ opo→ qrr→ stt→ uvw→ xyz
7 DMA→ UPS→ CPU→ CRT→ LCD→ IRQ→ KBD→ I/O

Practice Short Words and Tab
8 all→ ad→ cat→ cot→ dot→ lot→ rot→ not
9 be→ bit→ bat→ do→ to→ tot→ in→ the
10 if→ so→ then→who→ call→to→ tell→me
11 TO→ BE→ OR→ NOT→ TO→ BE→ THAT→IS

Practice Indenting with Tab
Key the following text as a paragraph. Use word wrap. To indent the paragraph, press Tab where you see the arrow.

12 →   Qatar is an independent Arab state
13 in the Middle East, bordering the
14 Persian Gulf. It is a major exporter of
15 oil and natural gas.

Inserting Clip Art (CONTINUED)

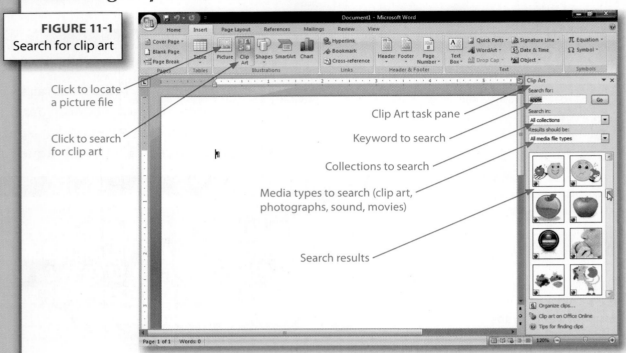

FIGURE 11-1
Search for clip art

Click to locate a picture file

Click to search for clip art

Clip Art task pane

Keyword to search

Collections to search

Media types to search (clip art, photographs, sound, movies)

Search results

To copy and paste an image into a document:

1. Locate a drawing or photograph from any source.

2. Copy the image. You can use your preferred copy method: click the Copy button on the Ribbon, press the keyboard shortcut Ctrl + **C**, or right-click the image and choose **Copy** from the shortcut menu.

3. Position the insertion point in your document.

4. Paste the image. You can use your preferred paste method: click the Paste button on the Ribbon, press Ctrl + **V**, or right-click the document location and choose **Paste** from the shortcut menu.

PRACTICE 11-1

Inserting Clips

1. Open the document **WP-Newton**.

2. Position your insertion point at the beginning of the third paragraph (beginning with "We expect this force").

3. From the **Insert** tab, click **Clip Art**.

4. In the Clip Art task pane, key **apple** in the **Search for** box. Click **Go**.

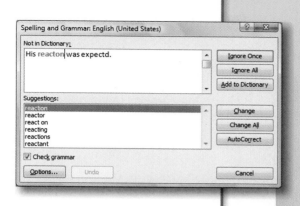

Function Keys

Function keys (F1, F2, and so on) are typically at the top of your keyboard. Use them to perform special tasks in the active computer program. For example, in Word:

- F1 Starts Help
- F4 Repeats the last action
- F7 Starts the spelling checker

Use Function Keys

Key the following sentence, including the misspellings.

        His reacton was expectd.

Using the mouse, click in the first misspelled word, "reacton." Press F7. In the dialog box, click Change to change to the correct spelling. Click Change again to correct the next misspelling. Click Close to close the dialog box.

TEST YOURSELF

Key each line twice: first slowly and then faster. Press Tab where you see an arrow. Press Enter after each line.

Names
1 Zailynne→   Kayanna→   Fabrizio→ Emanuel
2 Kathleen→   Ainsley→   Mikayla→   Brielyn
3 Demetria→   Guillermo→ Shirosama→ Calista

Left-Hand Sentences
4 Teressa craved a sweet sassafras tea.
5 Babbette's face was as red as a beet.
6 Gregg feeds a caged rat a treat: bread.
7 Rebecca Brewster's grades were great.
8 Greta Reeves wears a red taffeta dress.

 Spelling Check
Key the following with the spelling errors shown. Click in "Proverb," press F7 to start spell-checking, and correct the misspellings.

9 Proverb: The difcult is done at once;
10 The inpossible takes a little logner.

Improve Your Speed

Key the paragraph for one minute. Start with a tab and use word wrap. If you reach the end before time is up, start again from the beginning.

 TIME YOURSELF

11 →   Oil is a valuable natural resource.
12 Other resources that define the natural
13 wealth of a country are land, forests,
14 and water.

| 1 | 2 | 3 | 4 | 5 | 6 | 7 | 8 | WPM: 25

Work with Images

LEARN

Use Clip Art and WordArt

Images and other graphics make your documents more attractive and help to illustrate your ideas. Microsoft Office includes a gallery of drawings, photographs, and other files called *clip art* that you can insert in a document. These ready-to-use files are often called *clips*. You can also insert your own digitized photographs and scanned images into a document.

In this lesson you will insert and format clips. You will also use WordArt to create a graphic image from text.

Microsoft Word

Inserting Clip Art

You can insert images from several sources, including the clip art collection and pictures you have stored in folders. You also can copy and paste images from other documents or from the Internet.

To search for and insert clip art:

1. Position the insertion point in your document.
2. On the **Insert** tab, in the Illustrations group, click **Clip Art**. The Clip Art task pane appears.
3. Key text in the **Search for** box. To search within a specific collection, open the **Search in** drop-down list and choose an option. To search for a specific file type, set options in the **Results should be** drop-down list.
4. Click **Go** to begin the search. See Figure 11-1 on the next page.
5. Examine the clips that appear.
6. Click a clip to insert it in the document.
7. To close the Clip Art task pane, click its Close button ⊠.

To insert a picture from a file:

1. Position the insertion point in your document.
2. On the **Insert** tab, in the Illustrations group, click **Picture**.
3. In the Insert Picture dialog box, locate and select a file.
4. Click **Insert**.

CONTINUES

REVIEW

The keyboard shows the keys you have learned so far. This lesson focuses on the keys highlighted in purple.

WARM UP

Key each line twice. Press Enter after each line.

1 A diller a dollar, a ten o'clock scholar
2 Everyone's seen a movie, no? We did not.
3 a/b/c/d/e/f/g/h/i/j/k/l/m/n/o/p/q/r/s/t/
4 Del thinks he's all that. Al thinks not.

PRACTICE

Key each line twice. Press Enter after each line. Where you see an arrow, press Tab.

Practice Caps Lock

5 PHASE One; PHASE Two; PHASE Three; RESET
6 MONDAYS, WEDNESDAYS, and FRIDAYS AT NINE
7 Jamal: WISHING YOU A VERY HAPPY BIRTHDAY

Practice ?

8 Who said that? Why? Where is Paul going?
9 Well, which is it? What? You don't know?
10 How are you? Yes? No? Do you? Won't you?

Practice Tab

11 eucalyptus→hemlock→ sycamore→ larch
12 hickory→   dogwood→ chestnut→ willow

Practice Caps Lock ? and Tab

13 TO:→   FR:→ RE:→ CC:→ FAX:→EXT:→FL:→ DEPT:
14 VOL→   HIGH→LOW→ DATE→OPEN→CHG→ YTD→ INT
15 ADRIANA, did ALEJANDRO call the station?
16 Narrator: WHO KNOWS WHICH WAY THEY FLED?

BREAKING BAD HABITS

Do not look at your hands when keying. Look at your monitor or your book.

5. Insert a symbol that has something to do with art to the left of the first heading, "Address." If you cannot find an appropriate symbol, use an elegant shape instead. The symbol takes on the formatting of the heading line: bold with a shadow.

6. Change the font color of only the symbol to **Red** (from the Standard Colors row).

7. Copy and paste the colored symbol to the left of each of the remaining seven headings in the document.

8. Add a page border to the document. Choose a simple one from the **Art** drop-down list. Adjust the border width if needed.

9. Under "HOURS," align the tabbed text (the times) with a 1.5-inch tab.

10. Vertically align the entire document on the page.

11. Add a document footer containing your name.

12. Preview the document.

13. Save the document as *[your initials]*Test10-2.

14. Print and close the document.

TEST YOURSELF 10-3

America in the 50s

Research America in the 1950s. Determine the events and famous people that influenced this era. Create a one-page document with font effects, font color, symbols, borders, and shading that match the content of the document. Have fun and try several combinations, but remember not to clutter your document.

In writing your document, be sure to:

1. Add font effects to words that you want to stand out.

2. Use font, border, and shading colors that print well.

3. Vary font sizes of titles and headings.

4. Insert fun symbols that add to the content or message of the document.

5. Use paragraph and page borders.

6. Add a document header with your name (include a page number if it is more than one page).

7. Spell-check and preview the document.

8. Save the document as *[your initials]*Test10-3.

9. Print and close the document.

FIGURE 10-8
At 21 years old in 1956, Elvis Presley was about to become a pop music legend.

Geography

Over eons of time, the Earth has been formed and re-formed by the power of the wind, rivers, ocean tides, ice, and its own internal heat. Geography is all about the physical features of the Earth's surface and the distribution of life on the planet.

Do You Know...?

For each of the following questions, key the question, press Tab, key the answer in all capital letters, and then press Enter.

Monument Valley

```
Where is Monument Valley?
Which island is the largest on earth?
Which of the world's oceans is the youngest?
```

TEST YOURSELF

Key each line twice: first slowly and then faster. Press Tab where you see an arrow. Press Enter after each line.

Classic Television Shows

1	FRIENDS→	Good Times→	WHO'S THE BOSS?
2	FRASIER→	SEINFELD→	The Wonder Years
3	FELICITY→	Roseanne→	The Cosby Show
4	Full House→	The Nanny→	THE JEFFERSONS
5	Spin City→	Ally McBeal→	GROWING PAINS

Land and Water

6	LAGOON→	Estuary→	ISTHMUS→	Tributary
7	DESERT→	Continent→	VALLEY→	TUNDRA
8	BUTTE→	CANYON→	SWAMP→	Archipelago
9	PLATEAU→	STEPPE→	DELTA→	Waterfall

Homophones

10	GIBE/JIBE→	EWE/YEW→	lie/lye→	aisle/isle
11	IDOL/IDLE→	been/bin→	PEER/PIER→	ARC/ARK
12	flew/flu→	WRY/RYE→	SITE/CITE→	mean/mien
13	AD/ADD→	BAIL/BALE→	wet/whet→	chord/cord

 TIME YOURSELF

Improve Your Speed

Key the paragraph for one minute. Start with a tab and use word wrap. If you reach the end before time is up, start again from the beginning.

```
14 →    What do you want to do with your
15 life? Take time to analyze your skills
16 and decide what it is that you really
17 enjoy doing.
```

| | 1 | 2 | 3 | 4 | 5 | 6 | 7 | 8 | **WPM: 25** |

DID YOU KNOW?

If the wind chill falls below 0° F, exposed skin can freeze within 5 minutes or less. Frostbite most often affects fingers, toes, ear lobes, and the tip of the nose.

Wind Chill Factor

1. Open the file **WP-WindChill**. This document contains information about the wind chill factor.

2. Change the title "The Wind Chill Factor" to a 26-point serif font and center-align it.

3. Apply shading to the title, using a light shade of green.

4. Add a paragraph border to the title paragraph you just shaded. In the Borders and Shading dialog box, use one of the first three line styles. Make it a 2¼-point black shadow border.

5. Change the headings "What Is It?" and "Why Care?" to a green font color (use a darker color than the green you used for the title shading). Change the font size to 16-point and apply the same serif font as the title.

6. Justify the paragraphs below each of the headings. Change the font size for these two paragraphs to 12-point with 1.5 line spacing.

WORD TIP

Find the degree symbol by using the (normal text) font in the Symbol dialog box.

7. Add a degree symbol (°) directly after each temperature number in the paragraph below "What Is It?" There are five occurrences. Do not insert one after 25.

8. Add a document footer containing your name.

9. Preview the document.

10. Save the document as *[your initials]***Test10-1**.

11. Print and close the document.

DID YOU KNOW?

The Metropolitan Museum was built in 1895 in New York City. It has more than 2 million square feet of exhibit space.

The Metropolitan Museum

1. Open the file **WP-TheMet**. This document contains information about The Metropolitan Museum of Art in New York. The headings are formatted with Quick Styles. You will customize the formatting.

2. Apply **Dark Blue** shading (from the Standard Colors row) to the document title, which is the first two lines of text.

3. Add the Small Caps and Engrave font effects to the document title. Increase the font size to 22-point and then center-align the title.

4. Make the eight bold headings in the document 14-point all-caps with a shadow.

Alphabet Keys

WARM UP

Key each line twice. Press Enter after each line.

1. tub tiff tapped thrive trembled tranquil
2. urn unfit unique uplink unlucky unjustly
3. woe wave women whimsy wriggle winterized
4. owl onyx ought octopus oxidize overwhelm

PRACTICE

Key each line twice. Press Enter after each line.

Reaches and Shifts

5. coaxes waxes vinyl razors quotas quizzes
6. Axes Onyxes Lynxes Polyp Monopoly Coccyx
7. laxly coyly alpaca stucco piccolo lonely
8. P.O. Boxes pop. qt. pt. gal. ex. wk. mo.
9. Morocco; Waco, TX; Taxco, Mexico; Oxnard

 ## TIME YOURSELF

10. We took a walk around the lake.
| 1 | 2 | 3 | 4 | 5 | 6 | WPM: 25
11. Everyone liked seeing the boat.
| 1 | 2 | 3 | 4 | 5 | 6 | WPM: 25
12. They gave all ten of us a ride.
| 1 | 2 | 3 | 4 | 5 | 6 | WPM: 25
13. After that, we all took a swim.
| 1 | 2 | 3 | 4 | 5 | 6 | WPM: 25
14. I won the big race to the dock.
| 1 | 2 | 3 | 4 | 5 | 6 | WPM: 25

TIME YOURSELF

15. The water was so cold that day.
16. We got home in time for dinner.
| 1 | 2 | 3 | 4 | 5 | 6 | WPM: 25
17. It was really such a nice time.
18. When can we enjoy it all again?
| 1 | 2 | 3 | 4 | 5 | 6 | WPM: 25

15-Second Drills

Key each of these lines for 15 seconds. Press Enter at the end of each line. If you reach the end of a line before time is up, start again from the beginning of the line.

30-Second Drills

Key each pair of lines for 30 seconds. Press Enter at the end of each line. If you reach the end of a drill before time is up, start again from the beginning of the drill.

12. Click the **Width** box down arrow and choose **¾ pt**. The **Preview** section reflects your settings. Click **OK**.

13. Leave the document open.

PRACTICE 10-5

Apply Shading

1. Place the insertion point in the first heading (Wilson "Snow-flake" Bentley).

2. Click the Shading button 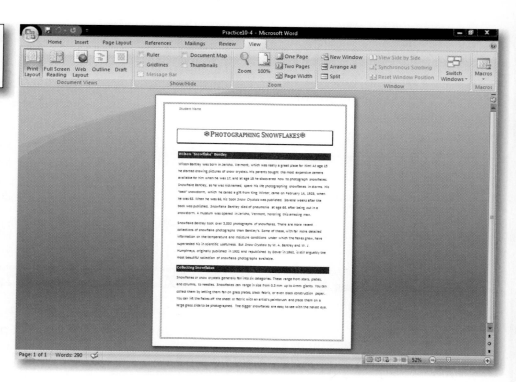 down arrow. Choose **Dark Blue, Text 2** from the palette.

3. Select the heading text (Wilson "Snowflake" Bentley) and use the Font Color button to change the text color to white.

4. Apply the same shading and font color to the second heading (Collecting Snowflakes).

5. Align the document text vertically on the page (**Page Layout** tab, Page Setup dialog box).

6. Add the **Blank** document header and key your name.

7. Save the document as *[your initials]***Practice10-5**.

8. Print and close the document.

WORD TIP

You can copy formatting from already-formatted text to other text. Select the formatted text, click the Format Painter button on the Home tab (Clipboard group), and then select the text you want to format.

FIGURE 10-7
Final document with all special effects

HISTORY TIP

Women were not given the right to vote until 1920—sixteen years after Anthony's death.

TEST YOURSELF

Working from Handwritten Material

The following text is from a speech given by Susan B. Anthony, the legendary civil rights activist, who was arrested for voting in the 1872 presidential election. Key the text. Use word wrap. Use a tab to indent the first line of each paragraph.

Friends and fellow citizens: I stand before you tonight under indictment for the alleged crime of having voted at the last presidential election, without having a lawful right to vote. It shall be my work this evening to prove to you that in thus voting, I not only committed no crime, but, instead, simply exercised my citizen's rights, guaranteed to me and all United States citizens by the National Constitution, beyond the power of any state to deny.

The preamble of the Federal Constitution says: "We, the people of the United States, in order to form a more perfect union, establish justice, ensure domestic tranquility, provide for the common defense, promote the general welfare, and secure the blessings of liberty to ourselves and our posterity, do ordain and establish this Constitution for the United States of America."

It was we, the people; not we, the male citizens; but we, the whole people, who formed the Union. And we formed it, not to give the blessings of liberty, but to secure them; not to the half of ourselves and the half of our posterity, but to the whole people - women as well as men.

The only question left to be settled now is: Are women persons? And I hardly believe any of our opponents will have the hardihood to say they are not. Being persons, then, women are citizens; and no state has a right to make any law, or to enforce any old law, that shall abridge their privileges or immunities.

PRACTICE 10-4

Apply Borders

1. Place the insertion point in the title "Photographing Snowflakes."

2. On the **Home** tab, click the Border button ⊞ down arrow to display the Border drop-down list. Click the **Bottom Border** option. This is an easy way to apply a bottom border to a paragraph. Now you'll create a more customized border.

3. With the insertion point still in the title, display the Borders and Shading dialog box. Click the **Borders** tab, if it is not already displayed.

4. Under **Setting**, click **Shadow**.

5. In the **Style** box, click the first border style, if it is not already displayed.

6. Click the **Color** box down arrow and choose **Dark Blue, Text 2**.

7. Click the **Width** box down arrow and choose **1 pt**. The **Preview** section reflects a 1-point dark-blue shadow border. Click **OK**.

WORD TIP

The Border button on the Ribbon reflects the most recent border applied with that button.

FIGURE 10-6
Borders tab in the Borders and Shading dialog box

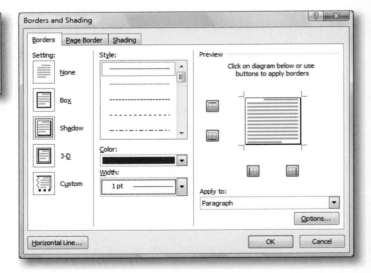

8. Display the Borders and Shading dialog box again and click the **Page Border** tab.

9. Under **Setting**, choose **Box**.

10. In the **Style** box, scroll down and select the first double line.

11. Click the **Color** down arrow and choose **Blue, Accent 1**.

Alphabet Keys

WARM UP

Key each line twice. Press Enter after each line.

1 egg exit effort enamel exceeded economic
2 rig rove rally resized roomfuls rejoices
3 paw play perks phoned position pipsqueak
4 icy ibex ivory ignite involve ill-suited

PRACTICE

Key each line twice. Press Enter after each line.

First-Row Emphasis

5 common, cinnamon, jammed, bobbin, banner
6 Zane, Zenda, Zenon, Zareb, Xenon, Xavier
7 Carmen, Cain, Chavez, Calix, Cecil, Coby
8 Viveca, Vernon, Vanna, Becca, Benny, Bob
9 Bambi, Neva, Mr. Nicol, Ms. Maxime Monez

⏰ TIME YOURSELF

10 →   When is the best time of the day to
11 enjoy a walk in the park?
| 1 | 2 | 3 | 4 | 5 | 6 | 7 | 8   **WPM: 25**

12 →   He told the truth, the whole truth,
13 and nothing but the truth.
| 1 | 2 | 3 | 4 | 5 | 6 | 7 | 8   **WPM: 25**

⏰ TIME YOURSELF

16 →   Each time he tried to bake muffins,
17 he used baking soda instead of baking
18 powder. This resulted in somewhat salty
19 muffins.
| 1 | 2 | 3 | 4 | 5 | 6 | 7 | 8   **WPM: 25**

20 →   Fernando makes the best pancakes,
21 and he doesn't use a mix. He adds sliced
22 bananas and tops with butter and real
23 maple syrup.
| 1 | 2 | 3 | 4 | 5 | 6 | 7 | 8   **WPM: 25**

30-Second Drills

Key each of these short paragraphs for 30 seconds. Start with a tab and use word wrap. If you reach the end of a paragraph before time is up, start again from the beginning.

60-Second Drills

Key each of these paragraphs for 60 seconds. Start with a tab and use word wrap. If you reach the end of a paragraph before time is up, start again from the beginning.

Applying Borders and Shading (CONTINUED)

3. To choose more border options, choose **Borders and Shading** from the bottom of the drop-down list to display the Borders and Shading dialog box.

4. Click the **Borders** tab, if it is not already displayed.

5. Under **Setting** at the left side of the dialog box, click the type of border you want.

6. Scroll through the **Style** box to choose a line style.

7. Click the **Color** box down arrow and choose a line color.

8. Click the **Width** box down arrow and choose a line width (thickness). The **Preview** section of the dialog box displays your chosen settings.

9. Click **OK**. The border is applied to the paragraph.

10. To remove a border, open the Border drop-down list and choose **No Border**.

To apply a page border:

1. On the **Home** tab, in the Paragraph group, click the Border button ⊞ down arrow, choose **Borders and Shading** from the drop-down list, and then click the **Page Border** tab. Or, on the **Page Layout** tab of the Ribbon, in the Page Background group, choose **Page Borders**.

2. Under **Setting** at the left side of the dialog box, click the type of border you want.

3. Scroll through the **Style** box and choose a line style. Or, open the **Art** drop-down list and choose a more decorative border style.

4. Click the **Color** box down arrow and choose a line color.

5. Click the **Width** box down arrow and choose a line width (thickness).

6. Click **OK**. The border is applied to the page.

7. To remove a page border, display the Borders and Shading dialog box again. On the **Page Border** tab, under **Setting**, choose **None**.

To apply shading to paragraphs:

1. Place the insertion point in the paragraph where you want to apply shading.

2. On the **Home** tab, in the Paragraph group, click the Shading button ⬛ down arrow. Choose a color. The shading appears behind the paragraph.

3. For more shading options, open the Borders and Shading dialog box and click the **Shading** tab.

4. Choose a fill color (for shading), choose **Pattern** options if desired, and click **OK**.

5. To remove shading, click the Shading button ⬛ down arrow and choose **No Color**.

Working from Unarranged Material

Key the first paragraph (which begins "Now that..."). Then key the next four paragraphs in the most logical order. Use word wrap. Use a tab to indent the first line of each paragraph.

Now that computers are a part of everyday life, keyboarding is an essential skill. No matter what your age or profession, if you can type, you have a valuable communication tool literally at your fingertips. Once you master this tool, it will help you at school, at home, and in your future workplace.

Keyboarding skills will help you perform better in the workplace. Today, businesspeople write their own letters, memos, and e-mails. They enter data in worksheets and create their own presentations. They need keyboarding skills for speed and efficiency. The person who has to hunt and peck at a keyboard will be left behind by more productive users.

For schoolwork, keyboarding skills allow you to type reports and do online research more quickly. You can write reports directly at the computer, correcting and editing your work as you go. Instead of wasting time searching for letters on the keyboard, your eyes are focused on your work. The faster you can type, the faster you can capture your thoughts on paper.

In the future, voice recognition and touch tablets might replace keyboarding. We do not know how technology will develop. But we do know that the keyboarding skills offer a fluency and freedom that helps us keep pace in our fast-changing world.

At home, you can answer your e-mail and instant messages quickly. You can surf the Web with ease. You can breeze through an online order form.

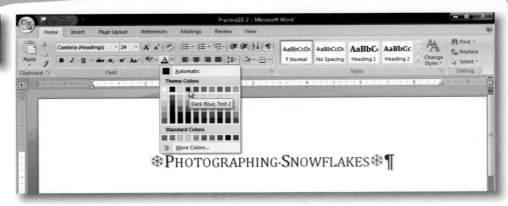

FIGURE 10-4
Choosing font colors

❈PHOTOGRAPHING·SNOWFLAKES❈¶

5. Apply the same color to all the text below the second heading (Collecting Snowflakes) through the end of the document.

6. Leave the document open.

Microsoft Word

Applying Borders and Shading

Borders add visual interest to documents, creating varying lines of color around paragraphs or an entire page. *Shading* creates blocks of color or shades of gray behind paragraph text.

To apply borders to paragraphs:

1. Place the insertion point in the paragraph where you want to apply a border.

2. On the **Home** tab, in the Paragraph group, click the arrow next to the Border button ⊞ . Choose an option from the drop-down list.

FIGURE 10-5
Border drop-down list

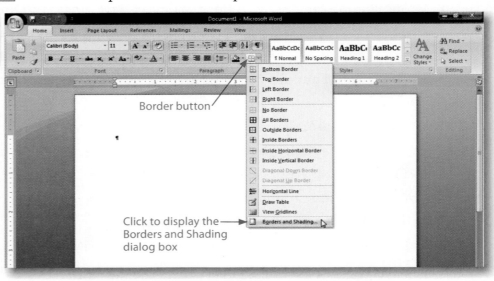

Border button

Click to display the Borders and Shading dialog box

CONTINUES

Alphabet Keys

WARM UP

Key each line twice. Press Enter after each line.

1 yew yolk yacht yonder yielded yellowtail
2 mop maze major muffler minerals mosquito
3 cub cave churn castle ceremony cityscape
4 gum gong guilt galaxy graphics gargoyles

PRACTICE

Key each line twice. Press Enter after each line.

Practice Punctuation

5 Color: Tan; Size: Medium; Quantity: Four
6 "Hello?" "Ciao." "Hola?" "Shalom." "Hi."
7 You'll join us, won't you? Yes/no/maybe?
8 The merry-go-round has an on/off switch.

 ## TIME YOURSELF

9 →   Greg had to choose between getting
10 a cat or a dog. After much thinking, he
11 decided on a bird. His hamster was very
12 grateful.

| 1 | 2 | 3 | 4 | 5 | 6 | 7 | 8 | **WPM: 25**

13 →   Mona has a rabbit that thinks it is
14 a dog. It follows Mona around, sits on
15 her lap, and sleeps by her feet. It even
16 snores.

| 1 | 2 | 3 | 4 | 5 | 6 | 7 | 8 | **WPM: 25**

 ## TIME YOURSELF

17 →   Never in her life has Leah seen a
18 sky as blue as the one in the Southwest.
19 There is no way to explain how a sky can
20 seem bluer in one place than in another
21 place. All Leah knows is that the sky
22 here is the clearest and truest blue she
23 has ever seen.

| 1 | 2 | 3 | 4 | 5 | 6 | 7 | 8 | **WPM: 25**

60-Second Drills

Key each of these short paragraphs for 60 seconds. Start with a tab and use word wrap. If you reach the end of a paragraph before time is up, start again from the beginning of that paragraph.

2-Minute Drill

Key the paragraph for 2 minutes. Start with a tab and use word wrap. If you reach the end of the paragraph before time is up, start again from the beginning.

WORD TIP

Recently used symbols will appear on the Symbols drop-down list.

5. Insert the same symbol to the right of the title. (You can click to the right of the title and press the **F4** key, which repeats the most recent action.)

6. Leave the document open.

Changing Font Color

Changing the font color can be a lot of fun. There are many colors to choose from, and the decision can sometimes be difficult. Pick a color that prints well and is easy to read. If you have a black-and-white printer, you'll want to use dark colors that print as darker shades of gray. Light colors print as lighter shades of gray. You can use the Font Color button **A** to quickly change the font color.

To change the font color:

1. Select the text to which you want to apply color.

2. Click the down arrow next to the Font Color button **A** on the Mini toolbar or on the **Home** tab in the Font group. A palette of colors appears below the button.

3. Point to one of the colors; the name of the color appears below the pointer. Click the color you want to apply. The text color is changed in your document and the Font Color button **A** changes colors to match the color you just applied.

4. Select other text and click the Font Color button **A** (not the down arrow) to apply the same color. Click the down arrow beside the button to choose another color.

5. To remove font color for selected text, display the Font Color palette and choose **Automatic** (the default font color, which is black).

WORD TIP

The first row of colors are Theme Colors, which are coordinated to look good together. If you like brighter colors, choose from the Standard Colors row at the bottom of the color palette.

PRACTICE 10-3

Change Font Color

1. Select the title of the document, including the symbols you inserted.

2. Click the down arrow next to the Font Color button **A**. Click **Dark Blue, Text 2** (the fourth choice from the left in the top row). See Figure 10-4 on next page.

3. Click somewhere else in the document to deselect the text. The entire title is dark blue.

4. Using the Font Color button **A**, apply the same color to the two paragraphs below the first heading (Wilson "Snowflake" Bentley).

Composing at the Keyboard

Topics:

Choose one of the following topics (or choose your own topic or one that your teacher recommends). Write a short essay in which you take a position on the topic.

➤ **The Space Program**—are we doing too much/too little?
➤ **The Ideal Pet**—is it cat, dog, or something else?
➤ **Instant Messaging**—r u using it 2 much?
➤ **Fast Food**—is it a good idea or a bad idea?
➤ **The Best Profession**—what do you think it is?
➤ **Your Favorite Book**—the book you think every middle-school student should read.
➤ **Working for Yourself or Working for a Company**—which do you think will be the best for you?
➤ **UFOs**—do they or don't they exist?
➤ **TV**—is it good/bad for us?
➤ **School Bullies**—what's the solution to the problem?
➤ **Your Role Model**—who do you look up to?
➤ **Dating**—what's the right age to start?

Are you a dog or a cat person?

In the first paragraph, present your position and a brief summary of your reasons. For example, suppose your topic was instant messaging and your position is that you do not use it too much:

Example:
```
I use instant messaging several times a day. I
don't overuse it—it actually saves me time.
```

In the second paragraph, explain one of your reasons in detail. For example:

Example:
```
Sending an instant message can be the easiest
and quickest way to connect with someone.
```

In the third paragraph, explain another reason in detail. For example:

Example:
```
If I see that a friend is online, that usually
means she can chat or answer a quick question.
I don't have to disturb her home with a phone
call or wait for an e-mail response.
```

In your fourth paragraph, summarize and restate your position. For example:

Example:
```
I end up spending less time chatting when I
instant message friends than when I call them,
and that means more time for homework.
```

Inserting Symbols (CONTINUED)

3. In the Symbol dialog box, click the **Symbols** tab.

4. Scroll the symbols for the current font, or choose another font from the **Font** list. The grid of available symbols changes based on the font you choose.

5. Locate the symbol you want to insert and click to highlight it.

6. Click **Insert** and click **Close**. The symbol is inserted into your document the same size as the text around it. You can change the font size of a symbol just as you would any other character.

PRACTICE 10-2

Insert Symbols

1. Place the insertion point to the left of the title "Photograph-ing Snowflakes."

2. Display the Symbol dialog box. Click the **Symbols** tab, if it is not already displayed.

3. Click the arrow next to the **Font** drop-down list and choose **Wingdings**.

4. Click the fifth symbol on the fourth row (this symbol looks like a snowflake), click **Insert**, and click **Close**. The symbol is inserted into the document with the same formatting as the text next to it.

FIGURE 10-3
Choosing symbols from the Symbol dialog box

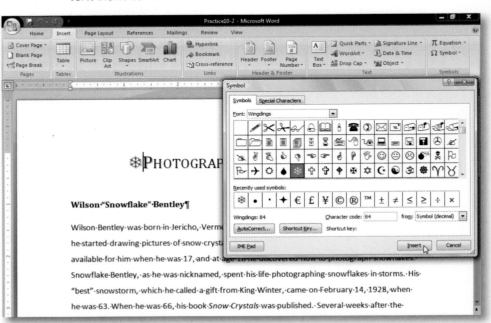

Learn $4 %5 ^6 and &7

Key each line twice. Press Enter after each line.

1 Jeff Jeffrey jitters jolly jelly jumbled
2 fry fit fray fries fire jut jug joy jury
3 fur falcon fitful fasting foists fumbles
4 jig jagged just-in-time jealously jostle

LEARN

Reach up and left with your F finger to key $4. Reach up and slightly right with the same finger to key %5. Keep your other left-hand fingers anchored on their home keys. Reach up and left with your J finger to key ^6 and &7. Keep your other right-hand fingers anchored on their home keys.

NEW KEYS

$4 Use the F finger.

%5 Use the F finger.

^6 Use the J finger.

&7 Use the J finger.

TECHNIQUE TIP

Adjust your chair so that your knees are slightly lower than your hips, and your elbows bend at right angles.

PRACTICE

Key each line twice. Press Enter after each line.

Practice 4 and 5

5 f ff fr f4 fr4 f4f 444 f4f 4/4 fr4f 4.44
6 f ff fr f5 fr5 f5f 555 f5f 5/5 fr5f 5.55
7 4 fry, 5 fear, 44 fume, 55 fray, 45 fret

Practice 6 and 7

8 j jj ju j7 ju7 j7j 777 j7j 7/7 ju7j 7.77
9 j jj jy j6 jy6 j6j 666 j6j 6/6 jy6j 6.66
10 6 jog, 7 joke, 66 jump, 77 hide, 67 join

Practice 4, 5, 6, and 7

11 fr f4 44 fr4; fr f5 55 fr5; f45 f54 4554
12 6 out of 7; telephone 555-4567; .75 inch
13 July 4; 7/4/65; June 7; 6/5/74; Route 66
14 6-year-old; 5 cents; 4-H Club; 7:45 p.m.
15 I will pick 7, 67, or 767. Add 466 more.

3. With the title still selected, display the **Home** tab and click the Font dialog box launcher . In the dialog box, make sure the **Font** tab is displayed.

4. From the **Size** list, change the font size to **24** points. Under **Effects**, click the check boxes for **Small caps** and **Shadow**. The **Preview** box shows you how the text will look with the effects applied.

5. Click **OK.** Center-align the title and then apply 24 points of spacing after it (from the **Page Layout** tab, Paragraph group).

6. Format the heading "Wilson "Snowflake" Bentley" with the Cambria font and the shadow effect.

7. Format the heading "Collecting Snowflakes" with the Cambria font and bold. Notice that bold looks better on the smaller size headings than the shadow effect.

8. Remove the shadow effect from the heading "Wilson "Snowflake" Bentley" and make the text bold. Leave the document open.

Microsoft Word

Inserting Symbols

The fonts you use contain *symbols* or characters that do not appear on your keyboard. There are also fonts such as Wingdings or Symbol that are made up entirely of symbols. Symbols include fractions (¼, ½), foreign language characters (Á, é, ö), international currency symbols (€, ¥), arrows, and decorative symbols.

To insert symbols:
1. Place the insertion point where you want to insert the symbol.
2. On the **Insert** tab, in the Symbols group, click **Symbol**. Choose a symbol from the drop-down list. To display additional symbols, click **More Symbols**.

FIGURE 10-2
Symbol drop-down list

Click to display the Symbol dialog box ⟶

CONTINUES

Seven Wonders of the Ancient World

As early as the second century B.C., historians began compiling a list of the seven wonders of the ancient world. The final list, compiled during the Middle Ages, appears below. It contains the seven most impressive structures built by humans—all were massive, yet beautiful. Only one survives.

The Great Pyramid of Giza is still standing.

The Great Pyramid of Giza	
The Hanging Gardens of Babylon	The Temple of Artemis at Ephesus
The Statue of Zeus at Olympia	The Mausoleum at Halicarnassus
The Lighthouse of Alexandria	The Colossus of Rhodes

Your Seven Wonders

Create your own list of seven wonders of the world, including still-existing ancient wonders or modern wonders. Key your list. (Do not use the wonders in Lines 4 and 5 below.)

TEST YOURSELF

Key each line twice: first slowly and then faster. Press Enter after each line.

Sentences with Numbers

1 All 4 girls paid 55 or 65 cents per bar.
2 It is 67.5 degrees, 4.75 percent warmer.
3 Of 5 pilots, only 4 flew a DC-6 or DC-7.

More Wonders

4 Machu Picchu, Stonehenge, Moai Statues
5 Great Wall of China, Borobudur Temple

Alternate Hands

6 55 cars, 44 dresses, 545 trees, 54 saves
7 67 pop up, 77 hop in, 767 poll, 677 jump
8 454 were safe, 555 are graded, 445 cars

TIME YOURSELF

9 You can get 4 of the 5 items.¶
10 Wait, 5 and 6 do not match 7.¶
| 1 | 2 | 3 | 4 | 5 | 6   WPM: 12

11 →   The Moai statues on Easter Island
12 average over fourteen feet tall. The
13 builders of these stone statues thought
14 they were sacred.
| 1 | 2 | 3 | 4 | 5 | 6 | 7 | 8   WPM: 26

Improve Your Speed

Each of these is a one-minute drill. For the first drill, press Enter at the end of each line. For the second drill, start with a tab and use word wrap. If you reach the end of a drill before time is up, start again from the beginning.

Applying Font Effects (CONTINUED)

To apply font effects by using the Font dialog box:

1. Select the text you want to change.
2. On the **Home** tab, click the Font dialog box launcher.

FIGURE 10-1
Applying font effects

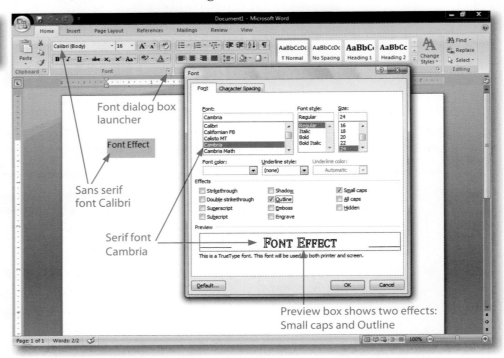

Font dialog box launcher

Font Effect

Sans serif font Calibri

Serif font Cambria

Preview box shows two effects: Small caps and Outline

3. In the Font dialog box, click the **Font** tab, if it is not already displayed.
4. Under **Effects**, click the check box next to the effect you want to apply. Sometimes you can apply two effects at the same time.
5. Click **OK** to apply.
6. To remove an effect, select the text, display the Font dialog box again, and clear the check box next to the effect.

PRACTICE 10-1

Apply Font Effects

1. Start Word and open the file **WP-Snowflakes**. This document uses Word's default sans serif font for body text, Calibri.
2. Select the title "Photographing Snowflakes" and change the font to Cambria. This is a serif font that Word uses for headings, by default.

WARM UP

Key each line twice. Press Enter after each line.

1   Koko; kicks; walks; whacks; banks; loans
2   polo; polka; polled; black holes; Poland
3   Good Luck; Book Club; King Lear; slacken
4   Walk the plank; Pile on; The yellow yolk

NEW KEYS

 Use the **K** finger.

 Use the **L** finger.

 Use the **;** finger.

LEARN

Reach up and left with your **K** finger to key . Reach up and left with your **L** finger to key . Reach up and left with your **;** finger to key . Keep your **J** finger anchored on its home key.

PRACTICE

Key each line twice. Press Enter after each line.

Practice 8
5   k kk ki k8 ki8 k8k 888 k8k 8/8 ki8k 8.88
6   l8r; Number 8, 888K; 888-888-8888; KIKI8
7   8 kin, 8 kits, 8 keys, keep 88, 888 know

Practice 9
8   l ll lo L9 LO9 L9 9 lbs. 9/9/99 Agent 99
9   Loren told 9 of the 99 funniest stories.
10 lop 9, 9 look, 9 like, 99 lope, 999 lose

Practice 0
11 ; ;; ;p ;0 ;p0 ;0; 00; ;0; 0/0 ;p0; 0.00
12 0-0 equals? 007, 008, and 009 are spies.
13 5000 pleas; .05 pints; Population: 7,000

Practice 8, 9, and 0
14 Pam was on the 8:09, which gets in at 9.
15 You have 8, 9, 80, 89, or 90 more plays.
16 890 Rolo Road, Apt. 80, Edison, NJ 08899

BREAKING BAD HABITS

Do not raise your elbows as you key. Keep your arms close to your body.

LEARN

Adding More Visual Interest

A document that has color, lines, or other special effects more easily attracts a reader's attention. It's important to apply these effects in a way that enhances the content of a document rather than cluttering it. Be creative and try a variety of combinations until you create a document that is visually pleasing.

Microsoft Word

Applying Font Effects

There are two types of fonts: serif and sans serif. A *serif* font (such as CAMBRIA) has decorative extensions at the ends of the lines that make up its characters. A *sans serif* font (such as CALIBRI) does not have these extensions. Sans serif means without serif. You can apply effects to both types of fonts by using the Font dialog box.

TABLE 10-1	Font Effects in the Font Dialog Box
Effect	**Example**
Strikethrough	Applies a ~~horizontal line~~ through text
Double strikethrough	Applies a ~~double horizontal line~~ through text
Superscript	Raises text ^{above} characters on the same line
Subscript	Lowers text _{below} characters on the same line
Shadow	Applies a **shadow** to text
Outline	Applies an outline to text
Emboss	Makes text appear raised off the page
Engrave	Makes text appear imprinted on the page
Small caps	Makes lowercase text SMALL CAPITAL LETTERS
All caps	Makes all text UPPERCASE LETTERS
Hidden	Text that appears on-screen only if Word's View options are set to display hidden text

CONTINUES

Endangered Species

In 1973, the U.S. Congress passed the Endangered Species Act (ESA), one of the strongest wildlife conservation laws in the world. The act conserves both endangered species and the ecosystems upon which they depend.

Extinct and Endangered Animals

Key the following lists of extinct and endangered animals. Tab once between columns to create two separate lists. Key the column headings in uppercase letters, as shown.

```
EXTINCT          ENDANGERED
Blue Pike        Jaguar
Eastern Elk      Leopard
Mammoth          Ocelot
Dodo Bird        Bighorn Sheep
```

Leopards are endangered.

TEST YOURSELF

Key each line twice: first slowly and then faster. Press Enter after each line.

Flowers
1 8 roses, 8 daisies, 8 lilies, 88 orchids
2 9 mums, 9 pansies, 99 asters, 99 poppies
3 80 carnations, 980 daffodils, 890 irises

Endangered Animals
4 Gorilla, Gazelle, Grizzly Bear, Wild Yak
5 Puma, Bobcat, Beaver, Condor, Blue Whale
6 Red Wolf, Woodland Caribou, Giant Panda

Double-Letter Words
7 8 books, 9 jeeps, 8 fillets, 9 dumbbells
8 80 cufflinks, affected 900, 980 patterns
9 4,890 gulls; 980 addresses; 80 different

Improve Your Speed

Each of these is a one-minute drill. For the first drill, press Enter at the end of each line. For the second drill, start with a tab and use word wrap. If you reach the end of a drill before time is up, start again from the beginning.

TIME YOURSELF

10 I let 9 kids make 8 tents at camp.¶
11 Jo hit 80 of 90 balls in the game.¶
    | 1 | 2 | 3 | 4 | 5 | 6 | 7   WPM: 13

12 →   The blue pike once swam the cool
13 waters of Lake Erie. With overfishing,
14 changes in habitat, and pollution, the
15 fish has become extinct.
    | 1 | 2 | 3 | 4 | 5 | 6 | 7 | 8   WPM: 27

TEST YOURSELF 9-3

Art Gallery Exhibit

You are in charge of an art gallery. Create a document with a multiple-column layout announcing a premiere art exhibit at your gallery. Research three or more present-day artists whose work you will display. Include background information on the artists and their work. The document should be at least one full page.

FIGURE 9-9
If you were in charge of an art gallery, what kind of art would you display?

In writing your document, be sure to:

1. Make the title of the document and some of the opening text one column and the remaining text in the document two or more columns.

2. Format the title in a font style that will emphasize the text.

3. Create paragraph headings throughout the second section in the document.

4. Format the paragraph headings in a font style that emphasizes them.

5. Include a small table in the document that relates to your topic.

6. Balance the columns in the second section of the document by using a continuous section break.

7. Proofread the document and add or delete text so the columns in the document are as balanced as possible.

8. Insert a document footer with your name (include a page number if the document is more than one page).

9. Spell-check and preview the document.

10. Save the document as *[your initials]*Test9-3.

11. Print and close the document.

WARM UP

Key each line twice. Press Enter after each line. Adjust your chair so your feet are well supported.

1 seat shoe gears strike sadly glad camels
2 stacks sassy brakes maker sweets rambled
3 chews dealings attached wears wash words

LEARN

NEW KEYS

 Use the **A** finger.

Use the **S** finger.

Use the **D** finger.

Reach up and left with your **A** finger to key. Reach up and left with your **S** finger to key. Reach up and left with your **D** finger to key. Keep your **F** finger anchored on its home key.

TECHNIQUE TIP

Position your monitor at eye level, about an arm's length away from you.

PRACTICE

Key each line twice. Press Enter after each line.

Practice 1
4 a aa aq a1 aq1 a1a 111 a1a 1z1 aq1a 1.11
5 1 at, 1 aqua, 1 aware, 11 are, 111 azure
6 1 quilt; 11:00; 11 to 14; 410 minus 111.

Practice 2
7 s ss sw s2 sw2 s2s 222 s2s 2sx sw2s 2.22
8 2-man. Swim 20 laps. Mia is 2. 2202 West
9 Liam is 21. Room 222. A 2-to-1 advantage

Practice 3
10 d dd de d3 de3 d3d 3d3 d3d 3dc dce3 3.33
11 3 cheers, 33 eggs, 33/hour, 33 deeds, 3D
12 3 CDs. 33 1/3. Number 23 scored over 33.

Practice 1 2 and 3
13 Quiz 12; Quasar 32 at 1:30; 23,231 hours
14 3-on-2; 1-on-2; 3 at 2:30; 3 blind mice;
15 I once caught 231 fish on a 21-day trip.

10. Select the entire table. On the **Table Tools Layout** tab, in the Cell Size group, change the row height from 0.16″ to 0.3″. Use the Center Align button ▤ to center all the text vertically and horizontally.

11. Format the document title ("Hurricanes") with the **Heading 1** Quick Style and center it. Format the title and the three paragraphs below it with 2.0 line spacing.

12. Insert the **Blank (Three Column)** footer in the document. Key your name, your class name, and the date in the placeholders.

13. Spell-check and preview the document.

14. Save the document as *[your initials]*Test9-1.

15. Print and close the document.

TEST YOURSELF 9-2

Gardening Newsletter

1. Open the file **WP-Gardening**.

2. Apply a two-column format from "**The History of Crop Rotation**" forward.

3. Apply the **Title** Quick Style to the document title "Gardening Tips."

4. At the blank paragraph mark above "Want More Information?" insert a 2-column by 5-row table.

5. Key the following text in the table:

Vegetable Family	Examples
Nightshade	Potatoes, tomatoes, peppers
Legumes	Peas, beans
Brassicas	Broccoli, cabbage, kale
Alium	Onions, chives, garlic

6. Apply a table style by choosing one from the third row of the gallery of styles.

7. Change the width of both columns in the table to 1.4″.

8. Balance the two-column format in the document by inserting a continuous section break at the end of the document.

9. Add a document footer that contains just your name.

10. Spell-check and preview the document.

11. Save the document as *[your initials]*Test9-2.

12. Print and close the document.

DID YOU KNOW?

Pests and diseases tend to affect vegetable groups and often remain in the soil for years. If you follow a crop rotation system, these pests and diseases can't build up in the soil.

Rate, Distance, and Time

When solving problems using rate, distance, and time, it is important to keep track of the units associated with each number and to work step by step.

FORMULA FOR RATE:

Rate = Distance/Time

Word Problems

Work out the solutions to the following problems. For each, key the problem and then the solution.

1. If you are driving at the rate of 1 mile in 45 seconds, how fast are you driving in miles per hour?

2. Alex and Kim start from the same point and ride their bicycles in the same direction. Alex travels at 8 mph; Kim travels at 12 mph. After 6 hours, how far apart are they?

TEST YOURSELF

Key each line twice: first slowly and then faster. Press Enter after each line.

Possessives
1 Ryan's 1 to Ana's 2; Elio's 2 to Nia's 3
2 the boy's 2 dogs; the crew's 213 workers
3 helper's, friend's, window's, neighbor's

Distance and Time

4 There are 315,360,000 seconds in 10 yrs.
5 1,000 miles equal exactly 5,280,000 ft.
6 1 mile equals 1,760 yards; 2 equal 3,520

Poisonous Snakes
7 1 pit viper, 1 copperhead, 1 coral snake
8 22 king cobras, 23 kraits, 33 boomslangs
9 1 green mamba, 2 tiger snakes, 3 taipans

TIME YOURSELF

10 There are 21 men and 3 women here.¶
11 I found 32 rocks on my trip today.¶
| 1 | 2 | 3 | 4 | 5 | 6 | 7   WPM: 14

12 →   Most students do not look forward
13 to exams. It feels great when an exam is
14 over, but the best feeling of all is
15 when you ace an exam.
| 1 | 2 | 3 | 4 | 5 | 6 | 7 | 8   WPM: 27

Improve Your Speed

Each of these is a one-minute drill. For the first drill, press Enter at the end of each line. For the second drill, start with a tab and use word wrap. If you reach the end of a drill before time is up, start again from the beginning.

WORD TIP

The AutoFit Window command extends a table to fit its current margins, whether in a one-column or a multi-column layout.

3. On page 1, click in the first paragraph of bulleted text (which begins "Cascade style"). Display the **Home** tab. In the Paragraph group, click the **Decrease Indent** button 📄. The bullets are now left-aligned in the column, with no indent.

4. Click in the table. Display the **Table Tools Layout** tab. In the Cell Size group, click **AutoFit** and choose **AutoFit Window**. The table now extends from the left to the right margin of the column.

5. Insert page numbers at the bottom of the document. Use the **Two Bars 1** style. Add your name to the right of the page number.

6. Preview the document by changing the zoom to **Two Pages** (**View** tab).

7. Make any adjustments needed to improve the final document.

8. Save the document as *[your initials]*Practice9-6.

9. Print and close the document.

TEST YOURSELF 9-1

DID YOU KNOW?

A hurricane can last for more than two weeks as it travels across the ocean and up a coastline.

Hurricanes

1. Open the file **WP-Hurricane2**.

2. Add a new paragraph at the end of the document. At this location, insert a table that is 3 columns by 6 rows.

3. Key the following text in the table:

Hurricane	Year	State
Great Labor Day Storm	1935	FL
Camille	1969	MS, LA, VA
Katrina	2005	LA, MS
Andrew	1992	FL, LA
Indianola	1886	TX

4. Position the insertion point in the first cell. Insert a row above this row.

5. Select the new row and merge the cells.

6. In the merged row, key the table title **MOST INTENSE HURRICANES IN THE UNITED STATES**

7. Apply the table style **Light Shading** (the second style in the first row of the gallery).

8. Clear the **First Column** table style option by unchecking the box.

9. Select row 2 (the column headings) and make the text bold.

Number Keys

WARM UP

Key each line twice. Press Enter after each line.

1 flew stew threw rust rumor port post toe
2 worth overt quart grate tired pride hope
3 gently partly mostly lately softly aptly
4 odious devious furious anxious obviously

PRACTICE

Key each line twice. Press Enter after each line.

Practice Numbers

5 1 on 1, 2 for 1, 7 or 8, 4 out of 5, 639
6 W-2, 3D, 4F, 5G, H6, J7, 8K, 9L, 00A-00Z
7 1 quart, 2 saws, 3 eels, 4 urns, 5 tires
8 1.02, 2.45, 3.76, 9.04, 6.55, 4.07, 8.85
9 4,250; 9,002; 4,523; 1,687; 6,085; 3,930

TIME YOURSELF

10 He has 2 birds, 4 dogs, and 1 cat.
   | 1 | 2 | 3 | 4 | 5 | 6 | 7   WPM: 14
11 Of the 63 hours, 20 were overtime.
   | 1 | 2 | 3 | 4 | 5 | 6 | 7   WPM: 14
12 All 8 students had 50 or 75 cents.
   | 1 | 2 | 3 | 4 | 5 | 6 | 7   WPM: 14
13 It is 85 or 90 degrees in the sun.
   | 1 | 2 | 3 | 4 | 5 | 6 | 7   WPM: 14

TIME YOURSELF

14 Of all the people in the public eye,
15 think of someone who you feel is a good
16 role model for you and your friends. It
17 might be someone in the arts, in sports,
18 or even in your town. It might be someone
19 you know. What is it about this person
20 that makes him or her special?
   | 1 | 2 | 3 | 4 | 5 | 6 | 7 | 8   WPM: 27

30-Second Drills

Key each of these lines for 30 seconds. *Do not look at the key-board*. Press Enter at the end of each line. If you reach the end of a line before time is up, start again from the beginning of that line.

2-Minute Drill

Key the paragraph for 2 minutes. Start with a tab and use word wrap. If you reach the end of the paragraph before time is up, start again from the beginning.

Balancing Columns

If you balance the length of columns, your document will be more visually pleasing. You can add or delete text to balance columns, or you can insert a continuous section break.

To balance columns:

1. Place the insertion point at the end of the document where you want to balance columns.
2. On the **Page Layout** tab, in the Page Setup group, click the **Breaks** command.
3. Choose **Continuous** from the drop-down list.

PRACTICE 9-6

Balance Columns

1. Move the insertion point to the end of the document (Ctrl + End).

2. Display the **Page Layout** tab. In the Page Setup group, click the **Breaks** command. Choose **Continuous** from the drop-down list. Word balances the length of the columns on page 2. Now you will make better use of the horizontal space in the two-column layout.

FIGURE 9-8
Balancing the length of columns

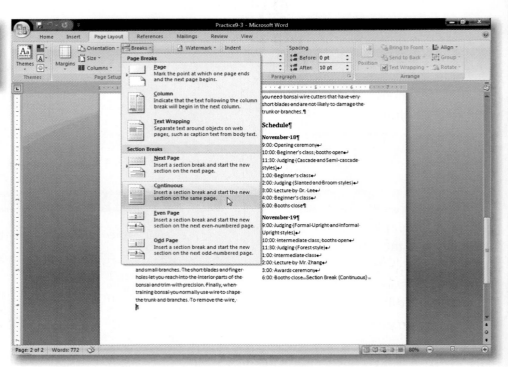

Lincoln gave his address in 1863 at the dedication of a Civil War battlefield cemetery in Gettysburg, PA.

Working from a Rough Draft

TEST YOURSELF

The following text is a rough draft of Abraham Lincoln's Gettysburg Address. Proofreading marks appear as corrections. Key the corrected text. Use word wrap. Use a tab to indent the first line of each paragraph.

Four score and seven

^ 87 years ago our fathers brought forth on this continent, a new nation, conceived in Liberty, and dedicated to the proposition that all men are created equal.

Now we are engaged in a great civil war, testing whether that nation, or any nation so conceived and so dedicated, can long endure. We are met on a great battle field of that war. We have come here to dedicate a portion of that field, as a final resting-place for those who here gave their lives that that nation might live. It is altogether fitting and proper that we should do this.

But, in a larger sense, we can not dedicate -- we can not consecrate -- we can not hallow -- this ground. The brave men, living and dead, who struggled here, have consecrated it, far above our poor power to add or detract. It is for us the living, rather, to be dedicated here to the unfinished work which they who fought here have thus far so nobly advanced. It is *rather* for us to be here dedicated to the great task remaining before us -- that from these honored dead we take increased *devotion* ~~loyalty~~ to that cause for which they gave the last full measure of devotion -- that we here resolve highly that these dead shall not have died in vain -- that this nation, under God, shall have a new birth of freedom -- and that government of the people, by the people, for the people, shall not perish from the earth.

The world will little note, nor long remember what we say here, but it can never forget what they did here.

Using Multiple-Column Layouts in Sections (CONTINUED)

To use a multiple-column layout:

1. Place the insertion point where you want to change the number of columns.
2. On the **Page Layout** tab, in the Page Setup group, click the **Columns** command. Choose **More Columns** from the drop-down list.
3. In the Columns dialog box, click one of the **Presets** options at the top of the dialog box, or key the number of columns you want in the **Number of columns** text box.
4. Click the down arrow next to the **Apply to** box and choose **This point forward**. This applies the new number of columns from the insertion point through the end of the document.

FIGURE 9-7
Creating a multiple-column layout

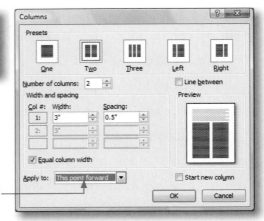

Use this setting to insert a continuous section break

5. Click **OK**. A continuous section break is automatically inserted at the insertion point, and the new section is formatted with the new number of columns.

PRACTICE 9-5

Use a Multiple-Column Layout

1. Place the insertion point to the left of the bold heading "**What is a Bonsai?**"
2. On the **Page Layout** tab, in the Page Setup group, click the **Columns** command. Choose **More Columns** from the bottom of the drop-down list.
3. In the Columns dialog box, click **Two** under **Presets**.
4. Set the **Apply to** box to **This point forward**. Click **OK**. A continuous section break is inserted before the heading. The first section is one column and the second section is two columns.
5. Leave the document open.

Learn $4 %5 ^6 &7 and *8

Key each line twice. Press Enter after each line.

1 fun funnels Fiji Fuji festival flapjacks
2 frijoles fan-jet fjords junks toy though
3 jaywalkers Jacksonville jack-o'-lanterns
4 Kilimanjaro khalif gill fish footlockers

LEARN

Press Right Shift and reach up and left with your F finger to key a dollar sign $4. Press Right Shift and reach up and slightly right with the same finger to key a percent symbol %5. Press Left Shift and reach up and left with your J finger to key a caret ^6 or ampersand &7. Press Left Shift and reach up and left with your K finger to key an asterisk *8.

PRACTICE

Key each line twice. Press Enter after each line.

Practice $ and %

5 fr 4r f4r f4$ f$ r f$$ $44 $45 $46 $47
6 f5 5rf f5f f5% f% %f% f%% 5% 55% 45% 56%

Practice & ^ and *

7 jj ju 7j j7j j7&j& T&E Q&A P&H S&L GBB&O
8 jj jy 6j j6j j6^j^ 2^3 3^3 2^4 equals 16
9 kk ki 8k k8k k8*k* 2*3 3*3 4*4 equals 16

Practice $ % ^ & and *

10 $4 fish, $47 fans, $48 flags, $745/title
11 45% off, 54% fees, 78% fat, 48.25% fines
12 Can you solve these: 6^3, 5^6, 8^4, 9^2?
13 Katz & Co. Home & Garden; 9*11 equals 99
14 **Note: AM&J will provide shoes & socks.

NEW KEYS

$4 Use the F finger.

%5 Use the F finger.

^6 Use the J finger.

The caret symbol is used to indicate exponentiation (for example: "2^3" is read as "2 to the third power," which is computed as $2 \times 2 \times 2$ or 8).

&7 Use the J finger.

*8 Use the K finger.

The asterisk is used to indicate multiplication. In text and tables, it is often used to indicate a footnote or special note.

SPACING TIP

Do not space after the dollar sign (example, $55). Do not space before the percent sign (example, 50%).

PRACTICE 9-4

Apply a Newspaper Column Layout

1. In the open document (which is one column, by default), click anywhere in the document text. Do not click in the table.

2. Display the **Page Layout** tab. In the Page Setup group, click the **Columns** command. Choose **Two** to change the document to a two-column layout.

FIGURE 9-6
Changing the number of columns

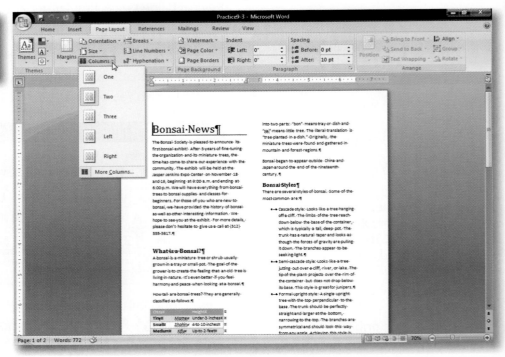

3. Using the **Columns** command again, change the document to a three-column layout. Notice the amount of text in three columns versus two columns.

4. Change the document back to one column. Leave it open.

Microsoft Word

Using Multiple-Column Layouts in Sections

To add even more visual interest to a document, you can create a multiple-column layout in which one section of the document has a different number of columns than another section. You do this by inserting a continuous section break. A *continuous section break* divides a document into sections without inserting a page break.

CONTINUES

Isolating Variables

When given an equation with two variables, first isolate one variable and solve it; then use that solution to find the second variable.

Word Problems

Jasmine works at a video rental store. In one week she earns $390 for working 47 hours, of which 7 hours are for overtime. The next week includes a holiday. Jasmine earns $306 for working 37 hours, of which 5 hours are overtime. Compute the solutions to the following questions and key the lines with the solutions.

```
Jasmine's regular pay rate is $     /hour.
Her overtime pay rate is $     /hour.
Her overtime pay rate is     % higher than her regular rate.
```

TEST YOURSELF

Key each line twice: first slowly and then faster. Press Enter after each line.

Left Shift

1 L.L.P., Manual, King John II, Mr. Jones:
2 J&J Logs, K&L Metal, M&N Pipes, L&L Owls
3 *JIM: How about Kim and Mike? *OK by me.

Variable Equations

4 x% of $20,000 equals $20; x^3 equals 27?
5 12^y equals 144? 50% of $39.00 equals?
6 ?^2 equals 16,900? 0.5% of 950 equals?

Semiprecious/ Precious Stones

7 diamond, rose quartz, amethyst, obsidian
8 emerald, garnet, jade, sapphire, crystal
9 topaz, citrine, tourmaline, amber, pearl

Improve Your Speed

Each of these is a one-minute drill. For the first drill, press Enter at the end of each line. For the second drill, start with a tab and use word wrap. If you reach the end of a drill before time is up, start again from the beginning.

TIME YOURSELF

10 It is $51.85 and is well worth it.¶
11 *Ann & Jim pay 8% less than we do.¶

| 1 | 2 | 3 | 4 | 5 | 6 | 7 | **WPM: 14**

12 →   For many companies, the overtime
13 pay rate is double the regular pay rate.
14 Some companies also pay a special bonus
15 for work on weekends.

| 1 | 2 | 3 | 4 | 5 | 6 | 7 | 8 | **WPM: 27**

FIGURE 9-5
Choosing a table style

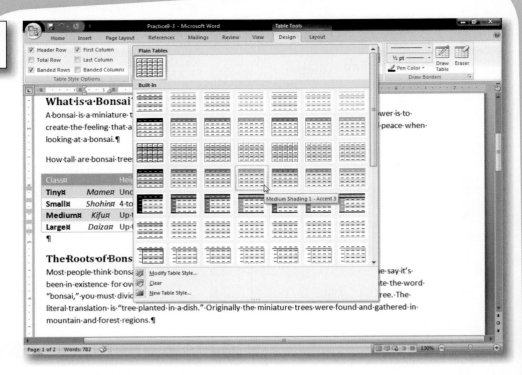

3. In the Table Style Options group, see if your table looks better with the option **First Column** checked or unchecked. (This option makes the first column text bold.) Experiment with some of the other options in this group to get the best result.

4. Save the document as *[your initials]***Practice9-3**. Leave it open.

Microsoft Word

Using Newspaper Column Layouts

By default, a document is formatted as one column. You can change the number of columns and flow text up and down on the page, as in a newspaper or newsletter. To decide how many columns to use, you might need to see the text a few different ways.

Using a newspaper column layout:

1. Place the insertion point anywhere in the document.

2. On the **Page Layout** tab, in the Page Setup group, click the **Columns** command. Choose an option from the drop-down list. The options **Two** and **Three** divide the text into columns of equal width. The options **Left** and **Right** divide the text into two columns of unequal width.

LESSON 29 Learn (9) (0) { [and }]

NEW KEYS

(9) Use the **L** finger.

(0) Use the **;** finger.

Use parentheses ( ) to enclose such items as explanatory material and references within a sentence.

{ [} Use the **;** finger.

{] } Use the **;** finger.

Use square brackets [ ] to insert explanatory material within text that is enclosed in quotation marks or parentheses.

{ { } Use the **;** finger.

{ } } Use the **;** finger.

Use curly brackets { } in mathematical functions, hyperlinks, and computer programming languages.

SPACING TIP

Space once before a left parenthesis or left bracket. Space once after a right parenthesis or right bracket unless it is followed by a period or comma.

WARM UP

Key each line twice. Press Enter after each line.

1 lips laps lampoon limpet limping lamplit
2 loop; lope; loopy; lop; lamprey; Lapland
3 lip-sync; apple's pulp; people populate;
4 Leopold: Lock up Paula's laptop, please.

LEARN

Press Left Shift and reach your **L** finger up and left to key a left (opening) parenthesis (9). Press Left Shift and reach your **;** finger up and left to key a right (closing) parenthesis (0). Reach your **;** finger up and right to key a left or right square bracket { [} {] }. Press Left Shift and use your **;** finger to key left or right curly brackets { { } { } }.

PRACTICE

Key each line twice. Press Enter after each line.

Practice ( )
5 lo l9 9(9(l9(((99 ((l((99ooll((((
6 ;p ;0 0) 0) p0))) 00)) p)) 00pp;;))))

Practice [ ]
7 ; ;; ;[[[[[[;[[;[; [;[;;[[;[;[[;[
8 ; ;; ;]]]]]] ;]] ;];];] ;;]] ;];]];]

Practice { }
9 ; ;; ;[[{ [{[;{{ ;{; {;[;;{{ ;{;{ {;{
10 ; ;; ;]]}]}] ;}} ;}; };} ;;}} ;};} };}

Practice ( ) [ ] and { }
11 (enclosed) (on p. 3) [2002] {a, b, c, d}
12 [90] {color: red} [sic] [emphasis added]
13 The price was low ($5.50), so I paid it.
14 "His birthday [1/2/80] was on a Monday."

11. Drag from "Mame" down to "Daiza" to select the Japanese names in the middle column. Use the Mini toolbar to make them italic.

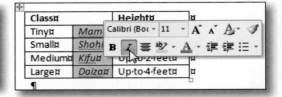

FIGURE 9-4
Using the Mini toolbar to format selected table text

12. With the cells containing the Japanese names still selected, click the Center Align button ▤ on the **Layout** tab in the Alignment group. The names are now centered in the cells.

Microsoft Word

Changing Table Design

To enhance the appearance of an entire table in one easy step, apply a preformatted table style from the **Table Tools Design** tab. You can preview what the table will look like before applying a style by just pointing to the style. After applying a style, experiment with the **Table Style Options** to see if your table looks best with banding (shading) of alternate rows or columns or with special formatting for the header row, first column, or last column.

To change the table design:

1. Click within the table.
2. On the **Table Tools Design** tab, point to a design in the Table Styles group. Use the scroll arrows to view more styles, or click the More button ▼ to see a gallery of all the styles.
3. Click a style to apply it to the table.
4. Select or clear a check box in the Table Style Options group to modify the table design as desired.

WORD TIP

Increase the zoom of the document to 130% so you can see more of the table with the Table Styles gallery open.

PRACTICE 9-3

Change Table Design

1. With the insertion point in the table, display the **Table Tools Design** tab. In the Table Styles group, click the More button ▼ to see the entire gallery of styles.
2. Move the pointer over some of the styles. Click to choose one of the styles that uses the color green (in the middle column of the gallery). See Figure 9-5 on the next page.

Mammals

Mammals are animals that have hair, are warm-blooded, and nourish their young with milk. People, dogs, mice, pandas, whales, and dolphins are all mammals. There are three types of mammals:

◆ Monotremes—primitive egg-laying mammals

◆ Marsupials—give birth to immature offspring that usually continue to develop in the mother's pouch

◆ Placentals—give birth to offspring that are in a more advanced stage of development

Mammal Types

Key the following mammals. Insert a tab between mammal names and press Enter after each line. Identify the mammals by putting parentheses ( ) around monotremes, square brackets [ ] around marsupials, and curly brackets { } around placentals.

Japanese snow monkeys are placental mammals.

Kangaroo	Bat	Spiny anteater
Koala	Dog	Duck-billed platypus
Numbat	Ape	Opossum

TEST YOURSELF

Key each line twice: first slowly and then faster. Press Enter after each line.

Fruit

1 (kiwi) (banana) (lime) (guava) (kumquat)

2 [peach] [lemon] [nectarine] [watermelon]

3 {lychee} {pomegranate} {papaya} {orange}

 Mammals

4 (Dogs/Cats) [Elephants/Mice] {Lion/Lamb}

5 {Cheetah/Sloth} (Pygmy Shrew/Giraffe)

6 [Bumblebee Bat/Blue Whale] {Bilby/Koala}

TIME YOURSELF

Improve Your Speed

Each of these is a one-minute drill. For the first drill, press Enter at the end of each line. For the second drill, start with a tab and use word wrap. If you reach the end of a drill before time is up, start again from the beginning.

7 "He [John] wants to go."¶

8 Can she (Jada) go there?¶

9 Section 1{a}(0) is open.¶

| 1 | 2 | 3 | 4 | 5   **WPM: 15**

10 →   The juice of one lemon supplies a

11 third of the vitamin C that you require

12 daily. Many people enjoy the flavor and

13 health benefits of lemons.

| 1 | 2 | 3 | 4 | 5 | 6 | 7 | 8   **WPM: 28**

PRACTICE 9-2

Change Table Layout

1. In the open document, make sure the **Table Tools Layout** tab is displayed.

2. Move the insertion point to the first cell. Select the entire row by clicking **Select** from the Table group and choosing **Select Row**. You will insert a new top row that will contain column headings.

3. From the Rows & Columns group, choose **Insert Above**. The table now has a new blank row.

4. Key the following column headings in the new row:

   Class   Japanese Name   Height

5. To adjust the width of the first column, click in the first cell ("Class"). In the Cell Size group, click the down arrow next to the Table Column Width 🗎 text box until the **2.2″** setting changes to **1.8″**.

6. To adjust the width of all three columns to fit the text, click **AutoFit** in the Cell Size group. Choose **AutoFit Content**.

WORD TIP

When you first insert a table, it extends from the left to the right margin and all columns are equal width. This is the default AutoFit Window setting.

FIGURE 9-3
Using the AutoFit Window command to resize the table

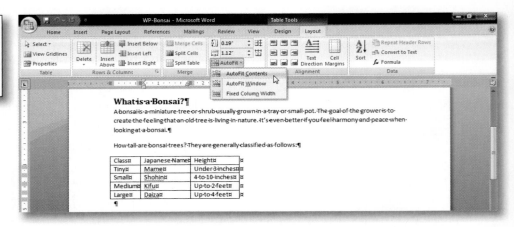

7. Drag over the first two cells in the first row, "Class" and "Japanese Name," to select them. (Position the I-beam to the left of "Class" and drag across.)

8. From the Merge group, click the **Merge Cells** command. The two cells are now one cell.

9. Delete the paragraph mark after "Class" and the text "Japanese Name," leaving only the word "Class" in the merged cell.

10. Drag across the cells in the first row to select them. Use the Mini toolbar to make the text bold.

Review $4 %5 ^6 &7 *8 (9)0 {[and }]

REVIEW

The keyboard shows the keys you have learned so far. This lesson focuses on the keys highlighted in purple.

WARM UP

Key each line twice. Press Enter after each line. Keep your shoulders down as you key.

1 fan-jet graceful gift-wrappings guffawed
2 grief glorify goofy grafting Guadalajara
3 Kipling kneeling kennels kernels Kampala
4 kibble lashes lathe Leroy larches launch

PRACTICE

Key each line twice. Press Enter after each line.

Practice
$ % ^ & *

5 $229.95 $0.03 $171.36 $105.00 or $106.00
6 2% 16% 0.003% 29.35% 10% salary increase
7 1^3 x^y .031^-3 A&B R&R *.doc 88*8 99*90

Practice
( ) [ ] { }

8 (a) (b) (c) (d) (e) (f) (1) 2) 3) 4) (5)
9 Decide on a size {small, medium, large}.
10 (The color [orange] was far too bright.)

Practice
$ % ^ & *
( ) [ ] { }

11 $1.99 .01% Abe & Sons *.* (12) [23] {34}
12 $435 $900 $502 $492 $807 $3.24 $12 & $22
13 100% 55% 39% 3.4% 92% 8*2 4%*15% {1,2,3}
14 (^) (%) ($) [&] [*] 6^6 [^a-f] [0-9] 1&3
15 (i.e., 9%) (1 meter) [65 tons] {1 liter}
16 (With inflation [5%], the price is $55.)

BREAK ING
BAD HABITS

Do not slouch. Sit up straight and center your body on J, about a hand's length from the keyboard, directly in front of your monitor.

Changing Table Layout

After inserting a table in a document, you can use the **Table Tools Layout** tab to modify the structure of the table. For example, you can insert and delete rows and columns, change cell size, and merge cells. You can also change the way text appears in the cells by changing the alignment or applying formatting to selected cells.

To add or delete rows or columns:

1. Click within the row or column. On the **Table Tools Layout** tab, in the Table group, click **Select**. Choose an option to select the row or column. (You can also use the mouse to drag over a cell, row, or column to select it.)

FIGURE 9-2
Select commands on the Table Tools Layout tab

2. With a row selected, choose **Insert Above** or **Insert Below** in the Rows & Columns group to insert a row above or below the selected row.

3. With a column selected, choose **Insert Left** or **Insert Right** to insert a column to the left or right of the selected column.

4. With the insertion point in any cell, click **Delete** in the Rows & Columns group. From the drop-down list you can choose to delete the cell, the entire row, the entire column, or the entire table.

To change row height, column width, or overall table size:

1. To change row height or column width, select the row(s) or column(s). In the Cell Size group, adjust the settings for row height 🔳 or column width 🔳.

2. To resize the table to fit the text, click within the table. In the Cell Size group, click **AutoFit**, and choose **AutoFit Content**.

3. To resize the table to extend from the left to the right margin, select the table, click **AutoFit**, and choose **AutoFit Window**.

To merge cells:

1. Click the left edge of the first cell and then drag across to include the other cell or cells you want to merge.

2. In the Merge group, choose **Merge Cells**. The selected cells become one cell.

The Scientific Method

Scientists use a type of reasoning called the *scientific method* in which they propose a hypothesis (a tentative assumption requiring testing to be proven true). Then they gather data to support or reject the hypothesis and arrive at a conclusion.

Testing a Hypothesis

Hypothesis: With modern medicine and improved nutrition and health care, people are living longer. Gather data to support or reject this hypothesis and arrive at a conclusion.

The table contains population data for 1900. Research the percentages for 2000. Key the Age Group column and the 2000 column. Use tabs to separate the columns. Then key your conclusion as a sentence below the data.

Age Group	1900	2000
Under 5	12.1%	?%
5-19 yrs	32.3%	?%
20-44 yrs	37.7%	?%
45-64 yrs	13.7%	?%
65 & over	4.1%	?%

TEST YOURSELF

Key each line twice: first slowly and then faster. Press Enter after each line.

Trees
1 (ash) (oak) [birch] [chestnut] {hickory}
2 {elm} (cedar) {fir} [hackberry] {gingko}
3 (cottonwood) (alder) [willow] {sweetgum}

Generation (Birth Years)
4 Echo Boom (1982-1995), Gen-X (1961-1981)
5 Boomers (1943-1960), Silent (1925-1942)
6 GI (1901-1924 [The Heroic Generation])

One-Hand Words
7 Lonny, I saw a free puppy in a pink car.
8 Fast cars were started. Crews are great.

TIME YOURSELF

9 It's now $5.50 per seat.¶
10 BB & BC are 100% agreed.¶
11 Is it a) up, or b) down?¶
| 1 | 2 | 3 | 4 | 5   WPM: 15

12 →   The hickory tree has a shaggy bark
13 and smooth leaves. The fruit of the tree
14 is the hickory nut, which is similar to
15 the pecan but not as large.
| 1 | 2 | 3 | 4 | 5 | 6 | 7 | 8   WPM: 29

Improve Your Speed

Each of these is a one-minute drill. For the first drill, press Enter at the end of each line. For the second drill, start with a tab and use word wrap. If you reach the end of a drill before time is up, start again from the beginning.

3. Position the insertion point at the blank paragraph mark on page 1, above the bold heading "**The Roots of Bonsai.**"

4. Display the **Insert** tab. In the Tables group, click the **Table** command.

5. In the grid, move the pointer three cells to the right and four cells down. Click the mouse button when the number above the grid is **3x4** to insert a table that is three columns across by four rows down.

FIGURE 9-1
Inserting a 3x4 table

WORD TIP

You can also drag the pointer in the grid and then release the mouse button to insert the table.

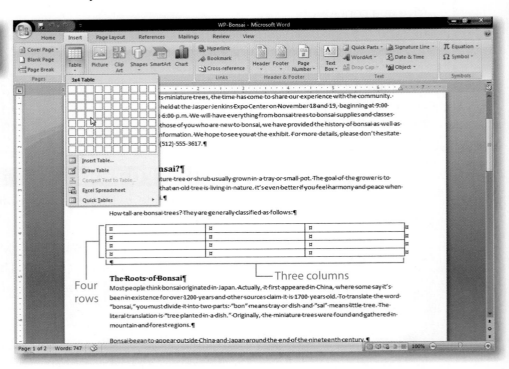

6. With the insertion point in the first cell, key the following table text. Press Tab to move from cell to cell.

Tiny	Mame	Under 3 inches
Small	Shohin	4 to 10 inches
Medium	Kifu	Up to 2 feet
Large	Daiza	Up to 4 feet

7. Leave the document open.

LESSON 31 Learn ~ !1 @2 and #3

WARM UP

Key each line twice. Press Enter after each line. Strike each key at a steady pace.

1 sensed staged stared seeded salted snare
2 waste water awesome assert ascend assess
3 squeezed squash squeegee squander squads
4 dancers dangles defeated dorsal deep-sea

NEW KEYS

~ Use the **A** finger.

~ Use the **A** finger.

The grave (`) and tilde (~) characters are used to show pronunciation. In math, the tilde indicates equivalency or similarity between two values.

!1 Use the **A** finger.

@2 Use the **S** finger.

The at symbol (@) is used in business forms (10 items @ $12 per item) or e-mail addresses (see next page).

#3 Use the **D** finger.

LEARN

Reach up and left with your **A** finger to key the grave ~ symbol. Press Right Shift and reach up and left with your **A** finger to key a tilde ~. Press Right Shift and reach up and left with your **A** finger to key an exclamation point !1. Press Right Shift and reach up and left with your **S** finger to key the at symbol @2. Press Right Shift and reach up and left with your **D** finger to key the number symbol #3.

SPACING TIP

Space once after the exclamation mark. Space before and after the @ symbol unless it is used in an e-mail address (when it has no space before or after).

PRACTICE

Key each line twice. Press Enter after each line.

Practice ` ~ !
5 aq qa a` a`a aq`a aq a~ ~a a~a aq~a a`~a
6 aq qa a1 a1a a1!a a!a a1!a A1! Ha! Aha!!

Practice @ #
7 sw ws 2s s2s s2@s s@s s2@s s@s @w@s s@s@
8 de ed 3d d3d d3#d d#d d3#d d#d de#d# #33

Practice ` ~ ! @ #
9 ~F11, ~sx file, (~), ~23, [~], [`], `560
10 Wow! Yes! Fantastic! Terrific! Let's go!
11 2 @ $2, 20 @ 2%, 200 gal. @ $12 per gal.
12 Inv. #213, Item #560, Apt. #3a, Ext. #12

LESSON 9
Word Processing

Use Tables and Columns

LEARN

Work with Tables and Columns

So far you have organized document text into paragraphs that run vertically down the page. This lesson shows you two ways to make document text more readable: by organizing it into tables or by formatting it in columns.

A *table* is a grid of intersecting rows and columns that you insert in a document. Tables are a great way to fit a lot of information into a small amount of space. A *column layout* often makes a long document easier to read. A familiar example is a newspaper. Text fills one column and then flows to the top of the next column.

Microsoft Word

Creating Tables

A table is useful for displaying text and/or numeric data. To create a table, you specify the number of rows and columns you want. You then key information in the table *cells*, which are the boxes formed by the intersecting rows and columns.

To create a table:

1. Place the insertion point where you want to insert the table.
2. On the **Insert** tab, in the Tables group, click the **Table** command.
3. In the grid, move the pointer to the right and then down to select the number of columns and rows you want.
4. Click the grid selection to insert the table in the document.
5. Key text in the first cell. Press Tab to move from cell to cell. Click outside the table when you finish keying text.

PRACTICE 9-1

Create Tables

1. Start Word and open **WP-Bonsai**.
2. Make sure you are working in Print Layout view with non-printing characters displayed.

E-Mail Addresses

Standard Internet e-mail addresses are composed of two parts separated by the at symbol (@). The part before @ is the *account name* or *user name*. The part after the symbol is the *domain name*. The account name identifies the particular e-mail account; the domain name identifies the e-mail server on which the account can be found. When spoken, the e-mail address "user@host.com" is read as "user at host dot com."

Your Favorites

Create a list of ten e-mail addresses. They can be real or made-up. Be sure to key the addresses with no spaces between letters or parts of the address. Examples of made-up e-mail addresses:

> yourname@yourschool.edu
>
> smokeythebear@forests.org

TEST YOURSELF

Key each line twice: first slowly and then faster. Press Enter after each line.

Exclamations

1 "Watson, come quickly! I need you!" Bell
2 "Alas, poor Yorick!" William Shakespeare
3 "A lifetime of happiness!" G. B. Shaw

E-Mail Addresses

4 president@whitehouse.gov; info@si.edu
5 cloisters@metmuseum.org; inquiries@un.org
6 hcinfo@parliament.uk; editor@nybooks.com
7 admission@howard.edu; webmaster@mfa.org

Symbols in Sentences

8 Buy 2 dozen eggs @ $1/dozen! A bargain!
9 Write to ej@isp.com. Ask for #14 & #13.

TIME YOURSELF

10 We are #1 on the charts. That is great!¶
11 E-mail her at rosa@ft.org and order #2.¶
| 1 | 2 | 3 | 4 | 5 | 6 | 7 | 8 | **WPM: 16**

12 →   The White House is open daily to
13 the public. By touring the staterooms,
14 you can learn how presidents and first
15 ladies lived there over the years.
| 1 | 2 | 3 | 4 | 5 | 6 | 7 | 8 | **WPM: 29**

Improve Your Speed

Each of these is a one-minute drill. For the first drill, press Enter at the end of each line. For the second drill, start with a tab and use word wrap. If you reach the end of a drill before time is up, start again from the beginning.

11. Insert a footer that contains your name and the page number.

12. Save the document as *[your initials]*Test8-2.

13. Print and close the document.

TEST YOURSELF 8-3

FIGURE 8-12
Researcher in laboratory

Research a New Medical Breakthrough

Research a topic on a new medical breakthrough. Use at least three sources. Write down your source information and outline your ideas. Write a rough draft of a report that is at least two pages long. The report should include a cover page, the body with parenthetical citations, and a bibliography. Proofread the report and create a final draft.

In writing your report, be sure to:

1. Insert a report header or footer that does not appear on the title page and begins with the correct page number.

3. Use font formatting and spacing that makes the report easy to read.

4. Insert parenthetical citations following any text you quote, summarize, or paraphrase. Include page numbers when applicable.

5. Enter the appropriate source information. Do a final pre-view of your source information before inserting your bibliography.

6. Spell-check the document.

7. Save the document as *[your initials]*Test8-3.

8. Print and then proofread the printed document.

9. Mark the document with proofreaders' marks and key these changes into your document.

10. Save the document again and print it.

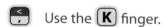 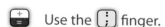
WARM UP

Key each line twice. Press Enter after each line. Hold your head straight without leaning it forward or backward.

1 point; poke; pike; kelp; keeper; kindly;
2 Kepler's, Kalli's, Kelvin's folks, kappa
3 Loki's, Lily's, lack, lackey, lurk, loop
4 low-key; lock-jaw; lockets; leathernecks

NEW KEYS

 Use the **K** finger.

 Use the **L** finger.

The less than symbol (<) and greater than symbol (>) are mathematical operators.

Use the **;** finger.

Use the **;** finger.

LEARN

Press Left Shift and reach down and right with your **K** finger to key the less than symbol. Press Left Shift and reach down and right with your **L** finger to key the greater than symbol. Reach up and right with your **;** finger to key the equals sign. Press Left Shift and reach up and right with your **;** finger to key the plus sign.

PRACTICE

Key each line twice. Press Enter after each line.

Practice < >

5 k kk k, k,k< k<k <<k kk< <kk k<k <<< <,<
6 l ll l. l.l> l>l >>l ll> >ll l>l >>> >.>
7 << >> << >> <56> <900> <12> <231> <4554>

Practice = +

8 ; ;[;= ;=; === ;=; ;;; =;= ;=; === ;[=;
9 ; ;= ;+; ;{+ +++; +;+ ;{+; ;+; ;=+; +=+;
10 = + = 1 + 2 = 3, 9 + 10 = 19, 6 + 8 = 14

Practice < > = +

11 22 < 23, 67 < 68, 899 < 900, 100.1 < 123
12 90 > 80, 75 > 63, 82 > 8, 0.175 > 0.0175
13 1 + 9 = 10, 22 + 22 = 44, 44 + 123 = 167
14 A = 3, B = 7, C = 999; A + B + C = 1,009

SPACING TIP

Space before and after the mathematical operators < > = +.

 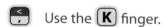 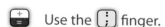

TEST YOURSELF 8-2

The Titanic

1. Open the file **WP-Titanic2**.

2. In the first paragraph, directly after the quote, insert a citation that refers to the following book. Use MLA style.

   Author: **Lord, Walter**
   Title: **A Night to Remember**
   Year: **2005**
   City: **New York**
   Publisher: **Henry Holt & Company, Inc.**

3. Edit the citation to include the page number **xii**.

4. On the second page, locate the paragraph that begins with "Titanic historian" and the quote that ends with "brilliant stars."

5. Insert a citation at the end of this quote, using the same source (Walter Lord). Edit the citation to include the page number **71**.

6. Format this entire paragraph (from "Titanic historian" through the citation) with the **Intense Quotation** Quick Style.

7. At the end of the last paragraph in the document, insert a citation using a new source, a Web site:

   Author: **Rowan, Beth**
   Name of Web Page: **Titanic Facts**
   Year: **2007**
   Year, Month, Day Accessed: Use today's date
   URL: **http://www.infoplease.com/spot/titanic.html**

8. Display the Source Manager dialog box and preview your sources, checking spelling and punctuation. From this dialog box, add a new source (to be included in the bibliography without a citation). The source is another Web site:

   Name of Web Page: **Titanic Nautical Society & Resource Center**
   Year, Month, Day Accessed: Use today's date
   URL: **http://www.titanic-nautical.com**

9. Insert the bibliography on a new blank page at the end of the document.

10. Insert a cover page for the report. Include the document title, your name, your teacher's name, the class name, and the date.

DID YOU KNOW?

In 1986, a deep-sea robot named J.J. explored the interior of the sunken Titanic, sending back pictures of the grand staircase, the gym, and artifacts strewn on the sea floor.

Roman Numerals

Roman numerals were the dominant numbering system through the first millennium. By the middle of the 16th century, most of Europe switched to Arabic numerals. Why the switch? Arabic numerals proved easier for multiplication, division, fractions, and advanced mathematics. Roman numerals are used today only for special numbering.

Comparing Roman and Arabic Numerals

In the table, determine whether the Roman numeral is less than, greater than, or equal to the Arabic numeral. On a separate line, key each Roman numeral, the appropriate symbol (<, =, or >), and the Arabic numeral. For example, for the first one, key L < 100.

Roman Numeral	< = >	Arabic Numeral
L	?	100
XXII	?	22
MCX	?	160
DCXIV	?	500

TEST YOURSELF

Key each line twice: first slowly and then faster. Press Enter after each line.

High School Radio Stations

1 WLTL 88.1 KASB 89.3 WMSS 91.1 KPHS 90.3
2 KCAC 89.5 WAVM 91.7 KDXL 106.5 WIQH 88.3
3 WHJE 91.3 KJHB 97.7 WHFH 88.5 KGAR 93.3

< = >

4 1.15 > 1.115; .99 < 9.1; 10% of 100 = 10
5 2% of .62 = .0124; .009 < .03075; 9 > .1
6 7 < 8; 75% of .008 = .006; 1.055 > 1.009

Math in Sentences

7 The formula used is = (A10 + B12) / C12.
8 If x = 10, and x + y = 102, then y = 92.

TIME YOURSELF

9 Bailey thought 405 + 695 + 532 = 1,632.¶
10 Jane showed how (x + y) > 8, but y < 5.¶
| 1 | 2 | 3 | 4 | 5 | 6 | 7 | 8   WPM: 16

11 →   Kelp is a type of seaweed. It is a
12 bit like a tree, anchored in the ocean
13 floor, growing up toward the surface of
14 the sea, always reaching for light.
| 1 | 2 | 3 | 4 | 5 | 6 | 7 | 8   WPM: 30

TECHNIQUE TIP

You can use Caps Lock when you have a lot of capital letters in a row. Numbers are not affected.

Improve Your Speed

Each of these is a one-minute drill. For the first drill, press Enter at the end of each line. For the second drill, start with a tab and use word wrap. If you reach the end of a drill before time is up, start again from the beginning.

5. Place the insertion point on the page after the cover page.

6. Display the Print dialog box again. Click **Current page** and click **OK**.

7. On the page you just printed (which should be the first page of the actual report), use proofreaders' marks to mark the errors in the second paragraph.

8. Working from your marked page, key the corrections into the second paragraph in your document.

9. Spell-check and proofread the entire document.

10. Save the document as *[your initials]***Practice8-5**.

11. Print the corrected pages of the document and close it.

TEST YOURSELF 8-1

The American Automobile

1. Open the file **WP-Automobile2**.

2. In the second paragraph of the report, key the corrections shown in Figure 8-11.

FIGURE 8-11

The beginning (1890s–1930) *(bold)*. The first gasoline-powered automobile was built in 1893 by *two* brothers who were bicycle mechanics. The *ir* automobile was actually a converted horse carriage with a Øne-cylinder engine. By 1989, some 3 0 manufacturers had produced 2,500 automobiles, with th*i*s number soaring to 8,000 by year's end. # Fewer than one-third of these automobiles were gasoline powered; most *ran on* ~~were~~ steam or electric *ity*.

DID YOU KNOW?

By 1923, more than 175 patents were granted to women for inventions related to automobiles, traffic signals, and turn indicators.

3. This report already has two bibliography sources in it. Insert a new blank page at the end of the document and then insert the bibliography. Use MLA style. (This will be a bibliography without citations in the body of the report.)

4. Add a footer with your name and the page number.

5. Spell-check the document.

6. Save the document as *[your initials]***Test8-1**.

7. Print the first page and the bibliography.

8. Close the document.

214

NEW KEYS

 Use the `;` finger.

The underscore (_) is used in e-mail addresses, filenames, and to create a fill-in line in a printed document.

 Use the `;` finger.

The backslash (\), not to be confused with the diagonal (forward slash /), is used in file paths to separate folder names and filenames.

 Use the `;` finger.

The vertical bar (|), also called a "pipe," is used to separate hyperlinks on a Web page. It is also used in programming language to join a series of commands.

BREAKING BAD HABITS

Do not favor your stronger fingers when reaching to key symbols and numbers. Use the correct fingers.

WARM UP

Key each line twice. Press Enter after each line. Sit up straight with feet flat and supported. Do not slouch.

1 papers; puppet; chipper; chopper; capped
2 "uppity" "yuppie" Lupa's Pepper's Opie's
3 pre-paid plans; Pre-Raphaelite paintings
4 up-to-date maps; 900-pound hippo; f-stop

LEARN

Press Left Shift and reach your `;` finger up and right to key an underscore ▭. Reach your `;` finger up and right to key a backslash ▨. Use Left Shift and your `;` finger to key a vertical bar ▨. On some keyboards, ▨ is located above `Enter`. On others, the key is located between `± =` and `Backspace`.

PRACTICE

Key each line twice. Press Enter after each line.

Practice _

5 ; ;- -_ -_-_-_ ;-_ _i_ ;-_i _i_ i_i ;-_i
6 ;_i _i_ ;_;_ a_b; b_c; c_data; sec I_(a)
7 l_p; (LP_) = (9_0) Pp_; Jo_Doe@ Ann_Lee@

Practice \|

8 ; ;; \ \\ ;\; ;\;\ ;\; ;\\; \;\ ;\; ;\\;
9 | ;| \ \| ;\;| ;|; ;\; ;||; |;| ;|; |\|;
10 files\old\homework| files\new| data\new|

Practice _ \|

11 ;_\| ;;;_ ;;;\ ;;;| ;_;\ ;\;| ;_\| ;_\|
12 A_Tate P_Sager M_Nesbit c: dir c:\ |more
13 Maria|Emma|Edward|Jean|Julian|Louis|Reed
14 jo_jamison@isp.com | c:\science\homework

Using Proofreaders' Marks (CONTINUED)

TABLE 8-1 **Proofreaders' Marks**

Proofreaders' Mark	Example	Outcome
Capitalize	jack	Jack
Apply bold	bright *(bold)*	**bright**
Apply italic	amused *(italic)*	*amused*
Apply underline	Science *(underline)*	Science
Move to the right	$45,670	$45,670
Move to the left	You can go.	You can go.
Stet	I am very glad *(stet)*	I am very glad

PRACTICE 8-5

Proofread and Print Specific Pages

1. In the second-to-last paragraph of the report, locate the text shown in Figure 8-10. Using Table 8-1 as a guide, make the corrections indicated.

FIGURE 8-10

Michelangelo was a sculptor as well as a painter. His most famous sculpture is David, the first major sculpture of the high renaissance. The huge figure was sculpted in 1510 as a patriotic symbol of the Florentine republic.

2. Click the Microsoft Office button. Choose **Print** from the menu.

3. In the dialog box, click **Pages** and key **p1s1, p3s2** in the text box to print the cover page, which is page 1 of section 1, and the bibliography, which is page 3 of section 2.

4. Click **OK**.

Emoticons

An *emoticon* (short for emotion icon) is a popular form of shorthand used to convey emotion in text messages. It was originally formed by keying certain letters and symbols that you then viewed by tilting your head to the left. The first emoticon appeared in 1982. It was the classic smiley. Programs such as Microsoft Word now convert text emoticons such as :) to ☺. Today, emoticons are more sophisticated graphics, often with animation and sound.

"Smiley," the first emoticon

Matching Emoticons

Match the following text emoticons below with their correct meanings. Then key the list of emoticons and meanings as a two-column list using Tab to separate the columns.

```
:-C          Winking
=8-0         Very unhappy
'-)          Yikes!
```

TEST YOURSELF

Key each line twice: first slowly and then faster. Press Enter after each line.

Similar Words

1 bases|basis defer|differ breath|breadth
2 exalt|exult occurs|recurs averse|adverse
3 genius|genus incite|indite later|latter
4 choose|chose lose|loose reverse|reverts

Emoticons

5 Surprised :-0 Foot in mouth :-! Duck .V
6 Shouting :-V Skeptical :-/ Sarcastic :->
7 Walrus :-< Frog 8) Robot [:] Hungry :0

 Improve Your Speed

Each of these is a one-minute drill. For the first drill, press Enter at the end of each line. For the second drill, start with a tab and use word wrap. If you reach the end of a drill before time is up, start again from the beginning.

TIME YOURSELF

8 Look in c:\work\proposal\new.¶
9 The address is mr_j@mail.com.¶
10 Part III_C_xx_e has the data.¶
   | 1 | 2 | 3 | 4 | 5 | 6 | WPM: 17

11 →   Nursery rhymes may or may not have
12 been based in fiction. For example, was
13 there an actual person named Peter Piper
14 who picked a peck of pickled peppers?
   | 1 | 2 | 3 | 4 | 5 | 6 | 7 | 8 | WPM: 31

Printing Specific Pages or Page Ranges (CONTINUED)

To print the current page:
1. Place the insertion point on the page you want to print.
2. Click the Microsoft Office button 🕮 and choose **Print**.
3. In the Print dialog box, click **Current page**. Click **OK**.

Microsoft Word

Using Proofreaders' Marks

The last step in creating a final draft is *proofreading* it to check content, formatting, spelling, and grammar. Word's spelling and grammar checkers do not catch all errors. When proofing a printed document you can apply handwritten corrections called *proofreaders' marks*. You can mark corrections on the printed page and then enter them in the Word document.

TABLE 8-1   Proofreaders' Marks

Proofreaders' Mark	Example	Outcome
Start new paragraph	That's great! How is	That's great! How is
Insert word/letter	noticable	noticeable
Insert period	The end	The end.
Transpose	beleive	believe
Change/delete letters	assistentance	assistant
Insert space	verygood	very good
Delete space	when ever	whenever
Lowercase	JAck	Jack

CONTINUES

LESSON 34

Review ~ ! @ # < > . = - and \

REVIEW

The keyboard shows the keys you have learned so far. This lesson focuses on the keys highlighted in purple.

WARM UP

Key each line twice. Press Enter after each line.

```
1  Aquila acquit sewn slaw stow sweets soul
2  queen king lot low par pew pry pug pails
3  paws perks pies pleas pouts props pastas
4  pickerel pocketful pumpernickel padlocks
```

TECHNIQUE TIP

Strike each key at a brisk and steady pace. Do not hesitate after pressing Enter.

PRACTICE

Key each line twice. Press Enter after each line.

Practice ` ~ ! @ #
```
5  a` a` a` xy~xy quest~ Yes! Okay! Thanks!
6  ~/UK #50! 3 @ $1 each! 8 miles @ 60 mph!
7  E-mail camp@isp.com Order #255 and #463!
```

Practice < > = +
```
8  600 < 700, 1,000 > 999.9, <500k> <650mb>
9  If a = 1, b = 6; a + b + c = 20; c = 13.
10 If (X + Y) < Z and Z = 5, is X > or < 4?
```

Practice _ \ |
```
11 c:\english\poets\hughes, d:\letters\work
12 8 underscores = _____. pair|pare|pear
```

Practice ` ~ ! @ # < > = + _ \ |
```
13 de`light ~user|mike jimmy_jarmon@isp.com
14 Correct! Bravo! #2 and #2.5 lead pencils
15 Explain how a + 9 = b, a < 8, and b > 9.
16 ~F_1, \~@comp, d:\docs\abc.html aa|bb|ab
```

5. Insert page numbers at the bottom of the document, excluding the cover page. Use the **Two Bars 2** style and start numbering at 1.

6. Leave the document open. You will do a final spelling and grammar check in the next Practice.

Microsoft Word

Printing Specific Pages or Page Ranges

Many printing options are available in Word. For example, you can print specific pages or page ranges. In a long report, you might want to print the bibliography only. You can also print the page where the insertion point is currently. You use the Print dialog box to print specific pages of a document.

To print specific pages or page ranges:

1. Click the Microsoft Office button and choose **Print** from the menu.

2. In the Print dialog box, click **Pages** and key the page numbers you want to print, separated by commas, in the text box. For example, to print pages 1, 3, and 6, key **1,3,6**. To print pages 1 to 3, key **1–3**.

3. Click **OK**.

FIGURE 8-9
Printing specific pages

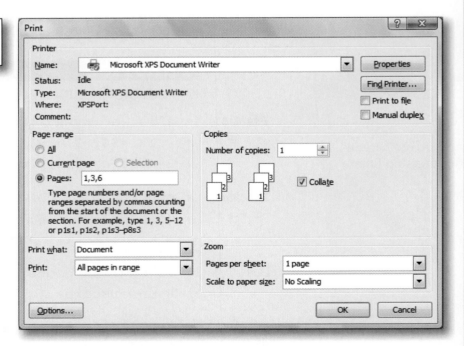

CONTINUES

Demonyms

A *demonym* (dem' a nim) is a name given to people of a particular city, territory, or country. For example, a person from Denmark is referred to as a Dane. ("Dane" is a demonym.)

Discover Demonyms

Find the correct demonym for each of the countries listed below. Then key the country, a vertical bar, and then the demonym.

Belgium
Finland
Luxembourg
Philippines

A person from Peru
is a Peruvian.

TEST YOURSELF

Key each line twice: first slowly and then faster. Press Enter after each line.

Fish Combos
1 `<bass + salmon>, <mullet + shrimp + cod>`
2 `<clams + lobster + scallops + oysters>`
3 `trout|catfish|snapper|grouper|flounder`

Demonyms
4 `United States|American, Guyana|Guyanese`
5 `The Bahamas|Bahamian, Switzerland|Swiss`
6 `Sweden|Swede, Kenya|Kenyan, Mali|Malian`

Right-Shifted Capitals
7 `Dr. Dean, B&B Auto, CSD Travel, F. Sales`
8 `Q&As, Western Wall, Fred's Diner, F.D.R.`
9 `Cleopatra, Romeo, April, Queen Elizabeth`

TIME YOURSELF

10 `Order #5 @ noon today. Great!¶`
11 `Your file address is c:\part.¶`
12 `The hint is that a + b > 100.¶`

`| 1 | 2 | 3 | 4 | 5 | 6 ` **WPM: 18**

13 → In chess, the queen is the most
14 powerful piece because she can move in
15 any direction. The king, however, is the
16 key piece. When he is captured, the game
17 ends.

`| 1 | 2 | 3 | 4 | 5 | 6 | 7 | 8 ` **WPM: 32**

Improve Your Speed

Each of these is a one-minute drill. For the first drill, press Enter at the end of each line. For the second drill, start with a tab and use word wrap. If you reach the end of a drill before time is up, start again from the beginning.

Inserting a Bibliography (CONTINUED)

To insert a bibliography:

1. Place the insertion point in a new blank page at the end of the document.
2. On the **References** tab, in the Citations & Bibliography group, click **Bibliography**.
3. Click the preformatted **Bibliography** at the top of the drop-down list. It contains the title "Bibliography."

PRACTICE 8-4

Insert a Bibliography

1. Press Ctrl + End to go to the end of the document. Press Ctrl + Enter to insert a page break.
2. On the **References** tab, in the Citations & Bibliography group, click **Bibliography**.
3. Point to the first built-in style, called **Bibliography**. Click to insert it.

FIGURE 8-8
Inserting a bibliography

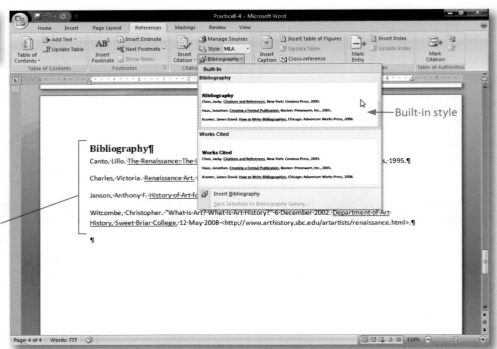

Bibliography in the document

WORD TIP

If you need to make changes to a bibliography after you insert it, simply reopen the Source Manager dialog box and make your edits. Then click the bibliography in the document and click Update Citations and Bibliography to apply the changes.

4. On the cover page of the report, replace the bracketed placeholders with your own information. Format the cover-page text and the title on page 2 as desired.

Symbol Keys

WARM UP

Key each line twice. Press Enter after each line.

1 opera Ohio optical Oliver outline Oxford
2 popcorn Peoria phobia Poe plywood Python
3 vest, zipper, hem; viola, oboe, clarinet
4 helper, yelp, gulped, sculpture, culprit

PRACTICE

Key each line twice. Press Enter after each line.

Practice Symbols

5 ($99.95) 85% [his & her] *.doc {1, 2, 3}
6 Okay! Look! **RSVP** #45 & #89 (^75) 1^4
7 3 @ $2 ea. = $6, (x < y), dr_lee@isp.com
8 \"Radio"\ </HTML> ~plans ~memos |x| M|N|

1-Minute Drills

Key each of these paragraphs for 1 minute. Start with a tab and use word wrap. *Concentrate as you key the symbols.* If you reach the end of a paragraph before time is up, start again from the beginning.

TIME YOURSELF

9 →   When Len (the CPA) said to leave an
10 18% tip on our $145 bill, Sue said
11 "Let's give $30!"

| 1 | 2 | 3 | 4 | 5 | 6 | 7 | WPM: 18

12 →   Key <FONT SIZE="+6">Jo</FONT> in
13 HTML to make "Jo" big. Key <B>Jo</B> to
14 make "Jo" bold.

| 1 | 2 | 3 | 4 | 5 | 6 | 7 | WPM: 18

TIME YOURSELF

2-Minute Drill

Key the paragraph for 2 minutes. Start with a tab and use word wrap. If you reach the end of the paragraph before time is up, start again from the beginning.

15 →   You can create your own home page
16 if you know the simple language of HTML.
17 It is called a language for lack of a
18 better word, but you do not have to
19 learn foreign words or letters. You
20 simply write text in plain English and
21 then mark it up by using common symbols.
22 A browser can then display the document
23 as a Web page.

| 1 | 2 | 3 | 4 | 5 | 6 | 7 | 8 | WPM: 32

FIGURE 8-7
Managing your sources

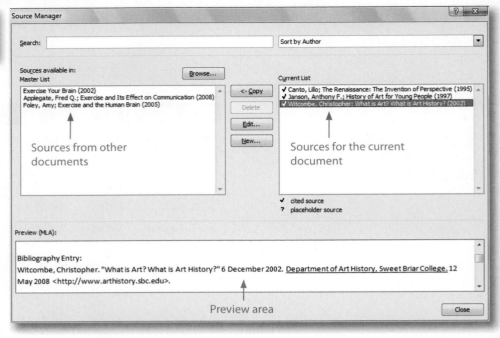

5. With the dialog box still open, click **New** to add a new source. This book was read for the report, but it does not require a citation in the text. Use the following source information:

   Author: **Charles, Victoria**
   Title: **Renaissance Art**
   Year: **2007**
   City: **New York**
   Publisher: **Parkstone Press**

6. Click **OK**. Preview the new source in the Source Manager dialog box. Preview the other sources in the document to check for spelling errors.

7. Close the dialog box. Leave the document open.

WORD TIP

When entering new source information, be sure to first choose the correct Type of Source.

Microsoft Word

Inserting a Bibliography

With your citations in place and your source information complete, now you can insert a bibliography. Your bibliography will include the sources for your citations as well as other sources you used in your report. You insert a bibliography on a new page at the end of the document.

CONTINUES

The following text outlines some of the historic events in the TV industry. Key the text. Use word wrap. Use a tab to indent the first line of each paragraph.

In 1923, the first TV transmission tube is patented. The first electronic TV image is transmitted in 1927. GE introduces a TV set with a 3″ × 4″ screen in 1928. The first TV is sold for $75.

By 1931, there are 40,000 television sets in the U.S.; 22% of them are in New York City.

In 1945, there are 13 commercial broadcast channels. The first World Series is televised in 1947. Cable TV comes to rural areas in 1949. Color TV is introduced in 1951.

By 1960, 90% of U.S. homes have TV. In 1962, the first transatlantic broadcast occurs via satellite. In 1965, ABC pays $32 million for Saturday afternoon football. The first "Star Trek" episode airs in 1966. Congress creates PBS in 1967. "Sesame Street" is introduced in 1969.

In 1972, "M*A*S*H" premieres, along with HBO (the first pay cable network). In 1977, the TV miniseries "Roots" draws an audience of 130 million.

Both CNN and MTV premiere in 1980. The Supreme Court allows TV cameras in the courtroom in 1981. The "Oprah Winfrey Show" hits national TV in 1986. By 1988, TV is in 98% of U.S. households.

By 1992, there are 900 million TV sets in use around the world; 22% are in the U.S. In 1996, HDTV (high-definition digital television) is introduced.

By 2005, new TV monitors are flat. Viewers have more choices. They can watch their favorite programs on home computers, on 52″ LCD screens, or on handheld mobile devices.

10. Edit the second Janson citation, adding the page number **290**.

11. Leave the document open.

Managing Sources

After completing the source information for a report, you can use the Source Manager dialog box to review all your sources, add or delete sources, or edit source information. The dialog box shows the sources you entered for the current document under **Current List**. It also shows all sources entered for other documents under **Master List**.

To manage sources:

1. On the **References** tab, in the Citations & Bibliography group, click the **Manage Sources** command.

2. To preview one of the sources you entered, click it in the **Current List** to select it.

3. To edit a selected source, click **Edit**. To delete a selected source, click **Delete**.

4. To use a source from another document, select it from the **Master List** and click **Copy**.

5. To enter a new source, click **New**.

6. Click **Close** when you have finished.

PRACTICE 8-3

Manage
Sources

1. In the current document, click the **Manage Sources** command on the **References** tab in the Citations & Bibliography group.

2. In the Source Manager dialog box, under **Current List**, click the Witcombe source. The **Preview** area shows exactly how it will appear in your bibliography. You need to make a correction to the URL. See Figure 8-7 on the next page.

3. Click **Edit**. At the end of the current URL, add the text **/artartists/renaissance.html**

4. Click **OK**. (If a message appears asking if you want to update the master list, click **Yes**.) Check how the edited source appears in the **Preview** area.

Learn Keypad: 4 5 6 and Enter

WARM UP

Key each line twice. Press Enter after each line

1 jut jog jug Joe June jump jury junk joke
2 kit kid Kim key kick kiln knot kite Kidd
3 law lit lot lop lug luck limb ladle look
4 jungle little kitten liter loom multiply

NEW KEYS

4 Use the 4 finger.

5 Use the 5 finger.

6 Use the 6 finger.

Enter Use the right-hand little finger.

BREAK ING
BAD HABITS

Do not use the Enter key on the regular keyboard when keying a list of numbers on the numeric keypad. Keep your focus on the numeric keypad keys and your right hand.

LEARN

The numeric keypad is a block of keys typically located at the right side of the keyboard. Use the keypad when entering numbers only. It contains keys for digits 0 through 9 and for addition, subtraction, multiplication, and division, as well as a separate Enter key. To use the keypad, first press the Num Lock key to turn on the indicator light on the keyboard.

4, 5, and 6 are the home keys on the numeric keypad. Position your right hand so your index finger rests on 4 and your second finger on 5. This key has a raised underscore that lets you feel when your finger is correctly placed. Your third finger rests on 6, and you strike Enter with your little finger.

PRACTICE

Key each of the following lists, one below the other. Start with list 5, pressing Enter on the numeric keypad after each complete number. Key list 6 below list 5, and so on. Key the lists twice.

Practice
4 5 6 Enter

5	6	7	8
444	555	666	456
464	565	556	654
454	545	656	664
455	544	655	446
454	545	645	465

9	10	11	12
4444	5555	6666	4565
4544	5455	6466	4665
4545	5566	6445	4654
4445	5556	4666	6565

3. In the Placeholder Name dialog box, key **Janson**. Click **OK**. This will serve as a temporary reference to a book by Janson.

4. Two paragraphs down, after the quotation that ends with "1556," insert another placeholder named **Janson** (you will be able to choose **Janson** from the **Insert Citation** drop-down list).

5. Now add source data for your new placeholders. Click the first Janson placeholder, click the down arrow, and choose **Edit Source**.

6. Set the source type as **Book**, and enter the following source information:

> Author: **Janson, Anthony F.**
> Title: **History of Art for Young People**
> Year: **1997**
> City: **New York**
> Publisher: **Prentice Hall**

7. Click **OK**. Both Janson placeholders are now citations with the new source data. Now you will add page numbers to the citations.

8. Click the first Janson citation, click the down arrow, and choose **Edit Citation**.

9. In the Edit Citation dialog box, key **245** in the **Pages** box. Click **OK**.

WORD TIP

Press Tab to move from one text box to the next as you enter source information.

FIGURE 8-6
Adding a page number to a citation

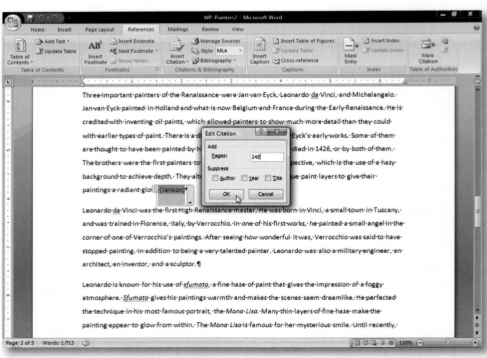

Binary Numbers

The decimal number system contains ten digits: 0-9. Computers use the binary number system, which contains just two digits: 0 and 1. In the decimal system, moving from right to left, the first place represents 1s, the second place 10s, the third place 100s, and so on. The number 123 means three 1s, two 10s and one 100. In the binary system, moving from right to left, each place represents the previous number times 2. As shown below, decimal number 123 is the equivalent of 64 + 32 + 16 + 8 + 0 + 2 + 1, which is binary number 1111011.

Converting Decimal Number 123 to a Binary Number	1	1	1	1	0	1	1
	64s	32s	16s	8s	4s	2s	1s

Convert Binary to Decimal

The following lines begin with a binary number and show the addition needed to convert the number to a decimal number. Key each line, including the decimal number answer. Use the number keys on the regular keyboard.

```
1101 = 8 + 4 + 0 + 1 = ___
1010101 = 64 + 0 + 16 + 0 + 4 + 0 + 1 = ___
11111 = 16 + 8 + 4 + 2 + 1 = ___
```

TEST YOURSELF

Key each line twice: first slowly and then faster. Press Enter after each line. Use the number keys on the regular keyboard.

Binary to Decimal

```
1  Binary 1000 = Decimal 8 (8 + 0 + 0 + 0)
2  Binary 1001 = Decimal 9 (8 + 0 + 0 + 1)
3  Binary 1010 = Decimal 10 (8 + 0 + 2 + 0)
```

Alternate-Hand Words

```
4  knew list hire liar hose more most lost
5  walk sail damp balk trip drum drip from
6  lugs lids pure love node pyre once lift
7  wail swim grip bail rain rein crop twin
8  mist hogs kids pose ooze plea live kite
```

Improve Your Speed

Key the paragraph for one minute. Use a tab and word wrap. If you reach the end before time is up, start again from the beginning.

TIME YOURSELF

```
9  →      The abacus is regarded as the first
10 computer. This ancient device, made of
11 wooden rods and beads, allows users to
12 add, subtract, multiply, and divide with
13 one hand.
```

| 1 | 2 | 3 | 4 | 5 | 6 | 7 | 8   WPM: 33

Inserting Placeholders (CONTINUED)

To insert a placeholder:

1. Place the insertion point at the end of the sentence or paragraph where you want to insert the placeholder.
2. On the **References** tab, in the Citations & Bibliography group, click the **Insert Citation** command.
3. Choose **Add New Placeholder** from the drop-down list.
4. Enter a placeholder name and click **OK**.

To add source information and citation page numbers:

1. Click in the placeholder, click the down-pointing arrow, and choose **Edit Source**.
2. Enter the source information and click **OK**.
3. To add a page number to a citation, click the citation, click the down-pointing arrow, and choose **Edit Citation**. Enter the page number and click **OK**.

PRACTICE 8-2

Insert Placeholders and Edit Information

1. Position the insertion point at the end of the next paragraph (after "radiant glow.").
2. Click the **Insert Citation** command on the Ribbon and choose **Add New Placeholder** from the drop-down list.

FIGURE 8-5
Inserting a placeholder

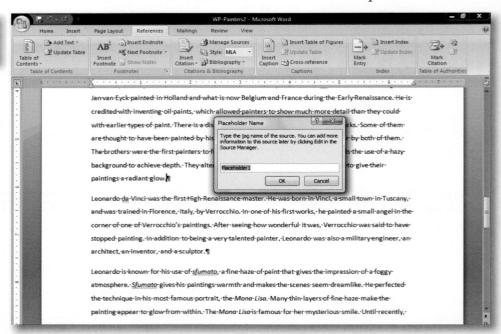

Learn Keypad: 7 8 and 9

WARM UP

Key each line twice. Press Enter after each line. Keep your shoulders down as you key.

1 pastry, nuance, happened, yearly, unable
2 low-key, knowing, ozone, lenient, proven
3 Jupiter, jasmine, junctions, IOU, Joplin
4 monsoons, Taj Mahal, moonlight, monument

NEW KEYS

7 Use the **4** finger.

8 Use the **5** finger.

9 Use the **6** finger.

LEARN

From the keypad home row, reach up with your **4** finger to key **7**. Reach up with your **5** finger to key **8**. Use your **6** finger to reach up and key **9**. Remember to press the Num Lock key to activate the numeric keypad.

TECHNIQUE TIP

After making a reach to the top row on the numeric keypad, bring your fingers back to keypad's home row: **4** **5** and **6**.

PRACTICE

Key each of the following lists, one below the other. Start with list 5, pressing Enter on the numeric keypad after each complete number. Key list 6 below list 5, and so on. Key the lists twice.

Practice 7 8 9

5	6	7	8
477	588	696	987
474	585	699	986
747	858	969	985
774	885	996	984
447	558	669	897
744	855	966	894
777	888	999	886
745	854	695	697

9	10	11	12
7679	8684	9594	8894
7798	8869	9975	8986
7998	8799	9884	9786
4798	6897	5978	7687
7874	8785	9497	9557

8. In the Create Source dialog box, click the **Type of Source** down arrow. Scroll down and choose **Document From Web site**. Key the information shown in Figure 8-4. For the year, month, and day accessed, use today's date.

FIGURE 8-4
Enter information for the new source.

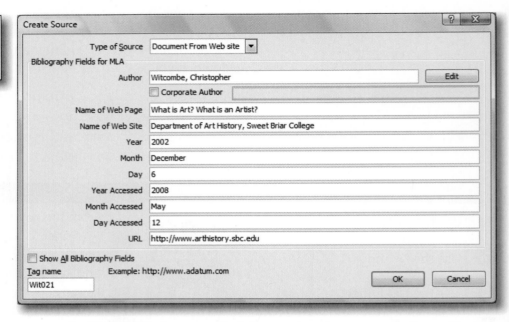

9. Click **OK** when you finish entering the source information. The citation "(Witcombe)" appears in the document.

10. Click at the end of the next paragraph (which ends with "optics."). You will insert another citation from the Witcombe source.

11. Choose the **Insert Citation** command on the Ribbon. From the drop-down list, click the source you just entered, "Witcombe, Christopher." A new citation using the same source is inserted in the document.

12. Leave the document open.

WORD TIP

Display nonprinting characters when inserting citations so you can see if you need to add a space character before or after the citation.

Microsoft Word

Inserting Placeholders

When writing a report, you can insert placeholders for citations until you are ready to enter the source information. When you're ready to convert your placeholder to a citation, you add the source information. If the source is a book or magazine, you also need to edit the citation to include a page number.

CONTINUES

Prime Numbers

A *prime number* is any positive number greater than one that can be divided evenly only by itself and by 1. Prime numbers play a large role in the science of encryption.

Determining Primes

Identify the prime numbers in the numbers below. Key the prime numbers as a list, pressing Enter after each number. Use the numeric keypad.

47 48 56 57 59 67 78 89 98 99

449 459 647 659 749 887 977

TEST YOURSELF

Key each line twice: first slowly and then faster. Press Enter after each line.

Acronyms and Abbreviations

1 CC, DNA, ZIP, PIN, FAQ, IMHO, SITCOM, IT
2 LOL, FYI, BTW, TMI, DNS, HTML, FTP, HTTP
3 CEO, AKC, SAT, BLOG, SPAM, OTOH, WYSIWYG
4 CD, ISP, DVD, URL, IOU, SKU, MIME, SCUBA

Speed Sentences

5 He is a good man. She is a fine singer.
6 Do you know if it is okay to go in now?
7 Kids and dogs like to play in the yard.
8 They said that it was the best of times.
9 Turn it up so we can all hear the music.

Prime Numbers

Use the numeric keypad to key each of these lines as a vertical list, pressing Enter after each complete number. Key the lists twice.

10 5 7 97 457 467 499 547 557 577 587 599
11 769 787 797 857 859 877 967 4447 4457
12 4547 4549 4567 4597 4999 5647 5657 6449

Improve Your Speed

Key the paragraph for one minute. Use a tab and word wrap. If you reach the end before time is up, start again from the beginning.

 ## TIME YOURSELF

13 →   The Taj Mahal is one of the eight
14 wonders of the world. This dazzling
15 monument of the finest white marble,
16 gemstones, and precious metal is the
17 most visited site in India.

| 1 | 2 | 3 | 4 | 5 | 6 | 7 | 8   WPM: 34

Insert Citations

1. Start Word and open **WP-Painters2**. This report already has a reference source and a citation.

2. To view the citation, scroll to page 2, the first paragraph. The first quotation ends with the citation "(Canto 5)." This refers to page 5 from a book by the author Canto.

3. To view the source information, click the citation. Click the down-pointing arrow and choose **Edit Source**.

FIGURE 8-3
Citation in the text

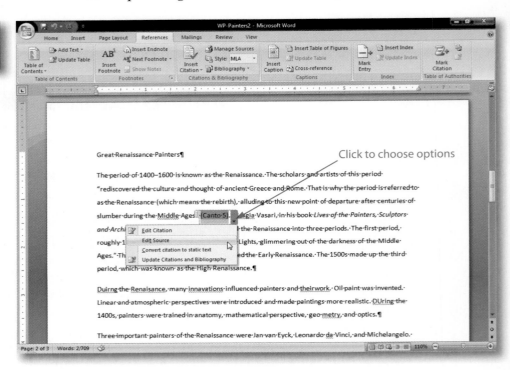

WORD TIP

There are different styles for representing citations and sources. Some use italics and some use underlining for source information. MLA and APA are popular for academic reports. Check your teacher's preferences.

4. Review the information already entered for this source; then click **Cancel** to close the dialog box. Now you'll enter your own citations and source information.

5. Display the **References** tab. In the Citations & Bibliography group, set the **Style** box to **MLA** (or whichever style your teacher prefers).

6. In the same paragraph, position the insertion point after the second quotation (before the sentence that begins "The second period").

7. Click the **Insert Citation** command. Notice the existing source is on the drop-down list. Choose **Add New Source**.

LESSON 37

Learn Keypad: 1 2 3 0 and Decimal Point

WARM UP

Key each line twice. Press Enter after each line. Keep your eyes on the page.

1 more, moray, money, moonstone, monoplane
2 noontime, normal, nominee, no-load, monk
3 Mona Lisa, smile, mill, milky, milligram
4 hominy, mollusk, mimic, monopoly, molten

NEW KEYS

1	Use the 4 finger.
2	Use the 5 finger.
3	Use the 6 finger.
.	Use the 6 finger.
0	Use the right thumb.

LEARN

From the keypad home row, reach down with your 4 finger to key 1. Reach down with your 5 finger to key 2. Reach down with your 6 finger to key 3. Reach further down with your 6 finger to key the decimal point. Use your right thumb to key 0. Bring your fingers back to the home row after reaching to the bottom row.

PRACTICE

Key each of the following lists, one below the other. Start with list 5, pressing Enter on the numeric keypad after each complete number. Key list 6 below list 5, and so on.

TECHNIQUE TIP

Keep the wrist of your right hand straight and comfortable as you move over the numeric keypad.

Practice 1 2 3 0 and Decimal Point

5	6	7	8
411	522	636	410
441	525	633	011
141	552	363	205
114	252	366	360
414	225	336	404

9	10	11	12
102	200	6.1	6.60
403	201	3.0	6.06
130	204	5.4	3.06
101	513	3.5	6.36
105	230	6.4	1.66
122	231	0.5	2.36
106	234	1.5	3.61
300	620	0.6	2.66

CHECKLIST

Source Information to Record

☑ For a book: Author name, title of book, publication information (this appears on the copyright page: place published, publisher name, year published), page numbers for parenthetical citations

☑ For a magazine: Author name, article title, magazine name, publication date, page numbers of article

☑ Online periodical: Author name (if available), title of the work, name of the periodical or Web site, publication date, date of access, Web address

Microsoft Word

Inserting Citations

You insert a citation at the end of a sentence or paragraph for content you have quoted, summarized, or paraphrased from a reference source. To insert a citation, you click where you want the citation to appear, and then enter the source information. Entering the source information builds a database that you will later compile for your bibliography.

To insert a citation:

1. Place the insertion point at the end of the sentence or paragraph where you want to place the citation.

2. On the **References** tab, click the **Insert Citation** command in the Citations & Bibliography group.

3. Choose **Add New Source** from the drop-down list.

FIGURE 8-2
Inserting a citation

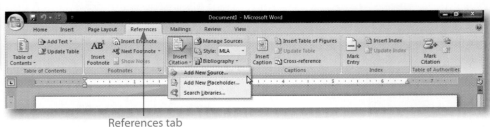

References tab

4. Enter the source information in the **Create Source** dialog box. Click **OK**.

Fibonacci

Leonardo Pisano (1170-1250), born in Italy but educated in North Africa, is better known by his nickname—Fibonacci (Fee-bo'-natch-e). Fibonacci is famous for his formulation of the numeric sequence 1, 1, 2, 3, 5, 8, 13, and so on, where each number is the sum of the previous two numbers. This sequence has since proven useful in the fields of genetics and mathematics.

Filling in a Sequence

Insert the missing numbers in the Fibonacci sequences below. Key each sequence as a vertical list, pressing Enter after each complete number. Use the numeric keypad.

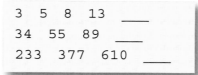

```
3   5   8   13   ___
34  55  89  ___
233  377  610  ___
```

TEST YOURSELF

Key each line twice: first slowly and then faster. Press Enter after each line.

Forests
1 Sierra, Black Hills, Yosemite, Allegheny
2 Bighorn, Saw Tooth, Lewis & Clark, Teton
3 Yellowstone, Shasta-Trinity, Six Rivers

Double-Letter Sentences
4 Nell sells sea shells in the Seychelles.
5 Dee spilled coffee on a yellow pillow.
6 Free cookies and coffee will thrill all.

Fibonacci Sequences
Use the numeric keypad to key the numbers in lines 7 and 8 as one vertical list, pressing Enter after each complete number.

7 610 987 1597 2584 4181 6765 10946 17711
8 28657 46368 75025 121393 196418 514229

Improve Your Speed

Key the paragraph for one minute. Use a tab and word wrap. If you reach the end before time is up, start again from the beginning.

⏰ TIME YOURSELF

9 →   The most admired painting of all
10 time is the Mona Lisa, created about
11 five hundred years ago. Who is she and
12 what's behind her famous smile? To this
13 day, no one really knows.

| 1 | 2 | 3 | 4 | 5 | 6 | 7 | 8 | WPM: 35

Create Final Drafts

LEARN

Create the Final Draft

To create a final draft of a report, you must credit any reference sources you used in your research. Sources can include books, magazines, and Web sites.

The way you credit a source in your report is to insert a *citation* in the text. For example, if you quoted from a book, you insert a citation after the quote. The citation shows the author's name and the page number, both in parentheses. Word provides tools for entering citations and source information. As a final step, you use this information to create a *bibliography*, which is a list of all of the sources you have read for your report.

FIGURE 8-1
Source entries as they appear in a bibliography

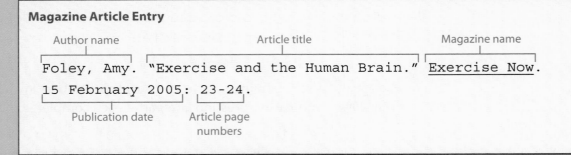

Book Entry

Author name — Applegate, Fred Q. *Exercise and Its Effect on Communication*. — Book title
Chicago: Marion Press, 2008.
Place published — Publisher name — Year published

Magazine Article Entry

Author name — Foley, Amy. "Exercise and the Human Brain." *Exercise Now*. — Magazine name
15 February 2005: 23-24.
Publication date — Article page numbers — Article title

Online Article Entry

Article title — Publication date — Web site name — Date of access
"Exercise Your Brain." 1 July 2002 *Web Workout*. 2 May 2008
<http://www.webworkout.com>.
URL address

Numeric Keypad

WARM UP

Key each line twice. Press Enter after each line.

1 Molly, novel, miner, noble, moon, nobody
2 under, image, oval, usable, ignite, only
3 purpose, yodel, polar, youngster, postal
4 koala, kangaroo, Katmandu, kazoo, kimono

PRACTICE

Key each of the following four lists, one below the other. Start with list 5, pressing Enter on the numeric keypad after each complete number. Key list 6 below list 5, and so on.

Practice the Numeric Keypad

5	6	7	8
714	981	1.7	9.21
485	783	2.6	8.03
596	857	3.5	7.04
684	749	4.8	6.54
753	156	5.9	5.26
951	354	6.1	4.37
248	486	7.3	3.83
327	116	8.0	2.19
196	371	9.6	1.01
274	842	0.6	0.03

TIME YOURSELF

2-Minute Drill

Key the paragraph for 2 minutes. Start with a tab and use word wrap. If you reach the end of the paragraph before time is up, start again from the beginning.

9 →   The beach is the perfect place on a
10 hot summer day. There is so much to do.
11 Kids build castles in the sand and look
12 for shells. Everyone warms up in the sun
13 and cools off in the water. Swimmers
14 ride the waves. Some folks play
15 volleyball or fly kites. Runners and
16 walkers enjoy the sound of the surf and
17 the fresh sea air. A good time is had by
18 all.

| 1 | 2 | 3 | 4 | 5 | 6 | 7 | WPM: 35

14. Format page numbering to start at 1.

15. Save the document as *[your initials]***Test7-2**.

16. Print and close the document.

TEST YOURSELF 7-3

Solar Energy

Research a topic on solar energy. Use at least two sources. Write a rough draft of a report that is at least two pages long. Create at least one bulleted or numbered list in the report. Your document file should include a cover page that you create manually.

In writing your report, be sure to:

1. Use a **Next Page** section break to create the cover page.

2. Vertically center the cover page text.

3. Add a report footer with your last name and the page number. The footer should not appear on the title page. Page numbering should begin at 1 on the first page of the body of the report.

4. Remember to create a bulleted or numbered list.

5. Spell-check and preview the document.

6. Save the document as *[your initials]***Test7-3**.

7. Print and close the document.

FIGURE 7-12
Harnessing the power of the sun could solve future energy needs.

Working from Statistical Material

Using the numeric keypad, key lists 1 through 4 one below the other. Add 5 to each of the numbers in the list before keying.

1	2	3	4
20	24	12	91
85	33	18	83
92	56	43	74
68	71	64	25
41	69	60	88

Key lists 5 through 8 one below the other. Subtract 3 from each of the numbers in the list before keying.

5	6	7	8
14	81	17	21
48	73	20	80
56	85	15	74
84	79	47	65
75	55	59	52

Key lists 9 through 12 one below the other. Multiply each number in the list by 10 before keying.

9	10	11	12
51	35	6.2	.97
28	48	4.3	.83
32	16	8.3	.12
96	71	9.6	.71
24	42	7.5	.43

Key lists 13 through 16 one below the other. Round each number up or down to two decimal places.

13	14	15	16
5.134	4.636	5.620	6.967
6.201	7.488	1.437	7.873
3.976	6.166	3.833	1.112
7.996	5.717	9.969	2.271
5.244	8.429	4.751	3.643
7.976	9.169	1.830	3.102

TECHNIQUE TIP

With your right hand over the numeric keypad, remember to use your thumb to press [0], your third finger to press the decimal point, and your little finger to press Enter.

WORD TIP

You can use the Different First Page option to remove a header from a cover page without working with sections.

DID YOU KNOW?

Winds of 50 miles per hour or more cause the Statue of Liberty to sway 3 inches and her torch to sway 5 inches.

WORD TIP

In Step 10, be sure to apply the vertical centering to the first section only.

9. Insert a header, using the **Stacks** style. In the Document Title placeholder, key your name.

10. Click in the header area. On the Ribbon, in the Options group, check **Different First Page**.

11. Double-click in the body of the document. Select the document (Ctrl + A) and change line spacing to **1.5**.

12. Save the document as *[your initials]* **Test7-1**.

13. Print and close the document.

TEST YOURSELF 7-2

The Statue of Liberty

1. Open the file **WP-Liberty2**. This is a different version of the Statue of Liberty report.

2. Change the font for the entire document to 12-point Book Antiqua.

3. Select the list of dated information beginning "July 1885" through "October 28, 1886" (five short paragraphs). Apply the numbering style that begins with 1).

4. On page 2, select the three-line list that begins with "Her crown contains" and apply the diamond bullet.

5. Format the page 1 title as 14-point bold.

6. Insert a new blank paragraph mark above the title.

7. Position the insertion point just below the new blank paragraph, to the left of the title text. Insert a **Next Page** section break.

8. In your new blank page, key cover page information: the document title ("The Statue of Liberty"), your name, your teacher's name, your class name, and the current date.

9. Apply double-spacing to the cover-page information. Center the text horizontally with the Center button ▤.

10. Center the cover-page text vertically by using the Page Setup dialog box (Layout tab).

11. Increase the text size of the title on the cover page to 18 points.

12. Click within page 2 (section 2). Unlink the section 2 footer from section 1 by clicking the **Footer** command, choosing **Edit Footer**, and then clicking **Link to Previous** on the Ribbon.

13. With the insertion point in section 2, insert the **Conservative** style footer.

Alphabet Keys

WARM UP

Key each line twice. Press Enter after each line.

1 aAa bBb cCc DdD EeE fFf gGg HhH iIi JjJj
2 kKk lLl MmM NnN oOo PpP qQq rRr SsS tTtT
3 uUu vVv WwW XxX YyY ZzZ asdf jkl; qwerty
4 G h I J K l m N O p q r s t u v w x y z.

PRACTICE

Key each line twice. Press Enter after each line.

Focus on Speed

5 one and two and three and four and seven
6 the boy the girl the dog the cat the dad
7 a red and a blue and a green and a black
8 to love to give to have to hold to reach
9 at lunch at play at work at home at once
10 in school in class in motion in the news
11 on time on ice on edge on hand on target

30-Second Drills

Key each of these paragraphs for 30 seconds. Start with a tab and use word wrap. If you reach the end of a paragraph before time is up, start again from the beginning of the paragraph.

TIME YOURSELF

12 →   A river is a natural stream of
13 water that empties into an ocean, lake,
14 or other river.
| 1 | 2 | 3 | 4 | 5 | 6 | 7   WPM: 35

15 →   A delta is a land mass that forms
16 at the mouth of a river by layers of
17 sand and gravel.
| 1 | 2 | 3 | 4 | 5 | 6 | 7   WPM: 35

60-Second Drill

Key the paragraph for 60 seconds. Start with a tab and use word wrap. If you reach the end of the paragraph before time is up, start again from the beginning.

TIME YOURSELF

18 →   A reef is a ridge of sand, coral,
19 or rock lying at or near the surface of
20 the water. Coral reefs are found in
21 tropical climates. They are made of the
22 remains of sea animals.
| 1 | 2 | 3 | 4 | 5 | 6 | 7 | 8   WPM: 35

FIGURE 7-11
Changing the starting
page number

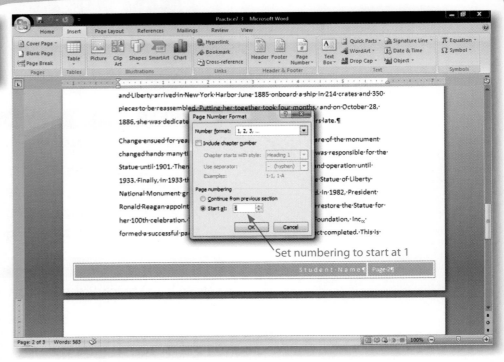

Set numbering to start at 1

5. Save the document as *[your initials]***Practice7-5**.

6. Print and close the document.

TEST YOURSELF 7-1

DID YOU KNOW?

The Titanic was 883 feet long (1/6 of a mile) and stood taller than most urban buildings of its time.

The Titanic

1. Open the file **WP-Titanic1**. This is a report on the Titanic.

2. Insert a hard page break (Ctrl + Enter) directly after "[Current Date]" on the first page.

3. Delete any extra blank lines after "[Current Date]" on the first page or before "The Titanic" on the second page.

4. Replace the information on the cover page with your name, your teacher's name, your class name, and the current date.

5. Format the cover page as follows: Apply the **Title** Quick Style to "The Titanic." Apply the **Subtitle** Quick Style to the text below the title. Format "Submitted by" and "Prepared for" as bold. Add 60-point paragraph spacing before the title and before "Submitted by."

6. Center the cover page text horizontally with the Center button ▤.

7. Format the title on page 2 as 18-point Cambria.

8. Apply round bullets to the timed account of the ship's sinking. The first paragraph in the list begins "11:39 pm:" and the last paragraph is "Four days later, the Carpathia reaches New York with 705 survivors."

WORD TIP

Remember, you apply paragraph spacing before or after from the Page Layout tab, the Paragraph group.

60-Second Drill

Key the paragraph for 60 seconds. Start with a tab and use word wrap. If you reach the end of the paragraph before time is up, start again from the beginning.

2-Minute Drills

Key each paragraph for 2 minutes. Start with a tab and use word wrap. If you reach the end of a paragraph before time is up, start again from the beginning of the paragraph.

 TIME YOURSELF

These are additional drills to build up your speed. Remember to sit with your back supported in your chair. Keep your eyes on the text.

```
1 →      Sally had to change a flat tire.
2 She had never done it before, but had
3 seen other people do it. She found the
4 spare tire and the tools, and made the
5 switch in twenty minutes.
```
| 1 | 2 | 3 | 4 | 5 | 6 | 7   **WPM: 35**

 TIME YOURSELF

```
6 →      How many hours a day do you spend
7 doing the things that you do? It could
8 be useful to keep track of the number of
9 hours you devote to such things as
10 schoolwork, sports, eating, and
11 sleeping. How many hours do you spend
12 online or watching TV or talking on the
13 phone? Think about how much time you
14 allot to hobbies and family. Is your
15 life in balance?
```
| 1 | 2 | 3 | 4 | 5 | 6 | 7   **WPM: 35**

```
16 →      Jerry always wanted to write a
17 mystery novel. He had all the details in
18 his head before he even sat down to
19 start writing. He knew the names of all
20 the people in the story. He had the plot
21 worked out. He knew how it would start
22 and end. When he began writing on his
23 laptop, the words flowed like water.
24 Before long he was ready to write the
25 sequel.
```
| 1 | 2 | 3 | 4 | 5 | 6 | 7   **WPM: 35**

4. Click the **Link to Previous** command on the Ribbon to break the link. Notice that "Same as Previous" is no longer in the footer area.

5. With the insertion point now in the section 2 footer, click the **Footer** command in the Header & Footer group on the Ribbon. Insert the **Tiles** footer style.

6. In the footer, click the company address placeholder and key your name.

7. Click the **Previous Section** command on the Ribbon. The section 1 footer is empty.

8. With the insertion point in the section 1 footer, press Tab and key **Draft** in the center of the footer pane.

9. Double-click in the document area and preview all pages of the document. Leave the document open.

Microsoft Word

Changing the Starting Page Number

When a report has a cover page, you can begin page numbering with "Page 1" on the first page of the actual report. You do this by changing the starting page number.

To change the starting page number in a header or footer:

1. Click on the page or in the section where page numbering begins.

2. On the **Insert** tab, click the **Page Number** command and choose **Format Page Numbers**.

3. In the Page Number Format dialog box, set the **Start at** option to **1**. Click **OK**.

PRACTICE 7-5

Change Starting Page Number

1. Click in page 2 (section 2) of the document. Notice that page numbering in the footer begins with "Page 2."

2. On the **Insert** tab, click the **Page Number** command. Choose **Format Page Numbers** from the drop-down list.

3. In the Page Number Format dialog box, click the button to the left of **Start at** and set the textbox to **1**. See Figure 7-11 on the next page.

4. Click **OK**. The page number in the section 2 footer now starts with "Page 1."

WARM UP

Key each line twice. Press Enter after each line.

1 It's great! You'll go? On/off, Good/evil
2 3 dogs, 5 geese, 7 mice, 2 sheep, 9 oxen
3 play 7, eat 5, ask for 4, give 3, use 30
4 2.5 grams, 63.9 acres, 10.4 feet, 45 MPH

PRACTICE

Key each line twice. Press Enter after each line.

Common Symbols

5 pay $95.60; earn $284.95/week; #1 seller
6 2 @ $1 (apiece), Jack & Jill, 73% filled
7 *Note: *Best guess. Hole-in-one Mid-life
8 Joan_Doe@herisp.edu, Lou_Ross@hisisp.org

Addresses

9 2960 West Rocks Road, Lockport, IL 60441
10 308 Powder Horn Hill, Hatfield, MA 01038
11 1457 Stonybrook Avenue, Novato, CA 94945
12 362 Pilot St., #5, South Salem, NY 10590

Numeric Keypad

Key each of the following four lists, one below the other. Start with list 13, pressing Enter on the numeric keypad after each complete number. Key list 14 below list 13, and so on.

13	14	15	16
914	181	0.7	9.45
465	723	9.6	8.65
597	853	7.5	7.04
284	449	8.8	1.54
736	176	6.9	2.26
950	358	5.1	3.07
245	286	1.3	4.83
307	106	2.0	0.09
894	370	4.6	6.01
107	802	3.6	5.03

Working with Headers in Sections (CONTINUED)

2. On the **Insert** tab, click the **Header** or **Footer** command. Click **Edit Header** or **Edit Footer**.

3. On the **Header & Footer Tools Design** tab, in the Navigation group, click **Link to Previous** to break the connection between the section headers or footers.

4. Create a header or footer in one section. Use the **Previous Section** or **Next Section** command in the Navigation group to go to the header or footer in the other section. Create a different header or footer in the other section.

PRACTICE 7-4

Create Headers in Sections

1. Place the insertion point on page 1 (section 1).

2. On the **Insert** tab, click the **Footer** command. At the bottom of the drop-down list, choose **Edit Footer**. The insertion point is now in the section 1 footer.

3. Click the **Next Section** command in the Navigation group on the Ribbon to go to the section 2 footer. Notice that it is labeled "Same as Previous."

FIGURE 7-10
Changing section footers

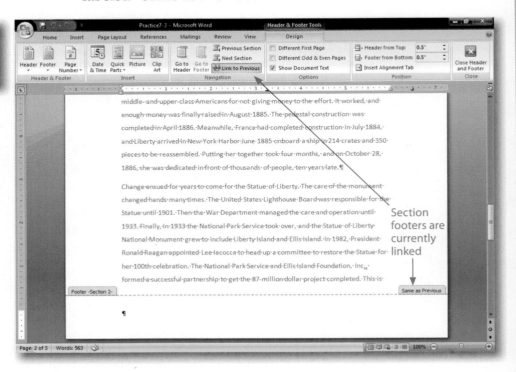

Section footers are currently linked

TEST YOURSELF

Name/ Address Blocks

Key the following name/address blocks. Where indicated, spell out or use the correct 2-letter state abbreviation. Press Enter at the end of each line. Double-space after each address block.

```
           International Tennis Hall of Fame
           194 Bellevue Ave.
           Newport, Rhode Island 02840        Abbreviate
                                              Spell out

           Rock & Roll Hall of Fame & Museum
     Spell 1 Key Plaza
      out
           Cleveland, Ohio 44114
                                        Abbreviate

           National Women's Hall of Fame
           76 Fall St.
           P.O. Box 335
           Seneca Falls, New York 13148
                                        Abbreviate
```

MATH SYMBOLS

* multiplied by
/ divided by
> greater than
< less than

Math Symbols

Key the numbers and symbols shown in line 1. Then key the line with the symbols translated into words (for example, "2 multiplied by 3 equals"). Do the same for line 2. Use the regular keyboard.

1 2 * 3 = 6; A9 / B4 = 653; 61.05 > 61.008
2 78 + 43 = 121; 286 < 465; 5% of 800 = 40

 TIME YOURSELF

3 →   Lee, Jean's in-law, bought 45% of
4 Jean's company, J&N Sox (which was
5 renamed to J&L Sox).

| 1 | 2 | 3 | 4 | 5 | 6 | 7   **WPM: 18**

6 →   If 20x = 92, then x = 4.6. But if
7 20 = 92x, then x = 0.2174. (How? Just
8 divide 20 by 92.)

| 1 | 2 | 3 | 4 | 5 | 6 | 7   **WPM: 18**

9 →   Tyrone loves music. He listens to
10 rock, pop, rap, hip hop, blues,
11 country, and R&B. He also likes Latin
12 jazz and salsa. He's not that fond of
13 classical music.

| 1 | 2 | 3 | 4 | 5 | 6 | 7   **WPM: 35**

60-Second Drill

Key each of the paragraphs for 60 seconds. Start with a tab and use word wrap. *Concentrate as you key the symbols.* If you reach the end of a paragraph before time is up, start again from the beginning of the paragraph.

WORD TIP

Changing margins in
section 2 will have no
effect on the margin
settings in section 1.
Remember, to change
margins, use the Page
Layout tab and choose
Margins.

8. If desired, add a blank line or two before "Submitted by."

9. On page 2 of the document, format the title as Cambria 14-point, bold, centered.

10. With the insertion point in page 2 (section 2), change the left and right margins to 1.25 inches.

11. Using the **View** tab, change the zoom to **Two Pages** and scroll through the document.

FIGURE 7-9
Viewing the two
sections

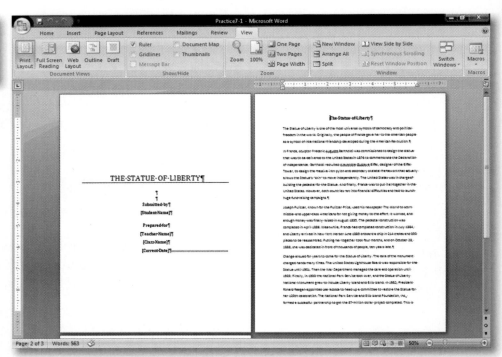

12. Change the zoom back to **100%**. Save the document as *[your initials]***Practice7-3**.

13. Leave the document open.

Microsoft Word

Working with Headers in Sections

You know how to create headers by using the **Header** and **Footer** commands on the **Insert** tab. When you create a section in a document, it affects the document's headers. You can have a header in section 1 that is different from the header in section 2.

To create different headers or footers between sections:

1. Place the insertion point in one section of the document.

CONTINUES

Word Processing and Communication

PRACTICE 7-3

Vertically Align Text

1. Delete any extra blank lines after "[Current Date]" on the first page or before the title "The Statue of Liberty" on the second page.

2. Place the insertion point anywhere in page 1, the title page.

3. On the **Page Layout** tab, click the Page Setup dialog box launcher ⬜. In the Page Setup dialog box, click the **Layout** tab.

FIGURE 7-8
Setting vertical alignment

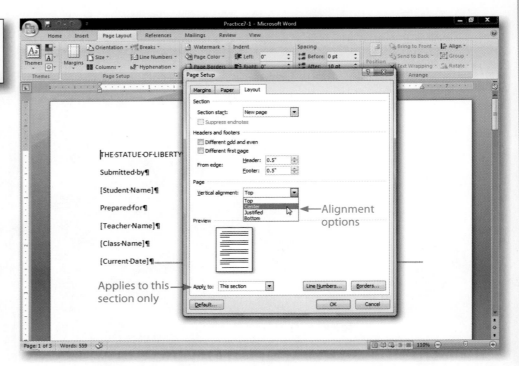

4. Under **Page**, click the down arrow next to the **Vertical alignment** box. Choose **Center**. The **Apply to** box should indicate **This section**. Click **OK**. The cover page text is now centered between the top and bottom margins.

5. Replace the placeholder text on the cover page with your name, your teacher's name, the class name, and the date.

6. Apply the **Title** Quick Style to the first line on the cover page. Apply the **Heading 1** Quick Style to the "Submitted by" and "Prepared for" lines. Apply the **Heading 2** Quick Style to your name, your teacher's name, the class name, and the date.

7. Select all the cover page text and use the Center button ≣ to center it horizontally.

LEARN

Create a Business Letter

You can create many types of documents in Word. A business letter is one example. Business letters usually contain the company letterhead. A *letterhead* includes a company's name and contact information. It can also display the company logo. In this lesson you will learn how to create a professional-looking letter. You will create a letterhead later in the course.

FIGURE 1-1
Parts of a business letter

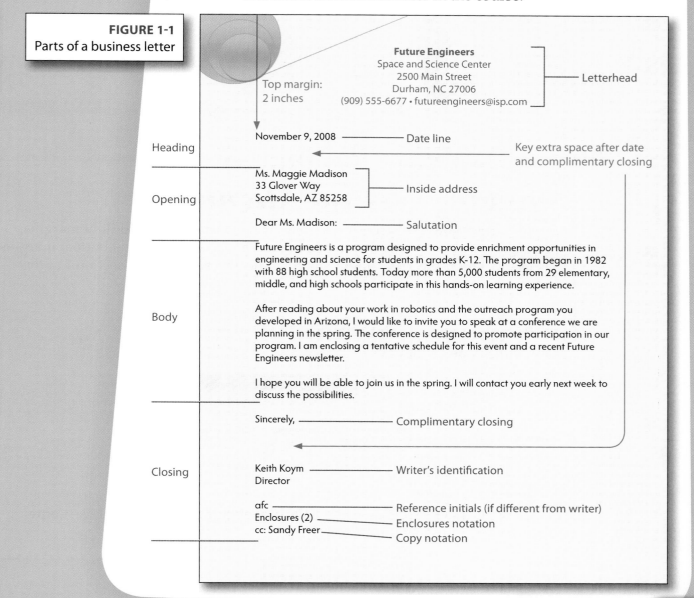

Future Engineers
Space and Science Center
2500 Main Street
Durham, NC 27006
(909) 555-6677 • futureengineers@isp.com
— Letterhead

Top margin:
2 inches

Heading

November 9, 2008 ——— Date line

Key extra space after date and complimentary closing

Opening

Ms. Maggie Madison
33 Glover Way
Scottsdale, AZ 85258
——— Inside address

Dear Ms. Madison: ——— Salutation

Body

Future Engineers is a program designed to provide enrichment opportunities in engineering and science for students in grades K-12. The program began in 1982 with 88 high school students. Today more than 5,000 students from 29 elementary, middle, and high schools participate in this hands-on learning experience.

After reading about your work in robotics and the outreach program you developed in Arizona, I would like to invite you to speak at a conference we are planning in the spring. The conference is designed to promote participation in our program. I am enclosing a tentative schedule for this event and a recent Future Engineers newsletter.

I hope you will be able to join us in the spring. I will contact you early next week to discuss the possibilities.

Sincerely, ——— Complimentary closing

Closing

Keith Koym ——— Writer's identification
Director

afc ——— Reference initials (if different from writer)
Enclosures (2) ——— Enclosures notation
cc: Sandy Freer ——— Copy notation

FIGURE 7-6
Inserting a section break

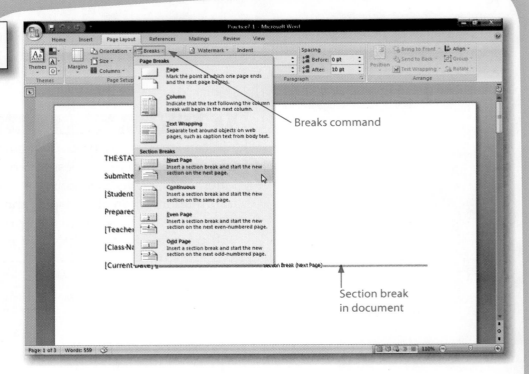

Breaks command

Section break
in document

Microsoft Word

Changing Vertical Alignment

You have learned how to align text horizontally between the left and right margins. *Vertical alignment* refers to the way text is aligned between the top and bottom margins. In this lesson, you use vertical alignment to vertically center text on section 1 of the document, the cover page.

To vertically align text:

1. Place the insertion point anywhere on the page.
2. On the **Page Layout** tab, click the Page Setup dialog box launcher 🔲.

FIGURE 7-7
Page Layout tab, Page
Setup commands

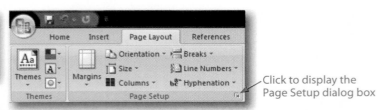

Click to display the
Page Setup dialog box

3. Display the **Layout** tab in the dialog box.
4. Click the down arrow next to the **Vertical alignment** box and choose **Center** from the drop-down list. Click **OK**.

Create a Personal Business Letter

Personal business letters, often called *personal letters*, have a slightly different format. The return address appears below the writer's name.

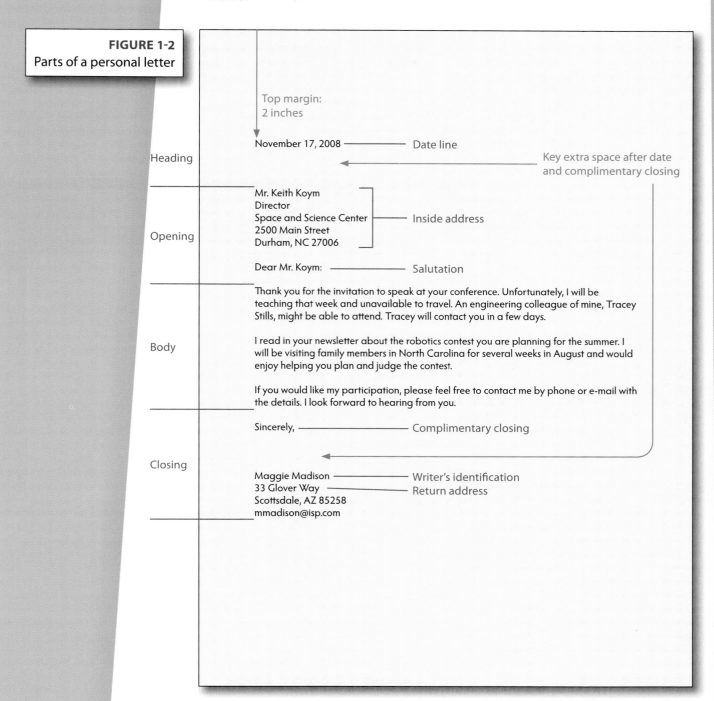

FIGURE 1-2
Parts of a personal letter

Top margin:
2 inches

Heading

November 17, 2008 ——————— Date line

←————————————————— Key extra space after date and complimentary closing

Opening

Mr. Keith Koym
Director
Space and Science Center ——— Inside address
2500 Main Street
Durham, NC 27006

Dear Mr. Koym: ——————— Salutation

Body

Thank you for the invitation to speak at your conference. Unfortunately, I will be teaching that week and unavailable to travel. An engineering colleague of mine, Tracey Stills, might be able to attend. Tracey will contact you in a few days.

I read in your newsletter about the robotics contest you are planning for the summer. I will be visiting family members in North Carolina for several weeks in August and would enjoy helping you plan and judge the contest.

If you would like my participation, please feel free to contact me by phone or e-mail with the details. I look forward to hearing from you.

Sincerely, ———————— Complimentary closing

Closing

Maggie Madison ——————— Writer's identification
33 Glover Way ——————— Return address
Scottsdale, AZ 85258
mmadison@isp.com

PRACTICE 7-2

Insert Page and Section Breaks

1. Make sure you are working in Print Layout view with non-printing characters showing.

2. Go to the first page of the practice document. The document begins with placeholder text for a cover page. You will create the cover page manually.

3. Place the insertion point on the blank line below "[Current Date]."

4. Press Ctrl + Enter to insert a hard page break. The cover page text is now on page 1 and the rest of the document continues on page 2.

WORD TIP

Remember to click Undo immediately after an action that you want to reverse.

FIGURE 7-5
Inserting a page break

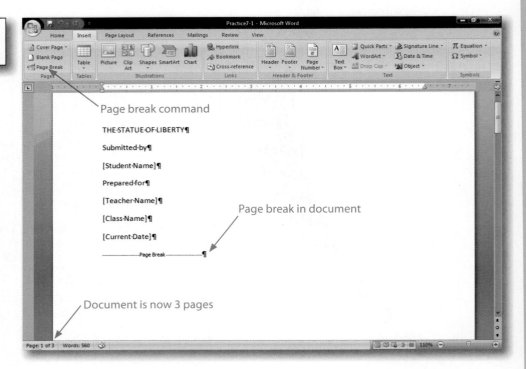

Page break command

THE·STATUE·OF·LIBERTY¶

Submitted·by¶

[Student·Name]¶

Prepared·for¶

[Teacher·Name]¶

[Class·Name]¶

[Current·Date]¶

————————Page·Break————————¶

Page break in document

Document is now 3 pages

5. On page 1, click at the beginning of the dotted page-break line to place the insertion point on the break. Press Delete to delete the page break.

6. Position the insertion point on the blank line below "[Current Date]." From the **Page Layout** tab, in the Page Set-up group, click the **Breaks** command. From the drop-down list, click **Next Page** to insert a section break. See Figure 7-6 on the next page.

7. Leave the document open.

Inserting Dates

The first line of text at the beginning of a letter is the date. When you begin keying the date in Word, the *AutoComplete* feature displays a suggested date you can insert by pressing Enter. You can also insert the date without keying it by using the **Date & Time** command on the **Insert** tab of the Ribbon.

To insert the date by keying it:

1. Key the current month. If you key the entire month and press the Spacebar once, Word displays the current date and a tip to press Enter to insert it.

2. Press Enter. The current date is inserted in the document.

To insert the date by using the Ribbon:

1. Display the **Insert** tab on the Ribbon. In the Text group, choose **Date & Time**. The Date and Time dialog box appears.

2. Under **Available formats**, choose the third date format in the list. This is the format you should use for letters.

3. Click **OK**. The current date is inserted in the document.

WORD TIP

If you key the wrong letter in the month, press the Backspace key to erase the letter and then key the correct letter. You can also key the first few letters of the month and press Enter when Word displays a suggested month.

PRACTICE 1-1

Insert Dates

1. Start Word. If you need to start a new blank document, click the Microsoft Office button and choose **New**. With **Blank Document** selected, click **Create**. Make sure you are working in Print Layout view.

2. With the insertion point at the top of the document, key the current month. Press the Spacebar after the month. Word displays a tip with the current date.

3. Press Enter to insert the date.

4. Select the date text. To do this, click to the left of the month, hold down the left mouse button, and drag to the right of the year. Release the mouse button. The selected text is highlighted in blue.

5. Press the Delete key to delete the date.

6. Display the **Insert** tab on the Ribbon. From the Text group, choose **Date & Time**. Choose the third date format and click OK.

7. Leave the document open for the next Practice.

Create Multiple-Page Reports

LEARN

Multiple-Page Reports

Any document that is more than one page should have page numbers. A multiple-page report, in addition to having page numbers, looks best when it begins with a *cover page*, also called a *title page*. A cover page is a separate page that contains the report title, your name, your teacher's name, the course name, and the date. Word provides many predesigned styles for cover pages and page numbers.

When you create a long report, you usually begin with a first draft. You'll learn how to mark the pages with the word "Draft" to indicate that the report is not finalized.

Microsoft Word

Inserting Page Numbers

Multiple-page reports need page numbers, especially if you intend to print the report. You can apply page numbering at the top or bottom of each page, or in the page margins. Word provides predesigned page-numbering styles. When you add or delete text, Word automatically renumbers your pages.

To insert page numbers:

1. Display the **Insert** tab on the Ribbon. In the Header & Footer group, click the **Page Number** command.
2. Choose a page number position (top, bottom, or page margins) from the drop-down list; then choose a page number option from the gallery of styles.

To remove page numbers:

1. Click the **Page Number** command.
2. Choose **Remove Page Numbers** from the bottom of the drop-down list.

PRACTICE 6-1

Insert Page Numbers

1. Start Word and open **WP-Painters1**. This is a draft of a report on great Renaissance painters.
2. Make sure the document is in Print Layout view, with rulers and nonprinting characters displayed.

Using Fonts

Fonts are type designs applied to all characters, including letters, numbers, symbols, and punctuation marks. A font is available in multiple sizes and is measured in points. When you start a new document in Word, the starting font is typically Calibri. The default font size is typically 11 points. You can change both the font and font size by using the **Home** tab on the Ribbon. A quick way to change the font and font size for selected text is to use the Mini toolbar.

To change a font by using the Ribbon:

1. Place the insertion point where you want to begin keying text.
2. Display the **Home** tab on the Ribbon. In the Font group, click the down arrow next to the Font box Calibri (Body) ▾.
3. Scroll down the list and locate the font you want. Each font name is displayed in the design of that font.
4. Click on the font name in the Font drop-down list to choose a new font.
5. Key your text.

FIGURE 2-2
Changing fonts by using the Ribbon

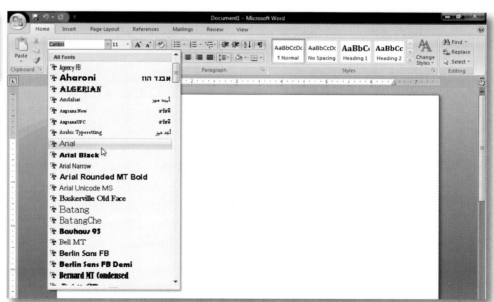

To change the font size by using the Ribbon:

1. Place the insertion point where you want to begin keying text.
2. Display the **Home** tab on the Ribbon. In the Font group, click the down arrow next to the Font Size box 11 ▾.
3. Scroll down the list and locate the font size you want.

CONTINUES

7. Locate the phrase "two poor actors." The wording could suggest that the actors were untalented. Use the thesaurus to find a better word for "poor."

8. Locate the word "dumped" and use the thesaurus to find a better word. Locate the words "stuff" and "famed" and find better words for both of them.

9. The word "trouble" is used repeatedly in one paragraph. Replace at least one instance with another word.

10. Study the fourth sentence in the first paragraph. Locate and correct the grammatical error not found by the grammar checker.

11. Study the second sentence of the last paragraph. Locate and correct the grammatical error not found by the grammar checker.

12. Save the file as *[your initials]***Test5-2** and print the document.

TEST YOURSELF 5-3

Lincoln, Kennedy, and King Speeches

The grammar checker can be a useful tool, but you should never rely on it completely. The grammar checker can miss errors. It also can falsely identify mistakes.

Locate copies of the following speeches: John F. Kennedy's inaugural address, Abraham Lincoln's Gettysburg Address, and Martin Luther King's "I Have a Dream" speech. Copy and paste these speeches into Word and use the grammar checker on them. Record the "errors" that the grammar checker finds in these speeches. In the King speech, determine how many times King uses the phrase "I have a dream."

Based on your findings, write a one-page report on the best use of the grammar checker. Give examples from the speeches you reviewed. Offer suggestions about how you should use the grammar checker.

In writing your report, be sure to:

1. Follow the general format for one-page reports.

2. Include introductory information (your name, your teacher's name, the class, and the date).

3. If you use quotations, use proper indentation for quotations of four lines or more.

4. Spell- and grammar-check your report.

5. Save the file as *[your initials]***Test5-3** and print the document.

FIGURE 5-7
Martin Luther King, Jr. delivering his famous "I Have a Dream" speech on the steps of the Lincoln Memorial in Washington D.C. on August 28, 1963

Using Fonts (CONTINUED)

4. Click the new font size in the Font Size drop-down list.

5. Key your text.

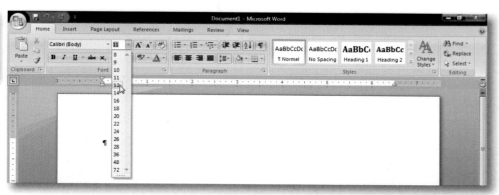

FIGURE 2-3
Changing font size by using the Ribbon

To change the font and font size for selected text by using the Mini toolbar:

1. Select specific text in your document. The Mini toolbar appears in semitransparent form next to the selected text.

2. Rest the pointer over the Mini toolbar to make the commands available. These commands are similar to those on the **Home** tab.

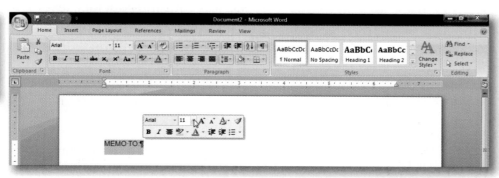

FIGURE 2-4
Changing font and font size by using the Mini toolbar

3. Just as you used the font commands from the Ribbon, choose a font and a font size from the Mini toolbar for the selected text. You can also use the Grow Font button ⒜ and Shrink Font button ⒜ on the Mini toolbar to increase and decrease selected text to the next font size.

PRACTICE 2-1

Use Fonts　1. Start Word. Use the Microsoft Office button 🔘 to start a new blank document. You'll start to create a memo by keying the heading with a new font and different font size.

2. Set a 2-inch top margin and 1.25-inch left and right margins.

TEST YOURSELF 5-1

DID YOU KNOW?

Civilization began to develop in the valley of the Nile River more than 7,000 years ago.

Egypt

1. Open the file **WP-Egypt**. It contains information about early civilization in Egypt.

2. Launch the Spelling and Grammar checker and correct the spelling and grammatical errors in the document.

3. Press Ctrl + Home to place the insertion point at the beginning of the document.

4. Display the **Home** tab on the Ribbon. In the Editing group, click **Find**. In the **Find what** text box, key **ancient Egypt**. Click **Find Next** until all instances of the phrase "ancient Egypt" have been located. Close the dialog box.

5. After locating all the phrases "ancient Egypt," right-click one instance of the word "ancient" and choose **Synonyms** to find a different word.

6. Launch the Find feature again by pressing Ctrl + F. Locate the word "commence" in the document.

7. Right-click the word "commence" and choose a synonym.

8. Locate the word "fertile." Click within the word and display the **Review** tab on the Ribbon. In the Proofing group, click **Thesaurus**. Choose a synonym to insert in the document.

9. Add your introductory text to the top of the report. Apply appropriate formatting to the document.

10. Save the file as *[your initials]***Test5-1** and print the document.

TEST YOURSELF 5-2

DID YOU KNOW?

In 1841, Edgar Allan Poe wrote the first detective story, "The Murders in the Rue Morgue." In his honor, the Mystery Writers of America presents the Edgar Allan Poe awards each year to the best mystery writers.

Edgar Allan Poe

1. Open the files **WP-Poe** and **WP-PoeWork**. Use these as the body of a report on Edgar Allan Poe.

2. Copy and paste the text of **WP-PoeWork** at the end of **WP-Poe**, making the copied text a new paragraph. Close the **WP-PoeWork** file without saving.

3. Apply the **No Spacing** Quick Style to the entire document and then apply double line spacing.

4. Key introductory information and a title for the report.

5. Apply the **Title** Quick Style to the title. Change the paragraph spacing for the title to 12 points before and after paragraphs.

6. Use the grammar check to correct the errors in grammar.

3. With the insertion point on the blank first line, use the Font box `Calibri (Body) ▾` on the **Home** tab of the Ribbon to choose Arial as the new font for the document.

4. Key the following memo heading, pressing Enter once at the end of each line. Key your name next to "FROM:" Key or insert the date, using the correct date format.

   MEMO TO: Sally Mason

   FROM: *[Student Name]*

   DATE: *[Current Date]*

   SUBJECT: Storytelling Day

5. Select the entire memo heading. Point to the semitransparent Mini toolbar that appears next to the selected text. Use the Font Size box `11 ▾` on the Mini toolbar to increase the font to 12 points.

6. Press Enter twice after the Subject line.

7. Leave the document open.

WORD TIP

Remember, to select text, you click in front of the text, hold down the left mouse button, move the pointer over the text, and then release the mouse button.

Microsoft Word

Applying Character Formatting

Bold, italic, and underline are examples of *character formatting* you can use to emphasize text. You can apply more than one format to text. For example, a word can have both bold and italic formatting.

You can apply bold and italic character formatting to selected text from the Mini toolbar. Additional formatting options are available on the Home tab of the Ribbon.

Normal	Sample text
Bold	**Sample text**
Italic	*Sample text*
Underline	<u>Sample text</u>
Italic, Underline	<u>*Sample text*</u>
Bold, Italic, Underline	<u>***Sample text***</u>

To apply character formatting to selected text by using the Mini toolbar:

1. Select existing text. Point to the Mini toolbar.

2. Click a character formatting command, such as Bold `B` or Italic `I`.

To apply character formatting by using the Ribbon:

1. Select existing text, or place the insertion point where you want to key new text.

2. Display the **Home** tab on the Ribbon. From the Font group, click the appropriate Formatting command, such as Bold `B`, Italic `I`, or Underline `U`.

CONTINUES

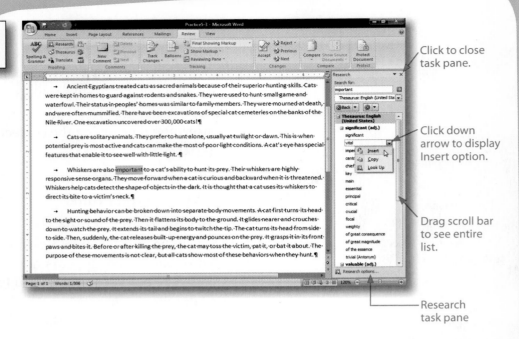

FIGURE 5-6
Using the thesaurus

Click to close task pane.

Click down arrow to display Insert option.

Drag scroll bar to see entire list.

Research task pane

Using Copy and Paste with Other Applications

You can copy and paste information from other programs to Word documents. Use this procedure when you want to copy information from a spreadsheet or a Web browser into a Word document.

To copy information from other running programs to Word:

1. Click the taskbar button for the window containing the text you want to copy.

2. Select the information to copy.

3. Right-click the selection. Choose **Copy** from the shortcut menu. The selected information is copied to the Clipboard.

4. Click the taskbar button to make the Word document window active.

5. Right-click the insertion point where you want to place the copied information. Choose **Paste** from the shortcut menu. The copied information is pasted in the document.

Applying Character Formatting (CONTINUED)

To remove character formatting from text:

1. Select the text with formatting.
2. Click the appropriate formatting command on either the Mini toolbar or the **Home** tab on the Ribbon.

PRACTICE 2-2

Apply Character Formatting

1. With the insertion point at the second paragraph mark below the Subject line, key the following text.

FIGURE 2-5

```
Our annual storytelling day is coming up! The theme this
year will be state folktales. We've asked the theater class
to perform the stories as they are being told. We'd like to
perform two in the morning and one after lunch.
```

2. Select "state folktales" in the first sentence. Use the Bold button B on the Mini toolbar to make the text bold.
3. At the end of this paragraph, start a new paragraph.
4. Key the following text. Select the folktale names and use the Italic button *I* and the Underline button U on the Ribbon to apply italic and underline formatting.

FIGURE 2-6

```
The first folktale we've chosen, The Coyote and the Colombia,
is from Washington. It's the story of how the Columbia River
began. Then we'd like to include Ohio's Johnny Appleseed.
Everyone should hear the story of the barefoot hermit wanderer
who traveled with a sack full of apple seeds to plant.
```

WORD TIP

The quickest way to select a single word is to double-click it.

5. Apply bold formatting to "Washington," "Ohio's," and "Everyone."
6. Remove the bold formatting from "Everyone."
7. Leave the document open.

FIGURE 5-5
Using the shortcut menu to find synonyms

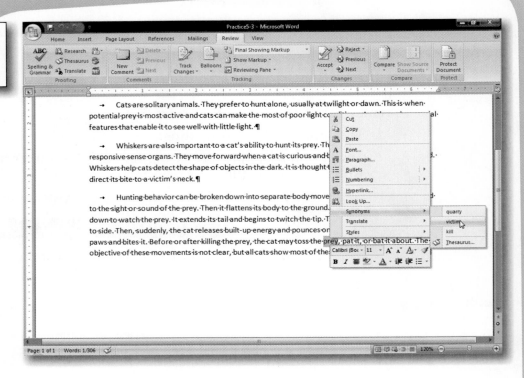

4. Choose **victim**. The word "prey" is replaced by "victim."

5. Right-click the word "objective" in the last sentence in the document. Use the shortcut menu to find an alternative word.

6. Use the **Find** command to locate the word "important" in the document.

7. Click within the word and then launch the thesaurus by displaying the **Review** tab and clicking **Thesaurus** in the Proofing group. The thesaurus appears in the Research task pane with several synonyms. Use the scroll bar to go through the list. See Figure 5-6 on the next page.

8. Point to the synonym you want in the list. Click the down-pointing arrow that appears, and then click **Insert**. The new option replaces "important."

9. Close the **Research** task pane by clicking its Close button ×.

10. Add your introductory text to the top of the document as you would for a one-page report. Apply appropriate formatting to the title. The report should fit on a single page.

11. Save the file as *[your initials]*Practice5-3. Print and close the document.

WORD TIP

Click any word listed in the task pane to look up synonyms for that word. Use the Back button to see previous searches. Words listed may be categorized by (n.) for noun, (adj.) for adjective, and (adv.) for adverb.

Using Command Keys

Command keys such as Ctrl and Alt can be used in sequence with other keys on the keyboard to accomplish tasks quickly. These command key sequences are called *keyboard shortcuts*. Some of the same tasks you accomplish by using Ribbon, toolbar, or menu commands can be accomplished by using keyboard shortcuts.

Keyboard shortcuts for formatting are sometimes called toggle commands because you use the shortcut once to turn on the formatting and then use the shortcut again to toggle off the formatting.

TABLE 2-1	**Common Keyboard Shortcuts**
Keyboard Shortcuts	**Outcome**
Ctrl + B	Applies bold formatting
Ctrl + I	Applies italic formatting
Ctrl + U	Applies underline formatting
Ctrl + Home	Positions the insertion point at the beginning of a document
Ctrl + End	Positions the insertion point at the end of a document
Ctrl + Shift + >	Increases font size
Ctrl + Shift + <	Decreases font size
Ctrl + A	Selects all the text in a document
Ctrl + S	Saves a document
Ctrl + P	Prints a document
Ctrl + W	Closes a document
Ctrl + Z	Undoes a recent action
Ctrl + Y	Redoes an action you have just undone

To apply character formatting by using command keys:

1. Select specific text, or place the insertion point where you want to key new text.

2. Use the appropriate keyboard shortcut, such as Ctrl + B for bold, Ctrl + I for italic, or Ctrl + U for underline.

To remove character formatting from text by using command keys:

1. Select the text with formatting.

2. Use the appropriate keyboard shortcut, such as Ctrl + B to remove bold, Ctrl + I to remove italic, or Ctrl + U to remove underline.

15. Click **Replace**. Word changes the word and moves to the next instance of "object."

16. Replace the next three instances of "object." Close the dialog box when "objective" is selected.

17. Leave the document open.

Using the Thesaurus

A thesaurus is a tool to help you improve the quality of your writing. Use the thesaurus to locate alternatives to words that are overused in a document.

To activate the thesaurus using the Ribbon:

1. Place the insertion point on the word for which you'd like a synonym.

2. Display the **Review** tab on the Ribbon. In the Proofing group, click **Thesaurus**. The **Research** task pane appears, with the thesaurus activated.

3. Position the pointer on one of the words in the task pane list box. Click the down-pointing arrow, and then click **Insert** from the drop-down list. The selected word is replaced with the synonym.

4. Close the Research task pane by clicking its Close button ☒.

To use a shortcut menu to locate a synonym:

1. Using the right mouse button, right-click the word for which you'd like a synonym. A shortcut menu appears.

2. Choose **Synonyms**. Choose the word you'd like to use or click **Thesaurus** to display the **Research** task pane with the thesaurus activated.

PRACTICE 5-3

Use the Thesaurus

1. Make sure the file *[your initials]***Practice5-1** is still open. In the last paragraph, locate the second-to-last sentence (which begins, "Before or after"). The word "prey" is used twice in this sentence. Place the insertion point in the second instance of "prey" (which occurs in "the cat may toss the prey").

2. Using the right mouse button, right-click the word. A shortcut menu appears.

3. Choose **Synonyms** from the shortcut menu. A short list of alternatives appears next to the shortcut menu. See Figure 5-5 on the next page.

WORD TIP

Instead of using the Ribbon, you can use the keyboard shortcut Shift + F7 to activate the thesaurus.

Use Command Keys

1. Add the following text at the end of the second paragraph. Use keyboard shortcuts to apply the bold, italic, and underline formatting shown.

FIGURE 2-7

Finally, we chose the **Hawaiian** folktale <u>The King of Sharks</u>. It's the story of *Nanave*, a part-human, part-shark boy who prevented local fishermen from catching any fish.

2. Select "*Nanave*" and use the keyboard shortcut to remove the italic formatting.
3. Key the following text as the third and final paragraph.

FIGURE 2-8

If you'd like more information on the folktales and the schedule we're proposing, I'd be happy to come by after class on Thursday. It should be quite a fun day.

4. Leave the document open.

Microsoft Word

Setting Tabs

A *tab* is a formatting feature you use to indent and align text. Default tab settings occur every half inch in a new document. If you want to change these tabs, you can set custom tabs by using the horizontal ruler.

The four most common custom tabs are left-aligned, right-aligned, centered, and decimal-aligned. When you set a custom tab, a *tab marker* (a symbol displaying the tab setting) appears on the horizontal ruler.

TABLE 2-2	Four Most Common Tabs
Tab	**Tab Marker**
Left	∟
Right	⌐
Centered	⊥
Decimal	⊥.

6. Continue locating all instances of "object." Word displays an information box telling you when the search is complete.

7. Click **OK**. The Find and Replace dialog box is still open. You can also have Word show you all instances of a word or group of words at once.

8. With the Find and Replace box still open, click the **Reading Highlight** down arrow and choose **Highlight All**. All forms of "object" are selected.

9. Close the dialog box. All forms of "object" are still selected. The word appears many times.

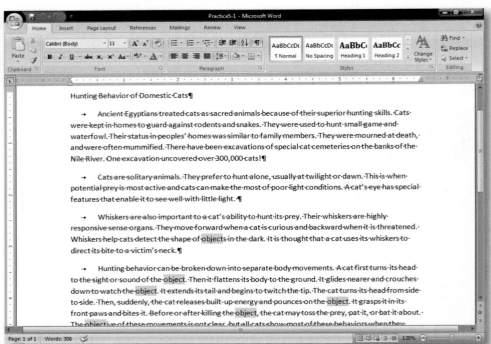

FIGURE 5-4
Displaying all instances of a word in a document

10. Press Ctrl + Home to place the insertion point at the beginning of the document.

11. Press Ctrl + **F**. This is the keyboard shortcut for displaying the Find and Replace dialog box. The **Find what** box still shows "object." Click the **Reading Highlight** down arrow and choose **Clear Highlighting**.

12. Click the **Replace** tab and key **prey** in the **Replace with** box.

13. Click **Find Next**. The first instance of "object" is in the word "objects" and shouldn't be changed.

14. Click **Find Next**. Word skips to the next instance of "object" (which is in the sentence that begins "A cat first turns").

Setting Tabs (CONTINUED)

To set, move, and delete a custom tab:

1. Click the Tab Alignment button on the left of the ruler to choose the type of tab alignment. The default tab alignment is left-aligned. Keep clicking until the alignment you want appears.
2. Click the position on the ruler for the new tab.

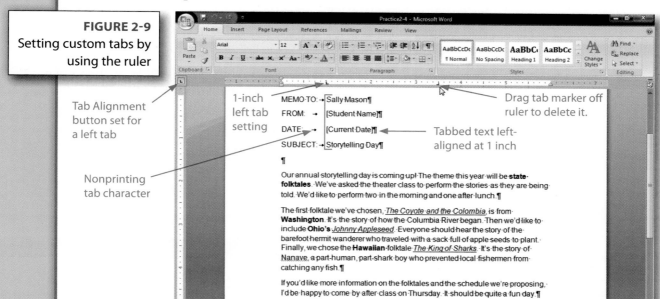

FIGURE 2-9
Setting custom tabs by using the ruler

Tab Alignment button set for a left tab

Nonprinting tab character

1-inch left tab setting

Drag tab marker off ruler to delete it.

Tabbed text left-aligned at 1 inch

3. To move a tab, click and drag the tab marker to a new location on the horizontal ruler.
4. To delete the tab, click and drag the tab marker off the ruler.

WORD TIP

The tab character is a nonprinting character that appears in your document as a right-pointing arrow. Showing nonprinting characters is very helpful when working with tabbed text.

PRACTICE 2-4

Set Tabs

1. Use the Show/Hide ¶ button ¶ on the **Home** tab to display nonprinting characters.
2. After each colon in the heading of the memo, replace the space characters with tab characters by selecting each space character and pressing Tab.
3. Select the entire memo heading, from "MEMO TO:" through "Storytelling Day."
4. Click the Tab Alignment button until the right-aligned tab ⌐ appears.

Using Find and Replace

Use the Find and Replace feature to find specific text in a document, such as a word or group of words, and replace it with other text.

To find and replace text:

1. Place the insertion point at the beginning of the document.
2. Display the **Home** tab on the Ribbon. In the Editing group, click **Find**. The Find and Replace dialog box appears.
3. Delete any text in the **Find what** text box, and key the word or group of words you wish to locate. Click **More**, if it is present, for additional search options.
4. To replace the specified text with a different word or group of words, click the **Replace** tab and key the new text in the **Replace with** text box.
5. Click **Find Next**. The first instance of the specified text is highlighted.
6. Click **Replace** to replace the selected text, **Replace All** to replace all instances of the text in the document, or **Find Next** to skip to the next instance of the specified text.
7. Click **OK** when Word finishes the search. Close the dialog box.

WORD TIP

You can use the keyboard shortcut Ctrl + **F** to display the Find and Replace dialog box.

PRACTICE 5-2

Find and Replace

1. With the file *[your initials]***Practice5-1** still open, press Ctrl + Home to place the insertion point at the top of the document.
2. Display the **Home** tab on the Ribbon. In the Editing group, click **Find**. The Find and Replace dialog box appears.
3. Key **object** in the **Find what** text box.

FIGURE 5-3
Finding a word in a document

4. Click **Find Next**. The first instance occurs in the word "objects." Word locates text containing any portion of the word.
5. Click **Find Next** again. Word locates the next instance of "object."

5. Click the 2-inch mark on the horizontal ruler. The tabbed text right-aligns 2 inches from the left margin.

6. Drag the 2-inch tab marker one inch to the right. The text moves over and right-aligns 3 inches from the left margin.

7. Point to the tab marker you just moved and drag it off the ruler to delete it. The text moves back to its original position.

8. Set a 1-inch left tab by using the Tab Alignment button ⌊L⌋ and the ruler.

9. Turn off nonprinting characters.

10. Spell-check the document.

11. Save the document as *[your initials]*Practice2-4.

12. Print and close the document.

TEST YOURSELF 2-1

DID YOU KNOW?

Mac is short for "Macintosh" computers. PC is short for "Personal Computers."

Mac versus PC Computers

1. Open the file **WP-Computers**.

2. Set the top margin to 2 inches and the left and right margins to 1.25 inches.

3. Press Tab after "DATE:" and insert the date.

4. Turn on nonprinting characters if they are not on. Select the entire memo heading. Set the Tab Alignment button to a left tab ⌊L⌋ and set a 1-inch left tab on the ruler.

5. Using the Mini toolbar, apply bold formatting to the heading text "MEMO TO:", "FROM:", "TO:", and "SUBJECT:"

6. Apply italic formatting to "The Benefits of Both" in the Subject line.

7. Use the keyboard shortcut Ctrl + ⌊I⌋ to apply italic formatting to "must" in the first paragraph.

8. Apply both bold and underlining to "Macs:" in the second paragraph and "PCs:" in the next paragraph.

9. Use the keyboard combination Ctrl + ⌊A⌋ to select all the text in the document. Increase the font size to 12 points.

10. In the memo heading, replace "Melinda Lawson" with your name.

11. Preview the document.

12. Save the document as *[your initials]*Test2-1.

13. Print and close the document.

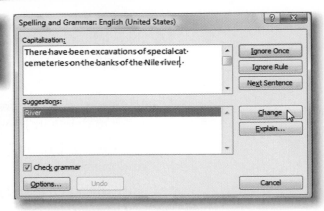

FIGURE 5-2
Spelling and Grammar
dialog box

8. Click **Change** to accept the suggested correction. The next error is highlighted (which is the sentence "Cats solitary animals."). This sentence lacks a verb. The grammar checker has no suggested corrections for this error. If you don't understand an error, you can read more about it.

9. Click **Explain**. Word Help appears with a brief description of a fragment. Close the Help window by clicking its Close ![x] button. You will need to manually edit this sentence.

10. With the dialog box still open (you can drag it to the side if it's in your way), click the sentence in the document. Place the insertion point after the word "Cats."

11. Key **are** after the word "Cats." The first button in the dialog box has changed from **Ignore** to **Resume**.

12. Click **Resume** in the dialog box. The grammar checker starts checking the document again. It stops at the next error (the sentence that begins "This is when"). This sentence contains another error in subject-verb agreement.

13. Make the correction by clicking **Change**.

14. Continue correcting the remaining errors in the document. Click **OK** when the grammar checker completes the check.

15. Examine the second sentence in the third paragraph, which begins "There whiskers are highly…." Notice the use of "there." The possessive adjective "their" should be used instead. The grammar checker failed to detect this mistake. The grammar checker is not foolproof. You should always proofread your documents carefully.

16. Make the correction by changing "There" to "Their."

17. Save the file as *[your initials]***Practice5-1**. Leave the document open.

DID YOU KNOW?

Australia is the sixth largest country in the world. It's about the same size as the 48 mainland states in the United States.

TEST YOURSELF 2-2

Visiting Australia

1. Open the file **WP-Australia**. Use this as the body of a memo.

2. Set the top margin to 2 inches and the left and right margins to 1.25 inches.

3. Use the keyboard combination Ctrl + Ⓐ to select all the text in the document. Change the font to Verdana. (If you don't have Verdana, choose another font that can be read easily.) Make the font size 11 points.

4. Start a new paragraph at the top of the document and key the following memo heading, using a 1-inch left tab. Key your name beside "FROM:". Key today's date in the Date line and apply correct spacing after the heading.

MEMO TO: **All Teachers and Students**
FROM: *[Student Name]*
DATE: *[Current Date]*
SUBJECT: **International Education Conference**

5. Apply bold formatting to the heading text "MEMO TO:", "FROM:", "TO:", and "SUBJECT:"

6. Apply italic formatting to "capital," "native people," "life expectancy," and "literacy rate" in the second paragraph.

7. Underline and italicize the last sentence in the last paragraph.

8. Spell-check and preview the document.

9. Save the document as *[your initials]***Test2-2**.

10. Print and close the document.

TEST YOURSELF 2-3

Currency Exchange Rates

Locate the currency exchange rates for three countries. Write a memo as the president of a travel agency to its staff, telling them about the exchange rates. Rank the countries as the first, second, and third best places to visit, based on the exchange rates and popular tourist attractions. Tell the staff these will be the top three travel packages for the summer.

In writing your memo, be sure to:

1. Follow the correct format for a memo.

2. Choose a font and font size that are appropriate for a memo.

FIGURE 2-10
The Euro is now widely adopted across Europe.

PRACTICE 5-1

Correct Grammar

1. Start Word and open the file **WP-Cats**. This file contains a number of grammatical errors. Word automatically marks the errors with green wavy underlines.

2. To see suggested corrections for an individual error, place the insertion point anywhere in the first marked error, "status in people's homes." This sentence has a problem with subject-verb agreement.

3. Using the right mouse button, right-click the error. A shortcut menu appears (along with the Mini toolbar). The first items on the shortcut menu show two possible solutions.

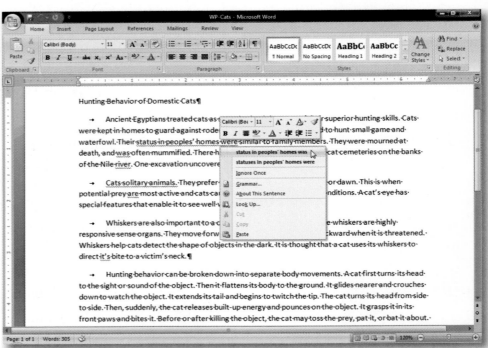

FIGURE 5-1
Using the shortcut menu to correct a grammatical error

4. Choose the first solution, **status in peoples' homes was**. The error is corrected.

5. Right-click the error in the next sentence ("was"). A shortcut menu appears.

6. Choose **were** from the shortcut menu to correct the error. In the next step, you'll have the grammar checker proceed through the rest of the document, displaying each error in turn.

7. Display the **Review** tab on the Ribbon. From the Proofing group, click **Spelling & Grammar**. The Spelling and Grammar dialog box appears. It shows a correction for the next error, "river." This word should be capitalized.

WORD TIP

Remember that the keyboard shortcut F7 starts a spelling and grammar check.

3. Use the following memo heading, inserting your name and the current date.

MEMO TO: **Staff**

FROM: *[Student Name]*

DATE: *[Current Date]*

SUBJECT: **Top Three Picks**

4. Key at least two paragraphs for the body of the memo.

5. Apply bold, italic, or underlining to words in the memo that need emphasis.

6. Spell-check and preview the document.

7. Save the document as *[your initials]*Test2-3.

8. Print and close the document.

Use Word Processing Tools

Work More Efficiently Your word processor has several tools that help you work more efficiently. The built-in grammar-checking program identifies grammatical errors. When you need to find a particular word in your document, you can have the word processor locate it for you. You can also replace every instance of a word with a different word. Your word processor also contains a thesaurus. A *thesaurus* is a tool that lists synonyms for a word. A *synonym* is a word with the same or nearly the same meaning.

Microsoft Word

Correcting Grammar

Word automatically shows possible grammatical errors by marking the text with a green wavy underline. You can check grammatical errors one at a time, or you can run the spelling and grammar checker on the entire document.

To check all grammatical errors in a document:

1. Place the insertion point at the beginning of the document.
2. Display the **Review** tab on the Ribbon. From the Proofing group, click **Spelling & Grammar**. The first spelling or grammar error is highlighted, and the Spelling and Grammar dialog box appears.
3. Click the dialog box command that applies to the error.
   - Click **Ignore Once** to ignore the error once.
   - Click **Ignore Rule** to ignore all instances of the error.
   - Click **Ne<u>x</u>t Sentence** after you've manually edited your sentence.
   - Click **<u>C</u>hange** to accept the suggested change.
   - Click **<u>E</u>xplain** to see an explanation of the error.

To correct individual grammatical errors:

1. Place the insertion point on the word or sentence containing a green wavy underline.
2. Using the right mouse button, right-click the error. A shortcut menu appears. Possible corrections appear as the first menu items.
3. Choose a correction from the shortcut menu if it is acceptable. The correction is applied to the text.

Write a One-Page Report

LEARN

Format a One-Page Report

A written report should always have a clear beginning, middle, and end. It should also be formatted in such a way that it is easy to read. A common format for school reports is called the *MLA style*. ("MLA" stands for the "Modern Language Association.") In this lesson, you'll learn to format a one-page report based on the MLA style.

FIGURE 3-1
Format for a one-page report

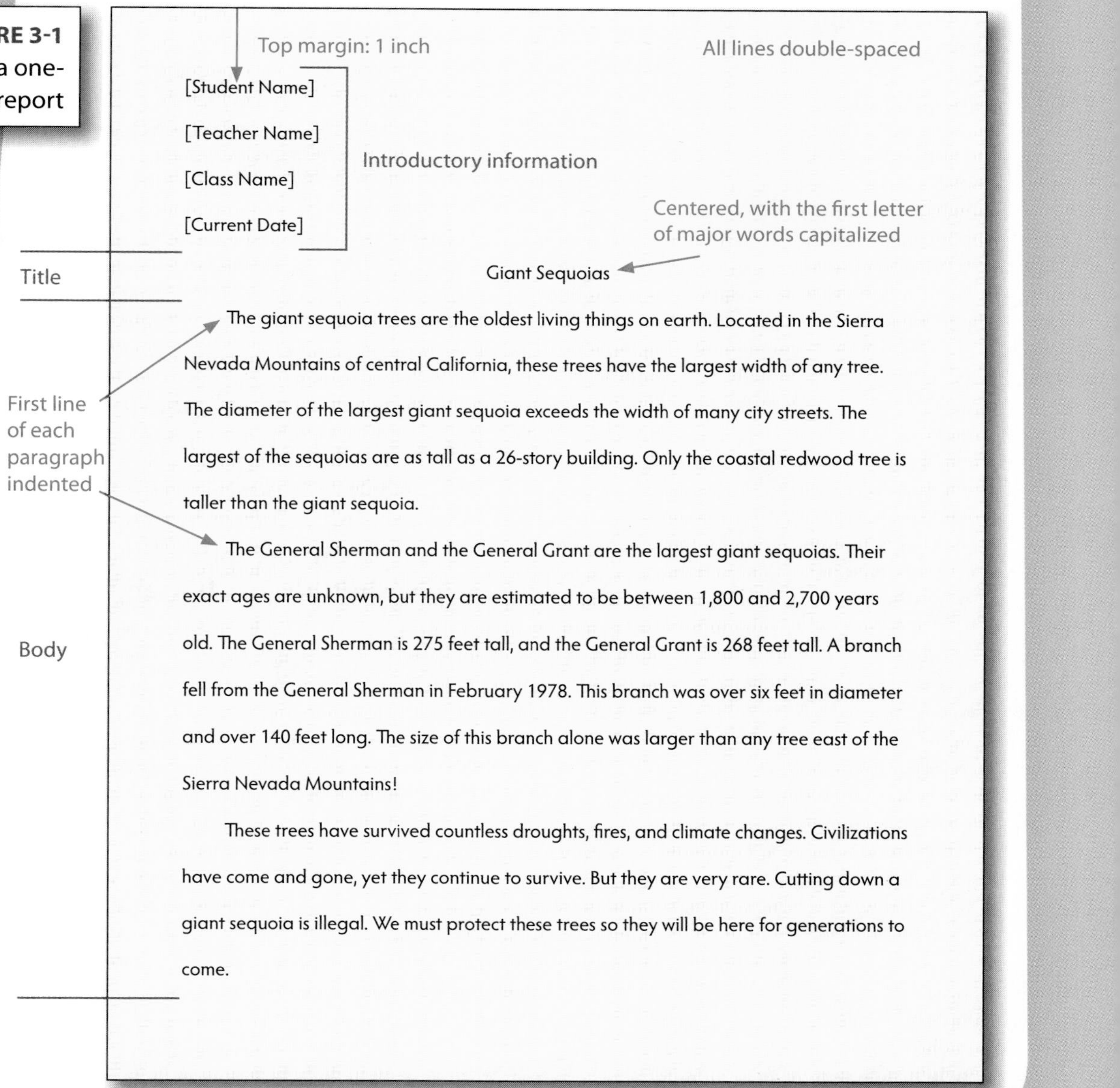

Top margin: 1 inch | All lines double-spaced

[Student Name]

[Teacher Name]

[Class Name]

[Current Date]

Introductory information

Centered, with the first letter of major words capitalized

Title

Giant Sequoias

First line of each paragraph indented

The giant sequoia trees are the oldest living things on earth. Located in the Sierra Nevada Mountains of central California, these trees have the largest width of any tree. The diameter of the largest giant sequoia exceeds the width of many city streets. The largest of the sequoias are as tall as a 26-story building. Only the coastal redwood tree is taller than the giant sequoia.

The General Sherman and the General Grant are the largest giant sequoias. Their exact ages are unknown, but they are estimated to be between 1,800 and 2,700 years old. The General Sherman is 275 feet tall, and the General Grant is 268 feet tall. A branch fell from the General Sherman in February 1978. This branch was over six feet in diameter and over 140 feet long. The size of this branch alone was larger than any tree east of the Sierra Nevada Mountains!

Body

These trees have survived countless droughts, fires, and climate changes. Civilizations have come and gone, yet they continue to survive. But they are very rare. Cutting down a giant sequoia is illegal. We must protect these trees so they will be here for generations to come.

8. Spell-check the report.

9. Close **WP-CurieQuote** without saving.

10. Locate a definition for radioactivity. Write a definition in your own words in one or two sentences. Insert your definition in the third paragraph, after the sentence containing the word "radioactivity."

11. Save the **WP-Curie** document as *[your initials]*Test4-2 and print it.

TEST YOURSELF 4-3

DID YOU KNOW?

A writer's reputation depends on his or her academic honesty.

Plagiarism Create a one-page report on plagiarism. Describe what it is. Give examples of types of plagiarism. Describe how to avoid it in writing reports.

In writing your report, be sure to:

1. Base the report on the MLA format: Start with the **No Spacing** Quick Style and then apply double line spacing. Center the title. Include your introductory information at the top of the report. Use Tab to indent the first line of each paragraph in the report.

2. Use left indentation for quotes.

3. Spell-check your report.

4. Save the report as *[your initials]*Test4-3a and print it.

5. Create another version of the report by using the **Normal** Quick Style. Apply an appropriate Quick Style to the introductory information, the report title, and quotes. Adjust spacing and formatting as needed. Save the report as *[your initials]*Test4-3b and print it.

CHECKLIST

One-Page Report (Based on MLA Style)

☑ Double-space all the text in the report.

☑ Use 1-inch top, bottom, left, and right default margin settings.

☑ Begin your report with introductory information: your name, your teacher's name, the class, and the date. Key each item on a separate line.

☑ Follow the introductory information with the title of the report. Capitalize the first letter of all major words in the title. Center the title.

☑ Indent the beginning of each paragraph half an inch. Use the Tab key to indent paragraphs.

Microsoft Word

Setting Line Spacing

Line spacing refers to the distance between lines of text within a paragraph. Word, by default, automatically adds space between lines in a paragraph. Single spacing is referred to as 1.0 line spacing, double spacing is 2.0 line spacing, and Word's default spacing is 1.15, which is a little more than single spacing. Reports usually use double-spacing.

When you create a new document, you can change the line spacing before you begin keying the text. You can also select text in an existing document and then change the line spacing.

To change the line spacing in a document:

1. Start a new document or select the text in an existing document.
2. On the **Home** tab of the Ribbon, in the Paragraph group, click the Line Spacing button. A drop-down menu appears.
3. Choose the desired setting, such as **2.0** for double-spacing.

FIGURE 3-2
Changing line spacing

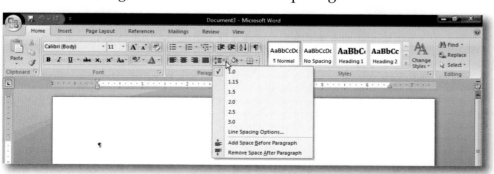

6. Select the last paragraph (which begins "In Lincoln's time"). Click the Cut button ✂ on the **Home** tab. Place the insertion point at the beginning of the second paragraph.

7. Click the Paste button 📋. It should now appear as the second paragraph.

8. Change the period at the end of the second paragraph to a colon so that it ends "his preparation in detail:" Press Enter to start a new paragraph, and add the quote by Lincoln's friend William Herndon, shown in Figure 4-6:

FIGURE 4-6

"Mr. Lincoln thought his speeches out on his feet walking in the streets: he penned them in small scraps--sentences, & paragraphs, depositing them in his hat for safety. When fully finished, he would recopy, and could always repeat easily by heart."

9. Select the new paragraph you keyed in the previous step. Display the **Page Layout** tab. Use the up arrows to change the **Left** and **Right Indent** settings to 1 inch.

10. Spell-check the report.

11. Save the document as *[your initials]***Test4-1** and print it.

TEST YOURSELF 4-2

Marie Curie

1. Open the file **WP-Curie**. Use this as the body of a report. You will format this report by using Word's Quick Styles.

2. Apply the **Normal** Quick Style to the report.

3. Add your introductory information at the top of the report, followed by a suitable report title.

4. Apply the **Heading 1** Quick Style to the title. Increase the font size of the title to 18 points.

5. Open the file **WP-CurieQuote**. It contains a quotation attributed to Marie Curie.

6. Copy all the text in the **WP-CurieQuote** document, and paste the text before the last paragraph in the **WP-Curie** document as a separate paragraph.

7. Start the quote as a separate paragraph. Apply one inch left and right indents to the quote and format it as italic.

FIGURE 4-7
Marie Curie is the only person to have won the Nobel Prize twice.

Setting Paragraph Spacing

Paragraph spacing refers to the amount of space before and after paragraphs. You have seen how Word, by default, automatically adds space after paragraphs. Paragraph spacing is measured in points, just like fonts. The default paragraph setting is 10 points of spacing after paragraphs. If a line of text is 11 points, that means Word adds almost the equivalent of a full blank line after paragraphs. This can be an attractive use of space and it makes documents easy to read. However, you might want to change this amount of space or remove it altogether.

To change the paragraph spacing in a document:

1. Start a new document or select the text in an existing document.
2. On the **Home** tab of the Ribbon, click the dialog box launcher to the right of Paragraph to display the Paragraph dialog box.
3. Increase or decrease the amount of spacing before or after paragraphs. You can also change line spacing settings in this dialog box.

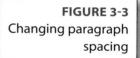

FIGURE 3-3
Changing paragraph spacing

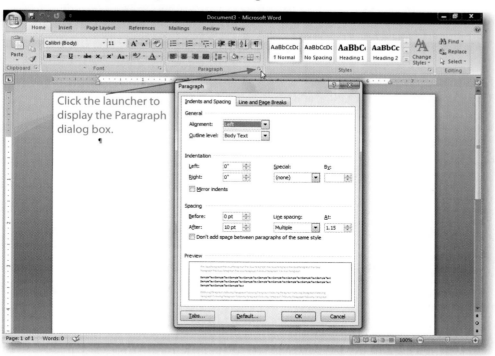

Click the launcher to display the Paragraph dialog box.

FIGURE 4-5
Using a shortcut menu
to paste text

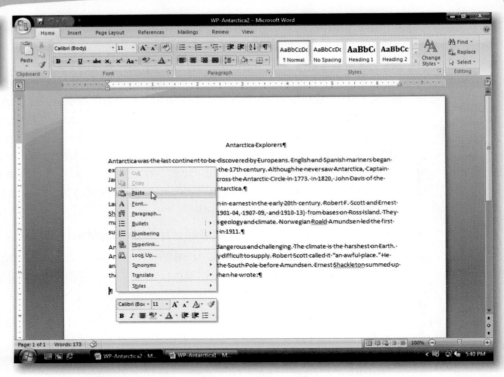

14. Choose **Paste** from the shortcut menu. The cut text is pasted into the second document.

15. Return to **WP-Antarctica1**. You can paste copied or cut text more than once.

16. Place the insertion point at the beginning of the last paragraph and click the Paste button 📋. The cut text is pasted into the **WP-Antarctica1** document again.

17. Save WP-Antarctica1 as *[your initials]***Practice4-3**. Print and close the document. Close WP-Antarctica2 without saving.

TEST YOURSELF 4-1

DID YOU KNOW?

Lincoln, one of the greatest orators in U.S. history, wrote his own speeches.

Abraham Lincoln

1. Open the file **WP-Lincoln**.

2. Press Ctrl + **A** to select the entire report. Apply the No Spacing style. The formatting for this report will be based on the MLA style.

3. At the beginning of the document, add introductory information (your name, your teacher's name, the class, and the date).

4. Apply the Quick Style **Heading 1** to the document title. Center the title and capitalize all the major words.

5. Select the entire report again and apply 2.0 line spacing

Removing Line and Paragraph Spacing

To remove extra line spacing in a document, you would set the line spacing to single spacing, or 1.0 lines. To remove extra paragraph spacing, you would change the setting to 0 space before and after paragraphs.

A quick way to remove all extra line and paragraph spacing is to change the document style from **Normal** to **No Spacing**. You'll learn more about Word's Quick Styles in the next lesson.

To remove all extra line and paragraph spacing in a document:

1. Start a new document or select the text in an existing document.

2. Choose **No Spacing** from the Style group on the **Home** tab.

FIGURE 3-4
Choosing the No Spacing style

PRACTICE 3-1

Set Line and Paragraph Spacing

1. Open the file **WP-Sequoia**. This document is using the default line and paragraph settings.

2. Press Ctrl + **A** to select the entire document.

3. To reveal the default settings, click the dialog box launcher to the right of Paragraph on the **Home** tab. In the Paragraph dialog box, in the **Spacing** area, notice the **After** setting is **10 pts** and the line spacing is **1.15** lines.

4. Change the **After** setting to **6 pts** by either keying in the text box or clicking the down arrow.

5. Click the down arrow next to **Multiple** and choose **Single**. Click **OK** to close the dialog box and apply the settings. The document is now single-spaced with 6-pt spacing after paragraphs.

6. With the text still selected, remove all extra line and paragraph spacing by choosing **No Spacing** from the Style group on the **Home** tab. The text is now all single-spaced, with no extra space after paragraphs.

WORD TIP

You can also change paragraph spacing from the Page Layout tab, in the Paragraph group.

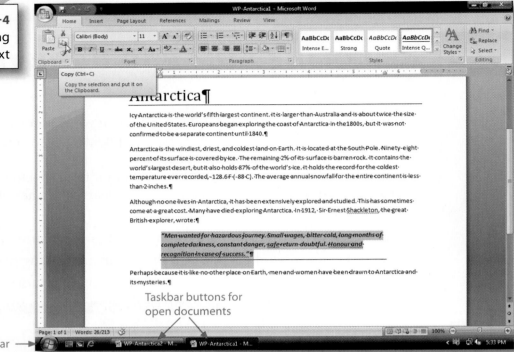

FIGURE 4-4
Copying and pasting text

Taskbar buttons for open documents

Taskbar →

4. Click the taskbar button for **WP-Antarctica2** to make that document the active window.

5. Go to the end of the document and press Enter to start a new paragraph. That is where you will paste the copied information.

6. Click the Paste button 📋. The text from the first document is pasted into the second document.

7. Display the **WP-Antarctica1** window. The selected text is still present and selected.

8. Return to the **WP-Antarctica2** window.

9. Click the Undo button 🔄 on the Quick Access toolbar to undo the paste. Next you'll perform a cut-and-paste.

10. Display **WP-Antarctica1**. Select the quote again if it is not still selected.

11. Click the Cut button ✂. The selected text is deleted when you use the Cut button ✂.

12. Display **WP-Antarctica2**.

13. Right-click at the end of the document. A shortcut menu appears. The Mini toolbar also appears with the shortcut menu. See Figure 4-5 on the next page.

WORD TIP

The Undo command button 🔄 has a down arrow that opens a list of commands recently executed in the document. You can use this list to undo a series of commands, not just the last command.

7. With the text still selected, click the down arrow next to the Line Spacing button 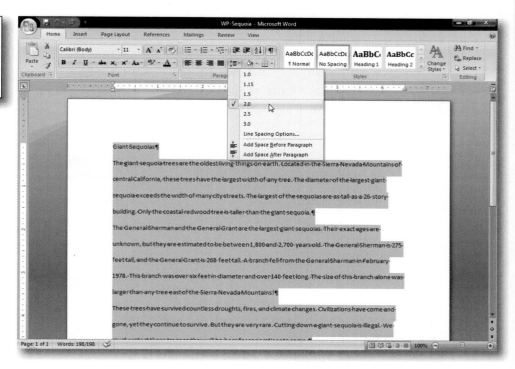 and choose **2.0**. Now the document text has double line spacing, with no additional space before or after paragraphs.

FIGURE 3-5
Document text double-spaced with no extra paragraph spacing

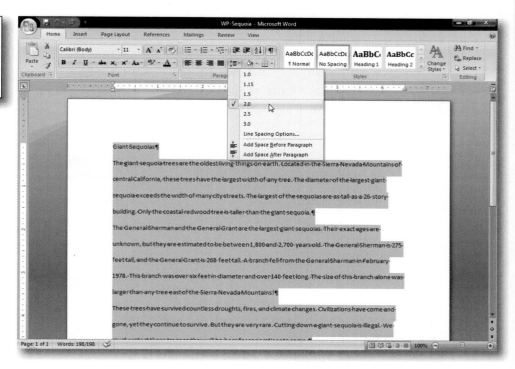

8. Click anywhere in the document to deselect the text. You can also change the spacing of individual paragraphs.

9. Place the insertion point in the second paragraph. Use the Line Spacing button to change it to **3.0** (triple-spacing).

10. Change the line spacing for the paragraph back to **2.0**. Leave the document open.

Microsoft Word

Setting Alignment

Alignment refers to the position of the text in relation to the margins. When you align text, all the text in the paragraph is aligned. There are four types of alignment.

◆ *Left-aligned* text is even with the left margin.

◆ *Right-aligned* text is even with the right margin.

CONTINUES

Using Undo and Redo

Two command buttons frequently used when editing text are the Undo 🔄 and Redo 🔄 buttons. Use the Undo button to reverse an action you have just done, such as cutting or formatting text.

   After using the Undo button, you can change your mind and use the Redo button. Undo and Redo are only available for immediately performed commands. Both command buttons are on the Quick Access toolbar at the top of the document window, and you can also access them with keyboard shortcuts.

TABLE 4-2	Undo and Redo	
Ribbon Command	**Keyboard Shorcut**
🔄 Undo	Ctrl + Z
🔄 Redo	Ctrl + Y

PRACTICE 4-3

Cut, Copy, and Paste

You can have more than one document open at a time. The active window is the window in which you are currently working. You use the taskbar at the bottom of the screen to switch from one document to another. It contains the Start button 🪟 and buttons for all the open documents.

1. Open the file **WP-Antarctica2**. Open the file **WP-Antarctica1** if it is not already open. You'll copy and paste information from one document to the other.

2. Click the taskbar button for **WP-Antarctica1** to make that the active window.

3. Drag to select the fourth paragraph (the formatted quote, which begins "Men wanted"). Click the Copy button 🔳 on the **Home** tab of the Ribbon. The selected text is stored on the Clipboard. See Figure 4-4 on the next page.

Setting Alignment (CONTINUED)

◆ *Centered* text is spaced evenly between the left and right margins.
◆ *Justified* text is even with both the left and right margins, with space added between words as needed.

The easiest way to change alignment is to use the alignment command buttons on the **Home** tab in the Paragraph group. You can specify alignment before you begin keying text, or you can select existing text and change the alignment.

TABLE 3-1	Text Alignment
Command	**Use**
▤ Align Left	Aligns text to the left margin
▤ Align Right	Aligns text to the right margin
▤ Center	Spaces text evenly between the left and right margins
▤ Justify	Aligns text to both the left and right margins

PRACTICE 3-2

Align Text

1. With your current document still open, start a new document. Set the font size to 14 pt.

2. Key the following text, with each sentence as a separate paragraph:

   This sentence is right-aligned.

   This sentence is left-aligned.

   This sentence is centered.

3. Select the first sentence and use the Align Right button ▤ in the Paragraph group on the **Home** tab to align the sentence to the right margin.

4. Select the third sentence and click the Center button ▤. The text is now evenly centered between the left and right margins.

5. Place the insertion point at the end of the third sentence. Press Enter twice. The insertion point is still centered on the page. Any new text you key will continue to be centered.

6. Key the following text:

   New text can be aligned before it is keyed.

WORD TIP

Notice that the second sentence is left-aligned automatically. This is the standard alignment Word uses when no other alignment is specified.

Using Cut, Copy, and Paste

When you *cut* selected text, you remove it from the document and place it on the Clipboard. The *Clipboard* is a temporary storage area in the computer's memory used to hold text or other information that is cut or copied. When you *copy* selected text, you place a copy of the selected text on the Clipboard.

After you have cut or copied selected text to the Clipboard, you can *paste* it in another location. This inserts the contents of the Clipboard at the location of the insertion point. You can cut, copy, and paste by using the Ribbon command buttons, keyboard shortcuts, and shortcut menus.

To cut text and paste it in another location:

1. Select the text to cut.
2. Click the Cut button ✂ on the **Home** tab of the Ribbon. The selected text is removed from the document.
3. Move the insertion point to the location where you want to place the cut text.
4. Click the Paste button 📋 on the **Home** tab of the Ribbon. The cut text is pasted in the new location.

To copy text and paste it in another location:

1. Select the text to copy.
2. Click the Copy command 📄 on the **Home** tab of the Ribbon. The selected text remains in the document.
3. Move the insertion point to the location where you want to place the copied text.
4. Click the Paste command 📋. The copied text is pasted in the new location.

TABLE 4-1	Ways to Cut, Copy, and Paste	
Ribbon Command	**Shortcut Menu Command**	**Keyboard Shorcut**
✂	Cut	Ctrl + X
📄	Copy	Ctrl + C
📋	Paste	Ctrl + V

7. Press Enter and click the Justify button 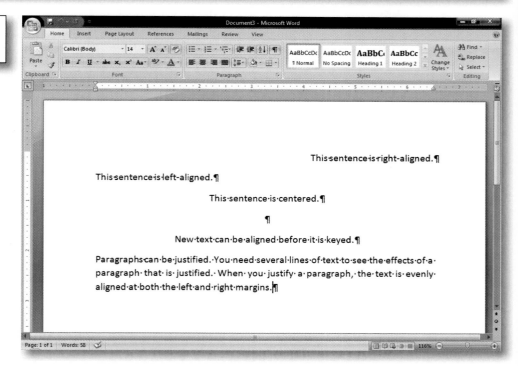. Key the following text:

FIGURE 3-6

```
Paragraphs can be justified. You need several lines of text
to see the effects of a paragraph that is justified. When you
justify a paragraph, the text is evenly aligned at both the
left and right margins.
```

FIGURE 3-7
Aligning text

8. Select the paragraph and left-align it. This is how it would look if you had used Word's default left-aligned setting.

9. Close the document without saving it.

10. In the Sequoia document, add your name, your teacher's name, your class, and the date on separate lines at the top of the document (refer to Figure 3-1 at the beginning of the lesson). All the lines should be double-spaced.

11. Center the title "Giant Sequoias." Place the insertion point at the beginning of the first paragraph and press Tab to indent the first line of the paragraph. Do the same for the remaining paragraphs.

12. Save the document as *[your initials]***Practice3-2** and print it.

If you apply incorrect formatting to a paragraph, click the Undo button 🔄 on the Quick Commands toolbar.

2. On the Home tab, click the Increase Indent button 📑 to increase the left indent by one-half inch.

3. Click Increase Indent 📑 again to increase the indent to one inch. The indent increases one-half inch each time you click the button.

4. Click the Decrease Indent button 📑 twice to return the text to the left margin. These commands control only the left indent.

5. Place the insertion point anywhere in the fourth paragraph (beginning "Men wanted").

6. Display the **Page Layout** tab. In the **Indent** boxes, use the up arrows to set the **Left** and **Right** indents to **.5**. The paragraph is indented .5 inch from each margin.

7. Display the **Home** tab. With the insertion point still in the fourth paragraph, open the Quick Styles gallery and apply the **Intense Quote** style. This overrides any previous indent settings and applies a dramatic quotation style that includes indents, bold, italic, and a bottom border.

8. Leave the document open.

Microsoft Word

Using a Shortcut Menu

A *shortcut menu* is a list of commands that are relevant to a particular item in a document. You can use shortcut menus in addition to Ribbon commands and keyboard shortcuts to perform an action.

You display a shortcut menu by right-clicking an item in a document, such as a paragraph or selected text. When you *right-click* an item, you point to it and quickly press and release the right mouse button. The Mini toolbar also appears when you display a shortcut menu.

To use a shortcut menu:

1. Point to the document item on which you'd like to perform a command.

2. Using the right mouse button, right-click the item. A shortcut menu appears near the item.

3. Choose the desired command on the shortcut menu.

DID YOU KNOW?

South America's Amazon River is the world's second longest river. It carries more water than any other river.

The Amazon River

1. Open the file **WP-Amazon**. The document contains information about the Amazon River.

2. Select the entire document. Apply the **No Spacing** style on the **Home** tab to remove extra line and paragraph spacing.

3. With the document still selected, click the Line Spacing button ⊟▾ and choose **2.0** to double-space the entire report. Click anywhere in the document to deselect the text.

4. Display the **Page Layout** tab of the Ribbon. Click **Margins** and make sure **Normal** is selected (the default setting for 1-inch top, bottom, left and right margins).

5. Add introductory information at the top of the report. It should include your name, your teacher's name, the class, and the date. Each of these items should appear on a separate line.

6. Use the Center button ≣ on the **Home** tab of the Ribbon to center the heading. Capitalize all the major words.

7. Add the text shown in Figure 3-8 to the end of the report as a new paragraph.

FIGURE 3-8

The Amazon River is also home to some of the world's largest and most exotic animals. The giant anaconda snake lives in the tropical waters of the Amazon. One of the world's most ferocious fish, the piranha, is found in the Amazon and its tributaries. Some catfish weighing over 200 pounds have been found in the Amazon. The Amazon is a river of extremes in many different ways.

8. The new paragraph should be double-spaced. Press Tab before the first word of the new paragraph to indent the line one-half inch.

9. Spell-check the report.

10. Save the document as *[your initials]***Test3-1** and print the report.

Setting Indents

Indentation or an *indent* refers to the distance between the sides of a paragraph and the left or right margin. Some Quick Styles apply indents to text. You can use the Paragraph command buttons on the **Home** tab of the Ribbon to indent text.

To indent the left side of a paragraph:

1. Click within the paragraph (or select multiple paragraphs).
2. On the **Home** tab of the Ribbon, click the Increase Indent button in the Paragraph group. This indents the left side of the paragraph by one-half inch.
3. Click the Decrease Indent button to decrease the left indent by one-half inch.

To indent the left and right sides of a paragraph:

1. Click within the paragraph (or select multiple paragraphs).
2. On the **Page Layout** tab of the Ribbon, in the Paragraph group, use the up and down arrows to change the **Left** and **Right Indent** settings.

FIGURE 4-3
Setting left and right indents on the Page Layout tab of the Ribbon

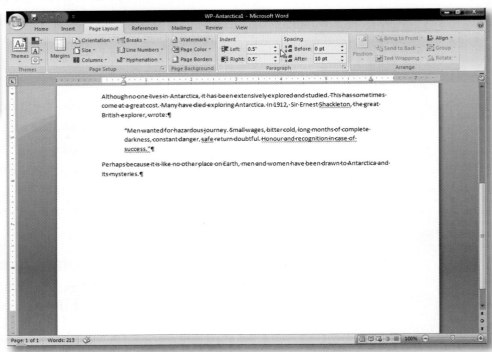

PRACTICE 4-2

Set Indents 1. In the Antarctica document, place the insertion point anywhere in the second paragraph.

DID YOU KNOW?

In 2005, Hurricane Katrina caused destruction as far as 100 miles from the storm's center, devastating hundreds of thousands of people along the Gulf Coast. It was the costliest hurricane in U.S. history, with more than $80 billion in damages.

Hurricanes

1. Open the file **WP-Hurricane**. It contains information about hurricanes and will be used as the body of the report.

2. Use the Paragraph dialog box to change the spacing after paragraphs to **0** and the line spacing to **Double** for the entire report.

3. Set the top, bottom, and side margins to the correct MLA-style margins.

4. Key introductory information for your report, including your name, your teacher's name, the class, and the date.

5. Add a title to the report. Use the correct alignment and capitalization.

6. Add the paragraph shown in Figure 3-9 to the end of the report as a new paragraph.

FIGURE 3-9

Scientists use the Saffir-Simpson scale to measure hurricane strength. It has five categories that measure wind speed and storm surge. A storm surge is a wall of wind-driven water that sweeps over the coastline when a hurricane strikes land. Category 1 hurricanes are the weakest. Maximum wind speed is no more than 153 kilometers per hour, but Category 1 hurricanes can uproot trees and cause minor building damage. Category 5 hurricanes are devastating storms. Wind speeds exceed 250 kilometers per hour, and the storm surge is more than 5.5 meters. Hurricanes of this strength destroy buildings and can cause great loss of life.

TEST TIP

You can find a conversion table for Celsius and Fahrenheit and other metric measurements on the Internet or in an encyclopedia.

7. Make sure all paragraphs begin with the correct indentation.

8. Convert the meters and kilometers to feet and miles. (*Hint:* 1 meter = 39.37 inches; 1 kilometer = 0.6 mile).

9. Convert the temperature from Celsius to Fahrenheit.

10. Spell-check the report.

11. Save the document as *[your initials]***Test3-2** and print the report.

PRACTICE 4-1

Apply Quick Styles

1. Start Word and open the file **WP-Antarctica1**. This document is created using Word's default style, Normal. Notice that **Normal** is selected in the Styles group on the **Home** tab.

2. Replace the introductory text at the top of the document with your own information (your name, teacher's name, class, and date).

3. Select the four lines of introductory text.

4. Click the More button ⬇ in the Styles group to open the gallery of Quick Styles.

5. Move the mouse pointer over the various gallery styles. Notice how they change your selected text.

6. Click the style **Subtle Emphasis** to apply it. Your text is italicized.

7. Select the document title, "Antarctica." Apply the **Title** style. This style changes the font, font size, and alignment of the text and adds a bottom border.

8. Leave the document open.

FIGURE 4-2
Applying a Quick Style to title text

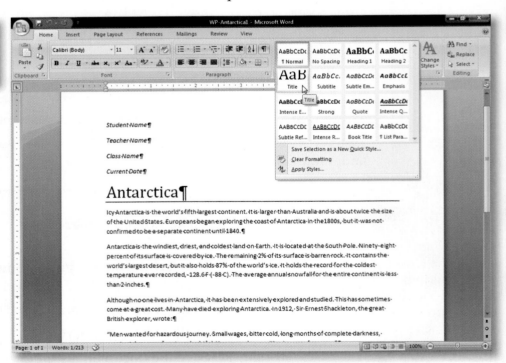

FIGURE 3-10
Mozart, shown here at 11 years old, was a child prodigy.

Famous Musician, Artist, or Writer

Create a one-page report on the life and work of a famous musician, artist, or writer from history. Be sure to include important personal information such as the date and place of their births, where they lived and worked, and where they died. Describe major works and important events in their lives.

In writing your report, be sure to:

1. Format the margins, spacing, and alignment to follow the MLA style for one-page reports.

2. Include introductory information for your report (your name, your teacher's name, your course or class, and the date). Use proper capitalization for the title.

3. Italicize the names of any compositions or paintings.

4. Spell-check your report.

5. Save the document as *[your initials]***Test3-3** and print the report.

LESSON 4

Enhance Reports

Word Processing

LEARN

Edit and Enhance Your Reports

One of the requirements for writing reports is to make sure the report contents are in the right order. As you edit your report, you might find it necessary to change the order of paragraphs. You might also want to emphasize certain text. For example, if your report contains a quotation, you can make it stand out from the rest of the text.

In this lesson, you'll learn how to cut, copy, and paste text. You'll also learn how to style paragraphs for special emphasis.

Microsoft Word

Applying Quick Styles

Quick Styles are formatting options created by Word for text and paragraphs. They are useful for specific parts of a document that you want to emphasize, such as headings or quotations. Quick Styles are located in the Styles group on the **Home** tab of the Ribbon.

When you begin a new document, the default style is **Normal**. This style has extra line and paragraph spacing, which you have already learned how to remove by applying the **No Spacing** style. Now you will apply Quick Styles to enhance text.

To apply Quick Styles:

1. Select the text you want to style.
2. On the **Home** tab, in the Styles group, click the More button ⊡ to display the gallery.

FIGURE 4-1
Quick Styles on the Home tab

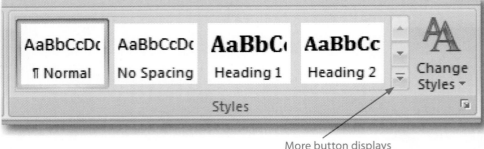

More button displays gallery of styles

3. Point to a Quick Style to see how it will format your selected text. Click the desired Quick Style to apply it.

Quick Reference Guide

Use the following tables as a quick reference when you don't remember how to do something in Microsoft Word or Windows. Use the screen representations and callouts to help you remember the various parts of Word and Window screens.

TABLE A-1   Mouse Terms

Term	Description
Point	Move the mouse until the tip of the pointer is touching the desired item on the computer screen.
Click	Quickly press and release the left mouse button.
Double-click	Quickly press and release the left mouse button twice.
Drag (or drag-and-drop)	Point to an object on-screen, hold down the left mouse button, and roll the mouse until the pointer is in position. Then release the mouse button.
Right-click	Quickly press and release the right mouse button.
Select	Hold down the left mouse button; move the mouse so the pointer moves from one side of an object to another. Then release the mouse button.

TABLE A-2   Mouse Pointers

Pointer	Description
⩗ Pointer	Used to point to objects
I I-beam	Used in keying, inserting, and selecting text
⇕ Two-headed Arrow	Used to change the size of objects or windows
✛ Four-headed Arrow	Used to move objects
�👆 Hand	Used in Window's Help system to display additional information

TABLE A-4 **Microsoft Office Menu Items**

Command	Description
New	Starts a new blank document
Open	Opens an existing document
Save	Saves a document
Save As	Provides options to save a copy of a document
Print	Provides options to print and preview a document
Prepare	Provides options to prepare a document for distribution
Send	Provides options to send a copy of a document to other people
Publish	Provides options to distribute a document to others
Close	Closes a document

TABLE A-3 **Tabs on the Ribbon**

Tab	Description
Home	Contains commands used to edit and change the appearance of document text.
Insert	Contains commands used to insert elements in a document, such as a hyperlink or picture.
Page Layout	Contains commands used to change the overall design of a document and how document elements occupy space on the page.
References	Contains commands typically used for creating reports, such as adding a table of contents or footnotes.
Mailings	Contains commands used to create envelopes and labels, and to perform mass mailings.
Review	Contains commands used to check the spelling or grammar in a document, and to perform an online document review by adding comments or suggesting revisions.
View	Contains commands used to change the way documents appear on the screen, and to display certain screen items such as the ruler.

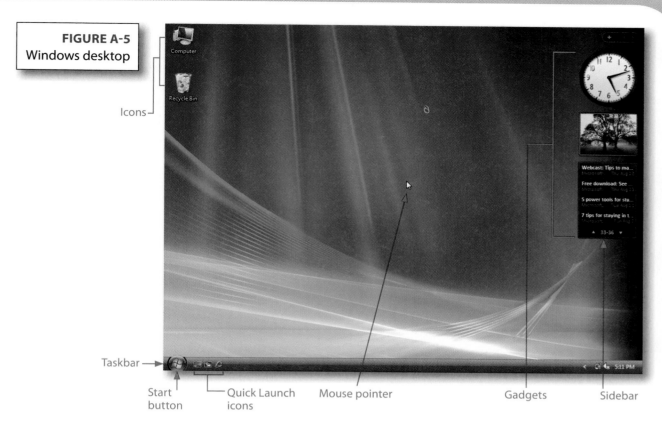

FIGURE A-5
Windows desktop

Icons

Taskbar →

Start button   Quick Launch icons   Mouse pointer   Gadgets   Sidebar

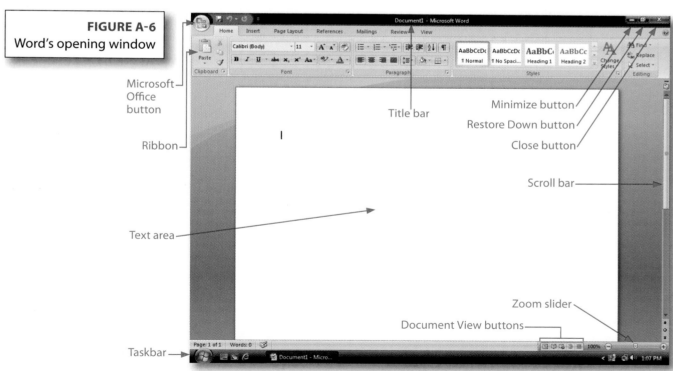

FIGURE A-6
Word's opening window

Microsoft Office button

Ribbon

Text area

Taskbar →

Title bar

Minimize button
Restore Down button
Close button

Scroll bar

Zoom slider
Document View buttons

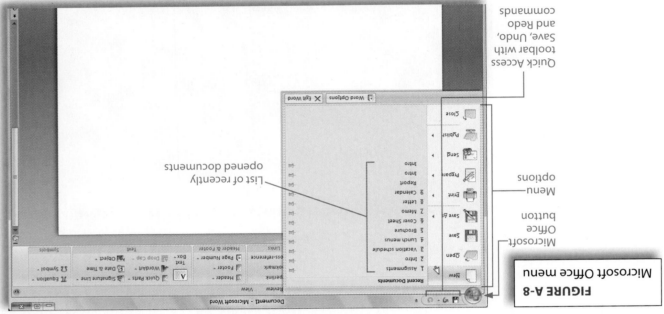

Quick Access toolbar with Save, Undo, and Redo commands

List of recently opened documents

Menu options

Microsoft Office button

Save As button

FIGURE A-8
Microsoft Office menu

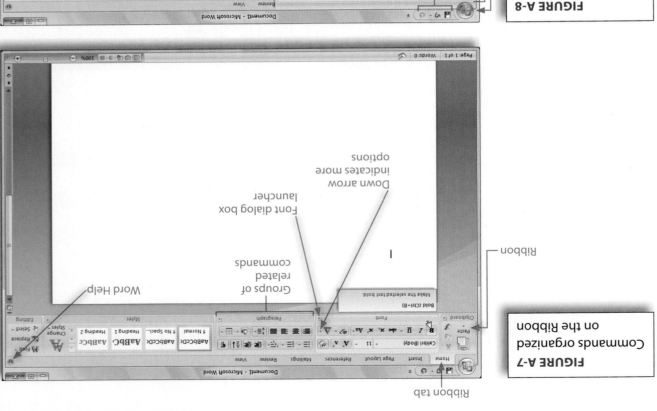

Word Help

Groups of related commands

Font dialog box launcher

Down arrow indicates more options

Ribbon

Ribbon tab

FIGURE A-7
Commands organized on the Ribbon

FIGURE A-9
Open dialog box

Click to display folders

Double-click filename

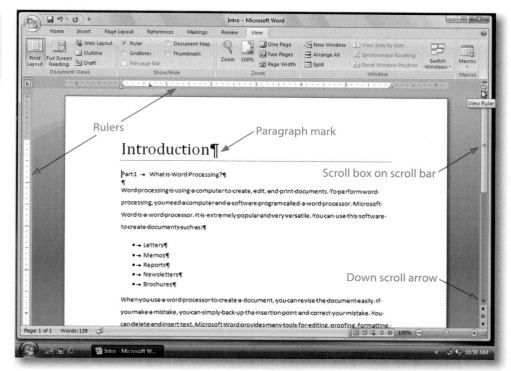

FIGURE A-10
Document in Print Layout view

Rulers

Paragraph mark

Scroll box on scroll bar

Down scroll arrow

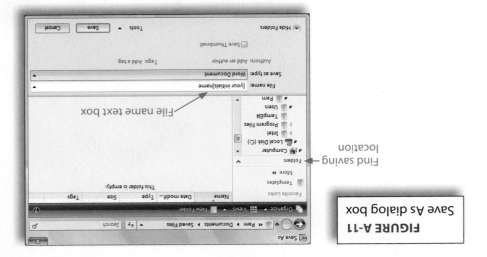

FIGURE A-11
Save As dialog box

File name text box

Find saving
location

Introduction

Active window Window in which you are working.

Click To quickly press and release the left mouse button.

Desktop Windows work surface containing graphical representations of programs or Windows features.

Double-click To quickly press and release the left mouse button twice.

Drag To point to an object on-screen, hold down the left mouse button, roll the mouse until the pointer is in position, and then release the mouse button.

File Basic unit of storage on a computer.

Filename Unique name given to a file when you save it. A filename can have up to 260 characters, excluding /\><*?":;|. It can include spaces and use uppercase or lowercase letters.

Filename extension Four-letter identifier that is automatically added to the end of a filename by an application, such as .docx for Word document files.

Folder Icon shaped like a manila folder that contains programs and files.

Four-headed arrow Mouse pointer used to move objects.

Gadgets Mini-programs that appear on the right side of the Windows desktop. They provide information at a glance.

Hand Mouse pointer used in Window's Help system to display additional information.

I-beam Mouse pointer used in keying, inserting, and selecting text.

Icon On-screen picture that represents a feature or a program.

Insertion point Vertical blinking line that marks a location at which you can enter text.

Mouse Pointing device that is typically attached to a computer by a cable.

Mouse pad Smooth pad on which a mouse rests or rolls.

Point To roll the mouse until the tip of the pointer is touching the desired on-screen item.

Pointer On-screen arrow that moves as you move the mouse and lets you accomplish specific tasks.

Ribbon Portion of the Word window just below the title bar that displays commands, organized by tabs, with each tab representing an area of activity.

Right-click To quickly press and release the right mouse button.

Rulers   Parts of the Word screen that show the size of the page and document formatting settings such as margins, tabs, and indents.

Scroll bars   Vertical bars used to move up or down and right or left in a document to display text that doesn't fit on a single screen. Scroll arrows appear at the ends of scroll bars.

Select   To hold down the left mouse button, roll the mouse so the pointer moves from one side of an object to another, and then release the mouse button.

Sidebar   Windows desktop feature at the right of the screen that contains information at a glance.

Taskbar   Bar at the bottom of the desktop. It contains the Start button and Quick Launch icons for opening programs and files. It lets you navigate among open programs or files by clicking their taskbar buttons.

Text area   Area of a document window where you enter text.

Title bar   Top bar in a window. It displays the window name.

Two-headed arrow   Mouse pointer used to change the size of objects or windows.

User password   String of letters, numbers, and symbols used to begin the Windows program.

Keyboarding

Adjective   Word that modifies a noun or pronoun, providing more detail. (16)

Adjective, comparative   Adjective that ends in "er" (taller, nicer) or is preceded by the word "more" (more attractive). When an adjective ends in "y," the "y" is changed to "i" before "er" is added (happy, happier). (16)

Adjective, superlative   Adjective that ends in "est" (tallest, nicest) or is preceded by the word "most" (most attractive). When an adjective ends in "y," the "y" is changed to "i" before adding "est" (happy, happiest). (16)

Adverb   Word that modifies a verb, an adjective, or another adverb. Adverbs are often used to emphasize or downplay something. (19)

City   Densely populated urban center whose inhabitants are engaged primarily in commerce and industry. A city is larger than a town. (9)

Cryptology   Science that deals with coded messages. Cryptology is used to code secret messages and to protect storage of data and transactions between computers on the Internet. (6)

Data, encrypted   Coded data. (6)

Demonym   Name given to people of a particular territory or country (American, Canadian). (34)

Double-line space   Space created by pressing Enter twice. (1)

Double-space   To add a blank line of space between two lines of keyed text by pressing Enter. (1)

Emoticons   Form of shorthand used to convey emotion in plain-text messages. To view an emoticon, you typically have to turn your head to the left and view the symbols sideways on the page. (33)

Haiku   The shortest literature form in the world, haiku are short poems, each consisting of 3 lines that together contain 17 syllables. The first line has 5 syllables; the second, 7; and the third, 5. Haiku usually focus on a subject from nature. (8)

Homophones   Words that sound the same but have different spellings. (4)

Hurricane   Tropical storm with winds of over 74 miles per hour (mph). The term "hurricane" usually refers to a storm that occurs over the North Atlantic Ocean. (14)

Keys, function   Keys (F1, F2, and so on) typically found at the top of your keyboard that perform special tasks in the active computer program. (23)

Keys, home   Starting keys on which the user's fingers rest: A, S, D, F, J, K, L, and ; (semicolon). (1)

Marks, proofreaders'   Handwritten corrections made to a page of text. The marks are combinations of symbols and short notations that are easy to understand. (5)

Method, scientific Type of reasoning in which scientists propose a hypothesis (a tentative assumption requiring testing to be proven true) and then gather data to support or reject the hypothesis and arrive at a conclusion. (30)

Metropolis Large or important city, such as the capital of a country or state. (9)

Name, account Part of an e-mail address that comes before the @ and identifies the particular e-mail account. Also known as the user name. (31)

Name, domain Part of an e-mail address that comes after the @ and identifies the e-mail server on which the account can be found. (31)

Noun Name of a person, place, or thing. (3)

Noun, abstract Name of a quality or concept. (3)

Noun, collective Name given to a group of persons, places, or things. (3)

Noun, common Name of a thing you can see, hear, or touch. (3)

Noun, proper Official name of a particular person, place, or thing. (3)

Number, prime Any positive number greater than 1 that can be divided evenly only by itself and 1. (36)

Participle, present Word, usually ending in "ing," that can be used as part of a verb, as the subject of a sentence, or as an adjective. (7)

Patent Property right granted by the United States to an inventor. (11)

Row, first Row of keys just below the home row. (1)

Row, home Row of keys containing the home keys. (1)

Row, third Row of keys just above the home row. (1)

User name Part of an e-mail address that comes before the @ and identifies the particular e-mail account. Also known as the account name. (31)

Verb Word that expresses action or a state of being. (7)

Word wrap Feature of word processing software that enables you to keep keying, without pressing Enter, while the word processing program automatically moves text to a new line. (2)

Word Processing

Alignment   Position of text in relation to the margins. (3)

AutoComplete   Word feature that suggests the completed word when you key the first four or more letters of a day, month, or date. (1)

Bibliography   Formatted list of all the sources used in a report, including the cited sources. (8)

Borders   Lines or boxes placed around paragraphs or entire pages for visual interest. (10)

Bulleted list   List used to organize details in a document. Items in this type of list are preceded by a bullet (•) or other character. (7)

Cells   In a table, the boxes formed by the intersection of columns and rows. (9)

Centered   Text that is spaced evenly between the left and right margins. (3)

Character formatting   Formatting such as bold, italic, and underline that is applied to characters to emphasize text. (2)

Citation   Author's last name and the page number of a source in parentheses following quoted, summarized, or paraphrased text in a report. (8)

Clip   Single file in a clip art collection. (11)

Clip art   Ready-to-use graphic images you can insert in a document. (11)

Clipboard   Temporary storage area in the computer's memory used to hold text or other information that is cut or copied. (4)

Column layout   Text layout option that formats text so it flows up and down on a page, as in a newspaper. (9)

Command keys   Keys such as Ctrl, Shift, or Alt used in sequence with other keys to accomplish tasks quickly. (2)

Continuous section break   Divides a document into sections without inserting a page break. (9)

Copy   Copies selected text to the Clipboard. (4)

Cover page   Page at the beginning of longer reports. It consists of a report title, your name, your teacher's name, the course name, and the date. Also called *title page*. (6)

Cut   Removes selected text from a document and places it on the Clipboard. (4)

Floating graphic   Image that can be moved freely in a document. (11)

Font   Type design of all characters, including letters, numbers, symbols, and punctuation marks. (2)

Footer   A separate area within the bottom margin of every page that is used for identifying text or graphic elements. (6)

Hard page break   Forces a page break to occur at a specific place. Inserted manually. (7)

Header   A separate area within the top margin of every page that is used for identifying text or graphic elements. (6)

Indentation   Distance between the sides of a paragraph and the left or right margins. (4)

Inline graphic   Image that aligns with a paragraph and is treated as a character. (11)

Inside address   Delivery address in a business or personal letter. (1)

Justified   Text that is even with both the left and right margins, with space added between words as needed. (3)

Keyboard shortcut   Command key sequence, such as Ctrl + C, used to accomplish tasks quickly. (2)

Landscape orientation   Page orientation that is wider than it is tall. (13)

Left-aligned   Text that is even with the left margin. (3)

Letterhead   Stationery containing a company's name, address, telephone number, fax number, and e-mail address. Letterhead can also include a company logo. (1)

Line spacing   Distance between lines of text within a paragraph. (3)

MLA style   Set of rules developed by the Modern Language Association to be used by students in writing reports and research papers. (3)

Margin   Distance from the edge of the paper to the edge of the text. (1)

Memo   Interoffice memorandum. Used to send written communication through an office. Similar to e-mail, but intended for more formal or detailed messages. (2)

Multilevel list   List that resembles an outline, in which text is organized by levels, using indents. (7)

Nonprinting character   Character, such as a paragraph mark or tab, that appears on-screen but not in the printed document. (1)

Numbered list   List used to organize details in a document. Items in this type of list are preceded by sequential numbers. (7)

Page orientation   Direction in which a page in a document prints or appears on-screen. (13)

Pagination   Flow of text from the bottom of one page to the top of the next. (7)

Paragraph spacing   Space before and after paragraphs. (3)

Paste   Inserts the contents of the Clipboard at the location of the insertion point. (4)

Personal business letter   Letter written on plain paper with the return address below the writer's name. It is often called a personal letter. (1)

Personal letter   Letter written on plain paper with the return address below the writer's name. (1)

Portrait orientation   Page orientation that is taller than it is wide. (13)

Proofreaders' marks   Handwritten corrections to text, using special symbols. (8)

Proofreading   Reading over a document to check its accuracy, formatting, spelling, and grammar. (8)

Quick Styles   Formatting options on the Home tab, created by Word for text and paragraphs. (4)

Right-aligned Text that is even with the right margin. (3)

Right-click Quickly press and release the right mouse button. (4)

Sans serif Type of font that is without serifs or extensions at the ends of the vertical and horizontal lines that make up its characters. (10)

Scale Changing the size of an image in proportion to its current or original size. (11)

Section break Divides a document into separate sections so you can apply different formatting to these areas. (7)

Serif Type of font that has decorative extensions at the ends of the vertical and horizontal lines that make up its characters. (10)

Shading Blocks of color or shades of gray behind paragraph text. (10)

Shortcut menu List of commands that is relevant to a particular item in a document. (4)

SmartArt Collection of diagrams composed of shapes, used for organizing information and communicating ideas. (12)

Soft page break Page break created by Word when text exceeds the length of a page. (7)

Style set Coordinated group of styles that are designed to work together to produce a professional document. (13)

Symbols Characters in font sets that do not appear on the keyboard. (10)

Synonym Word with the same or nearly the same meaning as another word. (5)

Tab Formatting feature used to indent or align text. The most common tabs are left-aligned, right-aligned, centered, and decimal-aligned. (2)

Tab marker Symbol on the horizontal ruler that displays a custom tab setting. (2)

Table Grid of intersecting columns and rows into which you key text. (9)

Text box Free-floating rectangle that contains text. (12)

Text wrapping Property of an image that determines how text flows around it. (11)

Theme Set of coordinated formatting choices that includes colors, fonts, and fill effects. (13)

Thesaurus Tool that lists synonyms for words. (5)

Vertical alignment Refers to the way text is aligned between the top and bottom margins. You can center text vertically between the top and bottom margins. (7)

Watermark Light-colored text, such as the word "Draft," that is applied to the background of a document. (6)

WordArt Graphic tool used for converting text into a decorative image. (11)

Communication

Attachment   Computer file that is sent with an e-mail message. (14)

Blog   Web site that appears as a personal online journal. The word blog comes from the words "web log." (17)

Blog post   Entry you publish to a blog site. Posts appear in reverse chronological order, with the most recent post first. (17)

Browser   Program used to access and interact with Web sites. (15)

Computer network   Group of two or more computers electronically linked together, using either special cables or wireless radio connections. (15)

E-mail   Electronic mail; a system used to send messages to one or more people over the Internet or over a private intranet. (14)

E-mail account   Electronic mailbox used to send and receive messages. (14)

E-mail service provider   Company that allows you to exchange messages with other e-mail users. (14)

Favorites   Bookmarks to Web pages that help you find the pages easily in the future. (15)

Hits   Web site addresses and descriptions that contain references to your search topic. (16)

Hyperlinks or links   Text or graphics that you click to go to another Web site location. (15)

Instant messaging   Also called IM or IMing; used to send messages to one or more people over the Internet in real time. (14)

Internet   Worldwide system of computer networks; sometimes called a "network of networks." (15)

Internet address   Unique location for a Web site on the Internet. You access the Web site by keying the Internet address into the browser's address line. (15)

Intranet   Private computer network within a company that uses Internet technology to provide information to employees. (17)

Keywords   Words or phrases that best describe your search topic. (16)

Pay-for placement sites   Web sites that pay search engines for high rankings so they appear first in a list of search results. (16)

Protocol   Set of rules or standards that allow computers to communicate with one another. (15)

Rank   Order the results of search from the most relevant to the least relevant. (16)

Search engines Indexes of information organized by categories. They contain hyperlinks to a variety of Web sites. You can use search engine Web sites to search for information about a specific topic. (16)

Search operators Keyword punctuation marks that instruct the search engine to include, exclude, or specify the order of your keywords. (16)

Spider Computer program that automatically collects information that is stored in a search engine. (16)

Web sites Collections of computer files that may contain text, pictures, sounds, and video. (15)

Photographs

Cover

J.W. Burkey/The Image Bank/Getty Images; Cossu/SIS; Scott Tysick/Masterfile; Jean-Yves Bruel/Masterfile

Section Openers

Section Opener 1: Jean-Yves Bruel/Masterfile; Section Opener 2: Jean-Yves Bruel/Masterfile; Section Opener 3: Cossu/SIS; Scott Tysick/Masterfile

Introduction

Page 21–22: Loudon Photography; Page 24–27: Loudon Photography

Keyboarding

Page 31: Corbis; Page 35: Getty Images; Page 37: Getty Images; Page 43: Getty Images; Page 47: Getty Images; Page 51: Getty Images; Page 53: Getty Images; Page 55: Getty Images; Page 57: Getty Images; Page 59: Corbis; Page 63: Ultimate Rollercoaster; Page 65: Getty Images; Page 71: Mary Evans Picture Library; Page 73: Getty Images; Page 77: Corbis; Page 83: Getty Images; Page 85: Corbis; Page 87: Getty Images; Page 92: Getty Images; Page 95: Getty Images; Page 99: Corbis; Page 105: Getty Images; Page 111: Getty Images; Page 113: Getty Images

Word Processing and Communication

Page 135: Corbis; Page 146: Corbis; Page 157: Mary Evans Picture Library; Page 166: Mary Evans Picture Library; Page 177: AP/Wide World Photos; Page 188: Getty Images; Page 201: Getty Images; Page 216: Corbis; Page 228: Corbis; Page 235: Corbis; Page 247: Getty Images; Page 272: Getty Images; Page 289: Corbis; Page 302: Corbis